REVOLUTION

NOMOS

NOMOS
VIII

REVO

LUTION

Yearbook of the American Society for Political and Legal Philosophy

Edited by CARL J. FRIEDRICH
Harvard University

ATHERTON PRESS   70 FIFTH AVENUE, NEW YORK   1969

"Revolution as a Problem in the Philosophy of
History," by Paul Schrecker, translated by R. B. Hamilton,
was first published in *The Claremont Quarterly,* Vol. 10,
No. 4, Summer 1963. It is reproduced with the permission
of Claremont Graduate School and University Center.

REVOLUTION: Nomos VIII
Carl J. Friedrich, editor

PREFACE

The volume on revolution here presented does not need any elaborate prefatory remarks. Its organization in terms of general conceptual problems, its relation to the emergent (we hope) international order, and the particular problems raised by Marxism and its revolutionary modes are clear enough in themselves. There are additional dimensions that might have been explored, especially on the concrete level of historical analysis, but the scope of the issues here presented is quite sufficient for a single volume. In a brief introduction I have sought to open up some of the issues; I did not give detailed references to the essays which follow, since it seemed pedantic and the links are obvious. I should have liked to have included a contribution from Crane Brinton and Eugen Rosenstock-Huessy who, together with George Pettee, have contributed most to the general discussion of revolution a generation ago. Unfortunately neither of them was able to do so, but I am glad that Pettee was interested in "revisiting" his old battleground.

The new volume of *Nomos* dealing with revolution is the eighth in the series. It is appearing with a slight delay, but will be followed this coming year by the volume on Equality. The new volume will be edited by Roland Pennock, a founder member of our society and a distinguished scholar in the field of political and legal theory and philosophy. I am very happy to be able to turn over the editorship to his capable hands. I have enjoyed the work, but felt that the time had come for a change. Scholarly publications should not, in my view, become too much linked with an individual, and the vitality of our society is such that our yearbook ought to continue to flourish.

CARL J. FRIEDRICH

CONTENTS

CONTRIBUTORS

DAVID BRAYBROOKE
Philosophy, Dalhousie University

RICHARD A. FALK
Political Science, Princeton University

CARL J. FRIEDRICH
Political Science, Harvard University

MANFRED HALPERN
Political Science, Princeton University

EUGENE KAMENKA
Philosophy, Australian National University

x   *Contributors*

C. B. MACPHERSON
Political Science, University of Toronto

GEORGE PETTEE
Political Science, Research Analysis Corporaticn

DAVID C. RAPOPORT
Political Science, University of California at Los Angeles

MELVIN RICHTER
Political Science, Hunter College

PAUL SCHRECKER (deceased)
Philosophy, University of Pennsylvania

ROBERT C. TUCKER
Political Science, Princeton University

GENERAL THEORIES OF REVOLUTION

1

AN INTRODUCTORY NOTE ON REVOLUTION

CARL J. FRIEDRICH

Ours is by all accounts a revolutionary age. The market place is filled with the clamor of voices proclaiming convictions which to be effective would require radical change in existing societies. While one ideology loses in appeal, another becomes more virulent in its call to action. There is no "end of ideologies" in the world, even though some of them may be more feeble in some countries.[1] What then could be a more appropriate topic for philosophers of politics and law to consider? Yet, any general statement on revolution, like any general etiology of war, implies a philosophy of history.

[1] Raymond Aron and Daniel Bell among others have, on the basis of the weakening of Marxist and generally Leftist ideologies in the West, advanced such claims.

"Revolution," as Eugen Rosenstock-Hüssy has written, "brings on the speaking of a new, unheard of language, another logic, a revaluation of all values."[2] At least, it does so, when it is comprehensive or total. Antecedent to revolution, there always is resistance in any society. It may be sporadic and marginal or it may be massive and concentrated, but wherever values, interests, and beliefs conflict, some kind of resistance is apt to appear. Nullification and crime are its familiar modes of operation. Revolutions are successful rebellions; they are also rebellions on a more comprehensive scale. To resistance, rebellion, and revolution correspond in turn the continuous changes, many gradual, some traumatic and violent, which the individual person undergoes as he grows from infanthood to senility.[3] And just as in the individual person, many small adjustments to a changing environment reduce the chance of traumatic experiences, so one might say that many small revolutions prevent a big one. As various detailed items of the political whole are "revolutionized" by way of a functioning political process, the tensions which would necessitate a violent and global transformation are channeled into promoting specific change. There is no better illustration of this contrast in the field of political experience than the comparison of the history of England and the continental countries in the eighteenth and nineteenth centuries, and the same may be said of the history of the United States. It is, in a sense, as has rightly been observed, the story of a "permanent revolution."

Trotsky once said that "revolutions are the mad inspiration of history."[4] Such a statement is a poetic way of calling attention to three important features of revolutions that go far beyond the strictly political dimensions, the creative and spiritual aspirations, involving values and beliefs, the historical setting and the highly emotional fervor of the revolutionaries. It is necessary, for purposes of political analysis, to bracket out these aspects of revolutions which are presumably characteristic of the "great" revolutions of Western history, and not, or not so much, of most other revolutions of a strictly political import. Aristotle's classical analysis of "limited" revolutions in the Greek polis permits the drawing of another sig-

---

[2] Eugen Rosenstock-Hüssy, *Die Europaeischen Revolutionen* (1931, 1951); English version (rev.), *Out of Revolution* (1938).

[3] The brief observations which follow are more fully developed in my *Man and His Government* (1963), ch. 34; resistance is there treated at some length.

[4] Leon Trotsky, *My Life* (1930), p. 320.

nificant distinction; namely, that between a revolution and a *coup d'état*—a stroke of force at the particular rulers of an established system of government, usually executed by members of the ruling group, but not aimed at changing the system.[5] (The removal of Khrushchev was an atypical *coup d'état* in that no manifest force was employed.) The *coup d'état* is frequent in unstable monocratic systems, especially dictatorships and tyrannies; it is far removed from Trotsky's mad inspirations of history; rather it is a coldly calculated maneuver in an ongoing power struggle.

Political revolution, then, may be defined as a sudden and violent overthrow of an established political order. Other revolutions, such as the industrial revolution, the scientific revolution, and the revolution of rising expectations, are quite gradual, as are the revolutions of the heavenly bodies. It may be limited or unlimited, as were the great revolutions, the English, the French, and the Russian, but its focal point is the alteration of political leadership and often that of political participation. The democratic revolutions, characteristically, have pretended to be preoccupied with securing for the people the participation in politics which a preceding authoritarian regime had denied them. Actually, they also have always been concerned with the leadership.[6] Some contexts seem especially favorable to revolutionary upheavals, e.g., Latin America and ancient Greece, while others, notably the constitutional regimes of Western Europe, particularly Great Britain and the Scandinavian kingdoms as well as Switzerland and the Netherlands, seem to have been singularly free of such sudden and violent alterations, as have been the United States and the British Dominions. The reason is to be seen primarily in the operation of constitutional mechanisms that allow and even promote social and political change, as contrasted with the Aristotelian tradition and its preoccupation with stability. Whether such devices as constitutional amendment, judicial interpretation and skillful manipulation could ward off the pressures which a "mad inspiration of history" might generate is an open question; there is

[5] Curzio Malaparte, *Coup d'État: The Technique of Revolution,* S. Saunders, tr. (1932); Vincenzo Gueli, "Colpo di Stato," *Enciclopedia dal Diritto* (1960); D. J. Goodspeed, *The Conspirators: A Study of the Coup d'État* (1962).

[6] The theory of modern parties (and movements tend to be like them) has brought this out clearly; cf. the definition of party, given *op. cit.* fn. 3, p. 508 which stresses (as have others) that a party "seeks to have its leaders become rulers. . . ." Cf. also Max Weber, *Wirtschaft und Gesellschaft* (1922), part I, par. 18, and part III, ch. 4.

at least a possibility that this might be the case. But if the constitutional morality—that is to say the belief in constitutionalism as such—became corroded, as it did in ancient Rome, presumably no constitutional device would continue to function effectively.

A number of writers, notably Crane Brinton and George Pettee, undertook some years ago to distill a kind of phenomenology of the revolutionary process.[7] They concentrated on the unlimited great revolutions in which they perceived a succession of stages which do not necessarily appear in the limited revolution, such as the American one. There is, however, one aspect which seems to be common to all revolutions and that is the re-establishment of more effective government; for it is the failure of government which is at the core of the political revolution. In the American Revolution, for example, we find neither the victory of the extremists, nor the terror, nor the Thermidor, nor yet the "tyrant" dictator who re-establishes a measure of order—all of these stages of the unlimited revolution. But a strong and more effective government did emerge from the Revolution. The absence of the other phases presumably is linked to relative weakness of the ideological factor.[8]

When we say that the problem of an effective government is at the core of a political revolution we have raised the problem of the causes of revolutions. The theory of revolutions since Aristotle has been focused on such an etiology (as contrasted with recent comparative analysis of the process). Aristotle thought, it will be remembered, that disputes about equality and justice and about property were the main grounds leading to revolutionary upheavals and the overturn of governments. These disputes he analyzed in terms of the feelings and motives of the revolutionaries and of the situations which give rise to them.[9] Modern writers have followed

---

[7] Crane Brinton, *The Anatomy of Revolution* (1938); George S. Pettee, *The Process of Revolution* (1938); R. B. Merriman, *Six Contemporaneous Revolutions, 1640–1660* (1938); cf. also the much earlier work by P. Sorokin, *The Sociology of Revolutions* (1925). Later, Harold Laski, *Reflections on the Revolution of Our Time* (1943), and Sigmund Neumann, *Permanent Revolution* (1962), undertook to relate the problem to the rise of dictatorship and totalitarianism. Cf. also more recently Hannah Arendt, *On Revolution* (1962).

[8] Ideology is here used in its specific political and functional sense; for this cf. my *op. cit.*, ch. 4.

[9] Aristotle, *Politics*, Bk. V. Although usually translated as "causes" of revolutions, *aitiai* are not merely efficient causes (the prevalent meaning of "cause" today), but grounds, nor is *stasis*, strictly speaking, merely a revolution, but any kind of overturn. Aristotle's discussion at 1301b would apply

this approach, but they have substituted other "basic values" such as freedom, security, and the like for equality and justice. But no particularly useful purpose is served listing such vague general terms as causes or grounds for revolutionary sentiment; they will of course always be invoked. Being very general values motivating all politics, they will necessarily enter into any revolutionary enterprise, as real motivations, as ideological slogans, and as rationalizations. This statement is not meant to argue for a "value-free" analysis of revolutionary process; far from it. Rather, it is meant to urge that these general values be specified in the concrete situation, while the causal relationship should be stated even more abstractly in terms of conflict over values, beliefs, and interests. Only a cumulation of stresses and strains, of frustrations and deprivations will, if they accumulate, build up into a revolutionary situation.[10]

Because European revolutions in the seventeenth to nineteenth centuries were directed toward the establishment of constitutional regimes, there has been a tendency for man to assume that such must be the natural thrust of a revolution. But in point of fact, many other revolutions, including quite a few in the twentieth century, were directed toward nothing but the alteration of the political order, not infrequently in the direction of a concentration of power rather than its constitutional division. Realistically considered, a revolution carried forward by a group which wants to establish a constitutional order (a constituent group, that is) is a different process from a revolution made by proponents of a concentration of power, more particularly totally unrestrained power.

More often than not, constitutional revolutions are limited. Such were the negative revolutions of the period following the Second World War in Europe;[11] such have been some of the revolutions in the formerly colonial world. These revolutions were and are preoccupied with the problem of how to organize an effective government of some sort. But when the government so established did not prove effective—as happened, for example, in France, in the Sudan,

---

to a modern election. He puts the problem in this very broad context by asking: (1) What is the feeling? (2) What are the motives of those who make overturns? (3) Whence arise political disturbances and quarrels? (1302a).

[10] Pettee, *op. cit., passim.*

[11] Cf. my chapter, "The Political Theory of the New Democratic Constitutions," in *Constitutions and Constitutional Trends Since World War II,* Arnold J. Zurcher, ed. (1951, 1955).

and in Pakistan—such a revolution was quickly followed by another which was not (or need not be, as in France) constitutional, but rather aimed at the establishment of a military dictatorship. A well-drawn constitution may anticipate the occurrence of such a limited revolution by so constructing the amending process that developing pressures for change can find expression in suitable alterations of the existing order, even to the point of a complete revamping, as happened in Switzerland in 1874. But this procedure, too, is aimed at providing more effective government. In other words, here too the objective is the remaking of the political order.

One more word about the negative revolutions just mentioned. They have been characteristic of recent constellations in both Western and non-Western countries. In these cases, we find no positive enthusiasm for constitutionalism, let alone a new order. These revolutions, rather, occur as the result of negating, of rejecting a past political order, because of its failure, its "immoral" leadership, and other defects. In France, Italy, and Germany, as well as in Japan, such negative revolutions occurred and produced new constitutions which do not possess popular support to any significant extent. Nor do the constitutions which result from them arouse much loyalty and understanding, affection or enthusiasm.[12] In Germany, Italy, and Japan the established regimes continue to exist largely because of an absence of viable alternatives and a widespread resigned skepticism regarding all politics. Frenchmen before the collapse of the Fourth Republic almost to a man agreed in condemning its constitution, and their view of the Fifth, General de Gaulle apart, is not much more favorable. In former colonial territories, constitutions have been fashioned on alien models and without any supporting beliefs.[13] Some residual political enthusiasm is expended upon unification movements—Pan-Arabism, Pan-Africanism, and a United Europe—but the revolutionary determination which the building of such novel structures requires is limited to quite restricted circles.

In conclusion, I would say that the phenomena of political revolution and resistance are endemic in any political order, and they are closely related to each other. To avoid them or reduce their menace to a minimum, effective change has to be organized to make possible recurrent adaptations of the institutions and processes of a po-

---

[12] John D. Montgomery, *Forced to be Free* (1957), *passim*.
[13] C. J. Friedrich, *Transcendent Justice—The Religious Foundations of Constitutionalism* (1964).

litical order to evolving values, interests, and beliefs by gradual transformation of such an order. Otherwise violence will take over, sporadically as resistance at first, globally and all-engulfing as revolution in the sequel. Political orders resemble forests and families. They contain the potentiality of self-renewal, but this potentiality does not exclude the chance of failure and ultimate extinction. Revolution, when successful, signalizes such passing of a political order. It is not in itself a good, as contemporary political romantics are inclined to feel, but it is better than the death of the society which such an order is intended to serve.

2

REVOLUTION—TYPOLOGY AND PROCESS

GEORGE PETTEE

Revolution is a most wide-ranging concept, inviting varied treatment. At the center of the subject we have a kind of political event, or process, of deep interest to historians, political thinkers, economists, and social scientists that involves areas of human concern ranging from science to religion. The search for its etiological and ontological bases has been active for a long time and has resulted in a series of quite different styles or fashions of thought, of exposition, of argumentation, of theory. A new book on revolution by several authors will exhibit evidence of this.

In attempting a rather general treatment we may well start with a brief treatment of our historical experience of revolutions, and of the course of development of the thought provoked by that experience. This may not inform so much as remind. There will follow thereafter some discussion of the different types of revolutionary occurrence, of the main features of the important types, of macro-processes, of implications for method, and of the current situation.

A GLANCE AT THE HISTORICAL BACKGROUND

Revolution has been a subject of interest to political philosophy ever since political thought in our Western tradition had its origins. The intensity of the interest has varied, however. It was strong in the classical period, when revolutions in the city-states were frequent, sometimes progressive or fruitful, often destructive or regressive, and commonly bitter and bloody. Interest lagged in the Middle Ages, but was reborn when the Italian cities renewed those conditions in which factional strife and intercity rivalry provided conditions conducive to political malaise. During this period revolution served sometimes as a corrective, but often only as an aggravation. Machiavelli, in his *Discourses*, is generally preoccupied with revolution, or with its opposite, the problem of political stability. Since his time revolution and stability have always rated the attention and effort of political thinkers.

The great period of strife which we call the Reformation widened the horizon. Political thought throughout Europe was at a most intense level of activity, and with or without the label "revolution," the problem of violent change of government, its justification or its lack thereof, its occasions and its causes, lay in the center of concern for the designers of just government, and for the factional arguments of monarchomachists and antimonarchomachists, Jesuits and Calvinists and Politiques.

The thinking of the Politiques, and such doctrines as those of Althusius on the social-political structure of the state, found a laboratory in England. Here the issue of the relative power of the Crown and Parliament became crucial to the solution of the clash of churches, and to the relationship between England and Scotland. This was the situation that called forth the principles of Hobbes, that the state is always necessary and always better than factional strife, and those of Locke, that government exists by basic constitutional agreement, with a right of revolution as redress for violation of the contract. Since then also, revolution has been subject to theoretical treatment by jurisprudence as well as by political thought.

The American Revolution passed with little fresh impact on

thought, partly because the men who conducted it were well aware of Locke, and able to translate the concept of the "right of revolution" into a highly pertinent interpretation of a new situation, as they did in the Declaration of Independence. It was the first major instance of separation of a colony of Europe from European authority; America was truly a colony, that is, a people derived by migration rather than by conquest. It was also an example of a case in which a people able to expel the government of the colonial empire was also well able to govern itself.

After the American Revolution came the French Revolution. Both bore the name of revolution. Beyond that, they had little in common. The French Revolution was an explosive release of energy, in a country growing in all its powers, destroying a system of authority that had failed to grow in capacity to function as a state. It brought not one but a dozen violent shifts of power. It brought the Rights of Man, and eventually the Code Napoléon. It released a reign of terror; drew upon itself the intervention of all conservative powers, and its military rejoinder shook the whole structure of Europe. In the world of thought it put forth doctrines that echoed Locke and Rousseau, and tried to echo Montesquieu on the design of a government. It left the fundamental repudiation of privilege and the affirmation of some sort of equality so established that they could not be effectively denied thereafter, though much more than a century has passed and practice has not yet come into full stride with those theories.

The French Revolution also provoked the thought of Burke and von Gentz. They saw the shallowness of its utopianism and its sham aspects, and its destructiveness to the fibers of stability and confidence in a well-ordered society. Burke confidently downgraded the physical power of Revolutionary France, seeing the wreck of its economy in its credit structure, and failing to see its booming growth of energy. But he also saw and lamented that "in ability, in dexterity, and in the distinctness of their views, the Jacobins are our superiors." (Second Letter on the Proposal for a Peace with the Regicide Directory of France.) After Napoleon had departed the scene and something called "Restoration" had occurred, there was left a strong residue of conviction that revolution can be necessary and justified, though also that its excesses can be deplorable.

There followed shortly the succession of revolutions in Spanish America that made all the area from Mexico to the Argentine free of rule by Spain. By 1830 there was a new round of outbreaks in Europe, and in 1848 a more pronounced one showed how powerful were the forces whose political character was *not* effectively geared to the half-modernized governments of that time.

On the side of political action there was an advance of parliamentary forms of government. This was overshadowed, however, by the implementation of nationalism, especially in Italy and in Germany. As an idea, nationalism was not a well-rooted branch of political theory; it was rather a necessary replacement for the Divine Right of Kings. It had the force of reality; a national people could be a new basis of political accounts. The growth of nationalism throughout Europe did as much to liquidate the stubborn residues of feudalism as did the idea of democracy.

Out of the experiences of 1830 and 1848 there arose seriously analytic considerations of the causes of revolution, and of a stable political system immune to revolution. The idea of stability had been dealt with at length by Aristotle and by Machiavelli, but not in the context of the industrial revolution. The idea of revolution similarly had lacked the insights afforded by the changes of property and production organization that occurred in the late eighteenth and early nineteenth centuries. Marx, Engels, and others wrote perceptive short historical accounts of several crises, as we would call them, in the middle of the century. At the same time Disraeli and his government were constructing an articulated system of power that made the English people a major organ of the English State and assured the State's continuing responsiveness. This work had started far earlier of course, as Namier has done much to show (*Crossroads of Power*, 1962, and other works on British political development), and it still awaited Bagehot to explain the design after the construction.

Marx went on, of course, to create a vast ideological superstructure founded on materialism as philosophic base, on the dialectics of action and reaction in historical sequence, on the role of the proletariat as the embodiment of virtue and enlightenment, and on revolution as the handmaid of progress.

This construction contained elements well suited to the needs and purposes of Lenin. Marxism was for him something like a staff college, where he learned to analyze a situation and mastered the tactics of revolutionary action. Here emerged the revolutionary technique, which could be combined with the intrinsic occasion and purpose for a true revolution, or could be separated from it as an effective instrument in a power struggle for the world, with little regard for the merit of an occasion for its use. Russia had a revolution, the greatest since the great French Revolution. It was preceded by a decay of effectiveness in government comparable to that in the Old Regime in France. Lenin was skillful and successful in seizing power, and then in consolidating the one-party Communist system, which hardened into Stalinism.

The period between the wars had much to teach about revolutions. The First World War had brought a great revolution in Russia and less drastic ones in several other nations, including Germany, Austria, Hungary, and Turkey. Soon there was the Kuomintang victory in China. Lawrence of Arabia had raised a revolution of national liberation among the Arabs, and found the truth that the expulsion of alien rulers can be accomplished by a people long before they can rule themselves. That lesson had been writ large in Latin America earlier, but it was not read and understood. It is still being written, and perhaps we have begun to read it. Meanwhile such writers as Laski went on examining the principles of revolution and finding the argument for the justice of revolution inescapable, given the possibilities of failure by an old regime and of lethargy and stupidity in a ruling class. One important new observation was made however, by Duguit and by Seldes. Each of them pointed out, though in different contexts and different idioms, that the modern industrial state is simply too delicate an organism to permit revolution à la France. The disruption of the modern social services would bring a paralyzing economic collapse that would make the luxury of such violence and disorder as in the classic revolutions impossible.

The last three decades have produced a new mass of experience, and new realms of thought. Hitler conducted a revolution in Germany, using the opportunity afforded by the great economic depression, and Nazism thoroughly alienated all those who had clung to the doctrine that revolution is probably just and necessary. The prosecution of revolutionary tactics by the Communists was all too evidently focused on world power, and all too evidently separate from the intrinsic needs or causes of historical revolution. Because of these obvious abuses of revolutionary technique, modern thinkers are more willing to lend a hand to the analysis of problems of counterinsurgency than their immediate predecessors were. Revolution seems farther away than ever before in those most advanced nations which, according to Marxism, should be most ripe for it. The means and methods of stable constitutional government, adaptable to changing problems, with an increasingly well-integrated linkage of government to people, seem to be making headway. Russian and Chinese Communists still conduct subversion, but not in full harmony. There are few books that offer clear theoretical propositions in this situation, but vast activities are predicated on the feasibility of conducting affairs generally in nations, and between them, so that all necessary measures can be taken. Weak regimes exist in many places, but they are not left to their own resources, economic or intellectual. One of the deepest tenets of the time is that the old-fashioned revolution is no longer needed as "the locomotive of history," that revolution leads only to tyranny, and that constitutional democracy need not fail. The Chinese Communists of course feel differently. The ideas that win will be those that win in the world of action.

TYPES

In order to discuss revolutions more clearly it is essential to define some classes. For initial purposes the following types serve fairly well to separate likes from unlikes.

A type that may be called the private palace revolution occurred many times in earlier history, but is less common today. The story told by Shakespeare of the murder of Duncan by Macbeth, and Macbeth's succession, is an illustration. It was conducted within one building; it involved very few people; the public had no information of it until after the fact. The general cultural circumstances were permissive, but the causes lay within the personalities of Macbeth and his wife.

Another type is the public palace revolution. These have occurred many times from our oldest to our most recent history. The event is more elaborate and much larger in scale than in the private type. Typically, there may be movements of troops about a city and a small battle at the palace. The public knows that something is going on, but it did not initiate the event, and takes little part in it. The causation is involved with economic and political issues, but at the level of organized factions. It is not linked to major economic and social contradictions. The new rulers are not altogether outsiders to the prevailing ruling class; and the new regime and old regime are not very different. Although the term *coup d'état* is used rather loosely, its most frequent and significant manifestations belong to this public palace revolution type. One need not look far away in time for good examples. They have occurred in Korea, in Vietnam, in Iraq, in Syria, in Brazil, and in several other countries.

Next in significance, of the recognized types, is the rebellion of an area against rule by the government of another country. Such a movement arises from large-scale social factors, involves large-scale military action, or at least the realistic threat of such action, and strong popular support. It is generally regarded as right and just. It reflects a considerable cultural advance by the rebellious people. A people submissive to foreign rule has become hostile to such rule, able to defy it, capable of expelling it, and to some unspecified degree, capable of providing a government for itself.

It is difficult to think of a case of rebellion that was not preceded either by the conquest of the rebellious people, or by true migratory colonization. Conquest is seldom mentioned in the context of revolution, yet it would seem as revolutionary, in the nonmilitary sense, for the conquered, as is rebellion for the liberated. Since history is predominantly told by the winners in such events, there is a bias here. We know of the conquest of Peru from Spanish sources rather than from Inca sources, and the violent revolution that was inflicted on the Incas passes as an incident of Spanish expansion. So for Clive in India, or Cecil Rhodes in South Africa. Yet these imposed revolutions are important, for they measure the condition of a people at one time as subjugable, just as their rebellion at a later time measures their emergence to a higher level of competence and activity.

The most important of the recognized types, however, is the type of which the French and the Russian Revolutions are the classic examples. They may be called the great national revolutions. One could almost regard one of them as a rebellion without spatial separation of the rebellious from the former rulers. Changes have occurred; a people that was subjugable has grown out of its passivity. A ruling class, separated from a formerly passive people by the privileges of power and property and culture, has remained isolated, has decayed in function, in leadership capacity, and in motivation toward measures needed for the growth and advancement of the society or community. Here we have a mass phenomenon, a people rejecting its government and the ruling class. It moves by plan, but the events constantly contradict the plans, and the results can be measured only long after the event. The social and political structure is drastically reorganized. Not every law is changed, but very great changes in the laws do occur, and public law is almost entirely changed. There is widespread violence, acute bitterness, brutality, and intense mass emotion. The process is in some respects like the business cycle, a mass action by a great number of individuals, with the course and outcome on a basis that is statistically and historically logical, *but not understood by the participants.*

There is one more class of historic event which is rarely mentioned in discussion of revolution, but which may deserve an important place in such a discussion. This I will call, for the sake of a label, a systemic revolution. The "system" referred to is not the internal social and political system; rather it is the system of state organization, the type state, for a wider human area than a single state.

Within Western history we have had several distinct state systems. In the earliest historical times there were tribes, and at quite an early time there were empires, originating in the Near or Middle East. Then there arose, in Greece and in nearby Asia Minor, and elsewhere about the Mediterranean littoral, the city-state. There were numerous examples of this type of political organization. The rise of the city-states reached a phase at which the Empire of Persia attempted to suppress the Greek cities. Persia was defeated. So for a time, some centuries before, and a little time after, there was the city-state system. Its strength, its progress, its growth, all led to conditions in which its supersession was inevitable. Great processes of change, with great wars and much violence, intervened between the time when the city-state flourished and the next time of stability, under the Augustan settlement of the Roman Empire. Thucydides recognized these civil wars as the first great revolutionary wars. They came in series, because the sides did not well understand what they were fighting about. So there were several Peloponnesian Wars, followed by several Punic Wars, and several Roman "social wars."

The change from the state system at the time of Pericles to that at the time of Augustus stands as the first great systemic revolution of which we know much detail. The second is the one we call "the fall of Rome." The third, oddly, we know as "the Renaissance and

the Reformation." The fourth we think of mainly by its wars, World
War I and World War II.

For each of these it is easy to identify an *ancien régime,* and
(except for the last case) easy to identify a postrevolutionary system.
Each involved exceptionally severe wars, recognized later as of civil
war character in many respects. Each was conducted to a great extent, including the conduct of its wars, under ideas and doctrines
that had little relevance to its main political effect. Each affected a
human area recognized as constituting a cultural community, though
a larger and less intense one than has generally been organized as a
single state (with the exception of the case of Rome). In each case,
a state system stood as the political order for the larger community,
as a single state may stand for a smaller and more closely knit area.

CHARACTERISTICS

The classes are not absolute, they make a continuum. Those
most typical of their own classes are markedly different. Those on
the margins are close to the nearest specimens in the next class.
There is a need to classify, but neither need nor reason for rigidity.

If the classification makes sense, then the characteristic features
of a revolution will vary a great deal according to class. The characteristic traits of the great national revolutions such as the French
or the Russian are more complex and significant than those of conquest, rebellion, or palace revolution.

Given a revolution and the hypothesis of social causation, we have
first to scrutinize the prerevolutionary society. This is not as easy
as it sounds and historians have given rather scanty effort to it. But
we do have the ordinary record of what may have seemed either a
dull period, as in France, or a period much concerned with ex-
traneous matters, as in Russia. In retrospect, however, a great deal
of memoir material is produced, and is added to evidence from
sources ignored in their own time, and recognized only by hindsight. Various men did say in France that the system was decrepit.
Madelin quotes Calonne, in the sharp language of a good policy
memorandum:

> France is a kingdom composed of separate states and countries,
> with mixed administrations, the provinces of which know nothing of
> each other, where certain districts are completely free from burdens
> the whole weight of which is borne by others, where the richest class
> is the most lightly taxed, where privilege has upset all equilibrium,

> where it is impossible to have any common rule or common will:
> necessarily it is a most imperfect kingdom, very full of abuses, and
> in its present condition impossible to govern.
> —Louis Madelin, *The French Revolution*, p. 11.

This is a description of the decay that created the opportunity for
new ideas to come in all at once, without earlier assimilation. Also,
note well, the faults in France that Calonne emphasized were most
definitely absent from the restored regime after the revolution was
over. The sheer disorder and the lack of power of reform had been
most thoroughly done away with. There is less than due emphasis
in the histories on these aspects of the revolution.

Less specifically, in a prerevolutionary society there is a general
alienation of public feeling. The state structure has failed to change
with the times; and regions and classes alike feel antagonism to the
government and to each other. Anomie is a good short name for it.
But anomie implies a lack of spirit. The lack of spirit is more apparent than real, as becomes all too evident when the backed-up
flood is released.

Low synergism, or high entropy, could also serve as terms for the
condition. The state of society is one of general frustration or cramp.
The system of laws and administration does not make it easy to do
constructive things. Enterprise is stifled. And enterprise is there; it
is not a passive or inert society. Among the important observations
is the fact that there is not less but more wealth than formerly,
though less than there should be. There is also more talent and
more education than formerly, though less than there should be and
less well employed than it should be. The society is ready for greater
economic and cultural progress, and needs a better order. Meanwhile the overt symptoms emerge, including the transfer of the
loyalty of the intellectuals, expressed in satire and criticism. The
Cahiers of 1789 and the elections for the Third Estate expressed the
downright depth of feeling.

In the same period, before the revolution, when the need for
reform is widely felt and widely recognized, various efforts at reform are made. But the issues involved are complex and contro-
versial, the sources of favorable power are prevented from making
the necessary changes. Needs are not clearly formulated or their
formulation gains little support. Political leaders of great talent and
energy appear, but they lose the support of the ruling groups and, in
turn, the support of the formal source of authority, the King or the

Czar. Strafford in England, Turgot and Necker in France, Stolypin in Russia, and others, all had careers that proved that the old system was past reform, even for a man of the highest caliber. While the legend is strongly laid that all prerevolutionary authorities are inept, incompetent, stupid, or frivolous, the record is also clear that the system did not fail without the struggle of one or a few great men to save it, and their defeat.

The failure of the great prerevolutionary reformer-conservative is of course a very important detail. This, if anything, measures the decrepitude of the ruling system, and the disparity between its effectiveness and the activities required.

Sometime after the defeat of the major reformer comes a breakdown of the state. A revolution may have been predicted by this stage; yet the real start comes unannounced. The incapacity of the state to deal with some simple fact brings a crisis; the demand that something be done reveals that some new agency must be created, and suddenly men know that a revolution has begun. In France, the financial breakdown of the treasury brought a need for new fiscal measures, so the Estates General had to be called, after more than a century without it. The immediate bargaining between the powers, the Estates and the Crown, brought the order for dissolution; and this order, in turn, brought the rebellious Tennis Court Oath, which Brinton identified as the real beginning of the revolution.

Just after a revolution has begun, and the participants have become aware of its onset, there has been a sort of era of good feeling. Enthusiasm and optimism and friendly feelings and mutual congratulations on the happy state of affairs are expressed on all sides. This lasts until urgent problems present themselves, new controversies emerge, and the struggle for policy turns into a struggle for power. The time of good feeling is brief.

Thereafter there is an extraordinarily energetic ideological period. The revolution has all the marks of being highly doctrinaire. The question is, Just what doctrine does it follow? In retrospect there is far more than enough doctrine, and an active, intellectually kinetic swarming of ideas. This ideological life serves the purpose of examining all relevant ideas, experimenting with many possible systems. Every possible speech is made. The influence of ideas is quite apparent afterward, but this is partly because hindsight has enabled us to select the influential speeches and writings and ignore the others. The French Revolution, with its succession of factions, its series of constitutions, and its numerous palace revolutions or *coups d'état,* is the best example of this. If they were all disciples of Rousseau or of the Encyclopedists, still they guillotined each other.

Every one of the great revolutions has seen more than one fundamental *coup d'état* to effect a shift in power. There were only a few of these in the English case, though Pride's Purge was clearly one. There were few again in the Russian Revolution, though there was a near success by Kornilov before the Bolshevik coup in October, and earlier, the Soviets had exercised power simultaneously with the regular government. In France there was a long succession of power shifts, of which the great coup of the 9th Thermidor ending the Reign of Terror, and the 18th Brumaire, when Bonaparte seized power, are only the most famous.

These mark a condition not anticipated in the first glow of success. The conduct of the revolution has become a subject for wide and bitter divergence. The illegal seizure of power is now a tactical measure. Civil war is at least latent, if not acute, and there may be several. Issues are regional as well as national, and where they are regional the territorial basis for civil war is good. So England fought a long and complex civil war, with established fronts through long winters; France fought a most savage civil war in the Vendée; the Russian Bolsheviks had to fight civil wars all around, in the Ukraine, in Siberia, in the Caucasus.

Civil wars have one certain effect: there is a winner and a loser. The winner retains the means to enforce his power over the loser and the terms are unconditional surrender. Some of the losers emigrate, some are dead, some are jailed, and some are pacified. There are many factors that can distort the result, but generally the side that can prove it is the stronger can win, and to the victor belong the spoils.

A period of foreign intervention frequently accompanies the civil wars. England and to some extent Russia are exceptions to this rule. In the case of England, Richelieu had enough to do in France and in Germany without attempting adventures in England, and most of the rest of Europe was busy with the Thirty Years' War during the early years of the Great Rebellion. In Russia, the Bolsheviks were in power for a year before the Armistice ended World War I. The victorious Western allies had ample means to intervene in Russia in 1919, but little clarity of policy or motivation to do so. There was intervention, but not to much effect. France was quite a different case. The revolution in France challenged the foundations of all the European order. The concept of nationalism was useful; but republicanism, the abolition of feudalism, regicide, and expropriations were scandalous and subversive. France found herself at war with all Europe from 1792 intermittently until 1815. Those wars made the revolution more European, and less exclusively French. And they served to motivate the organization of effort that left France the most unified of nations.

During civil wars there is a great deal of violence, and much of it is not conducted by the rules of civilized warfare. Civilians murder troops; ambush is commonplace; conspiracies are everywhere, and are suspected even where they don't exist. Methods of the police state are added to the partisan or guerrilla warfare; the argument for terror and counterterror is raised and followed. The system of investigation and trial is overloaded, and special courts and procedures of summary nature are instituted. The French Revolutionary Tribunal and the Russian Cheka are matched in other revolutionary crises, as in Spain in 1936. This period of partisan strife and terror contributes to the strength of the apparatus available to the victorious regime thereafter, and for the readiness of all concerned to abate the struggle.

At last there is a postrevolutionary society. The new regime is securely founded, and has proven its ability to make good its power by force. The fulfillment of a revolutionary plan is only started, if ever there was one. The greatest changes are the elimination of a vast mass of old abuses and old barriers to economic life, the reshuffling of property, and the replacement of nearly all the former ruling class by a new one. It distorts the point to call this a ruling class. It is surely the class composed of those who take part in ruling the society, but it may be drawn from various classes by any other definition. At any rate, the new men have made good their claims in a stiff competition; they are not there because their fathers were. Then there can be a restoration, as in France, but the restoration is only of an apparent form of government. The new linkage between government and society, once established, cannot be quickly done away. A regime in the *old* form can more or less govern the *new* state, but the ills that Calonne described cannot be brought back.

When the revolution is past men are not hesitant to describe it in definite terms. They recount its causes and purposes, identify the ideas that influenced it, see the result of the trial of power, the successes and mistakes of leaders. There is one difficulty. They go on writing books about the revolution, and as soon as there are many books there are many variations in the account given. Paul Farmer's study of the history of the French Revolution as written by French historians constitutes one of the most important observations on revolution that can be made. He shows that each of the successive schools of French opinion that have existed since it occurred has produced a different version of it, and that an objective history, therefore, has yet to be written. Perhaps it needs greater events than the Revolution to release the enduring tensions that distort interpretation. But history is conducted in extensional life and reality, and the simply true history may well be a Utopian illusion, without at all implying that history is thereby devalued. One of the most important aspects of the French Revolution or any other event is, for us, its effect on ourselves and our circumstances. So we may still find history useful, though it go on changing forever.

The great changes of state system have not been type classified in any familiar school of thought. However, when examined they have surprisingly many of the traits that might be expected.

In each of them there has been a mighty series of wars. In the first, those wars went on from the time of Pericles to the time of Augustus; then there were the wars we call the barbarian invasions. The third systemic change was the religious wars of the Reformation, and in the most recent case we have, so far, World War I and World War II.

Each of the systemic revolutions started from a well-defined general political system of a very wide human area. In some respects the cultural level of the whole area was similar. The area involved in the revolution has been cognate with the type of culture area with which Spengler and Toynbee have been concerned. Only in the case of the Roman Empire was a state system established in the form of a single formally organized state and government.

In each case the need for a change of system was somewhat apparent before the change occurred. Thucydides was filled with a sense of the vast and tragic alteration of the Greek community in the Peloponnesian Wars. He also saw the curious lack of decision in the first war, and the unrecognized, unresolved tensions that required the second phase of what he insisted was a single war divided only by a "treacherous truce." So with the Punic Wars, they were fought in series because the issue was not understood in the first one.

With the social wars of Rome too, only the succession of several wars could bring a final settlement.

The last phase of the classical systemic revolution that submerged the city-state in the Roman Empire has been very well portrayed by Ronald Syme, in his too little known book *The Roman Revolution* (1939). The evidence he offers shows how a new state arose, displacing the city of Rome itself as a community, as a state, and as a government.

The exceptional case of course is the fall of Rome. That has been given a degree of attention as great as it deserves, but scarcely yet in the manner of modern analytic social science. There was of course a decay in Rome, in discipline and capability. There was also a rise of capability in the barbarians; they were more formidable than the Gauls, whom Caesar defeated so handily. Yet they were of lower organization and technology than Rome. (A striking fact is that, though the Romans made bricks throughout the period of the Empire, medieval Europe was without new brick for centuries.)

So there was a systemic revolution. It adapted a state system suitable to the new peoples planted on the remains of Rome, from Britain to the Balkans. This system, which we call feudalism, linked the administration of land, to the administration of territory; *dominium* was what we think of as property ownership and government combined, and it was qualified by the higher dominium of an echelon of power, from baron to count to duke to king to emperor. There was also the parallel power of the Church. This is not the place for any extended treatment. It is only necessary to identify this as a state system, different from Rome, and different because its peoples could not operate the Roman one, and needed one fitted to their competence.

The Renaissance and Reformation is the set of words with which we obscure the revolution or transition from the medieval to the modern state system. Before it there was the *ancien régime,* the medieval system; after it there was the Europe of the Baroque, the Europe of the Peace of Westphalia, the Europe of Cromwell, of Richelieu, of Shakespeare, of Galileo and Newton, and of Bodin and Locke and Hobbes.

These great changes have not been classified as have the great national revolutions, and they have been immune to some of the tendencies exhibited in interpreting the others. It has not been charged that they were planned and executed by a conspiratorial faction. They have not been conducted by men preaching relevant theoretical doctrine. Not that theoretical doctrine was absent, it was rife enough in all cases. The speeches in Thucydides, the memoirs of Caesar, the vast outpourings of books and pamphlets of the eighteenth century, and the flood of divergent doctrines in this century are ideological and doctrinaire and theoretical, but for the most part they do not even talk about the major effect of all the events with which they are concerned. It was only long afterward that men recognized that a new system had replaced Rome or that the nation-state was a new thing replacing the system of medieval Europe.

The great civil wars of the unrecognized systemic revolutions have had many of the traits that set other great civil wars apart from ordinary wars between states. They surpass international wars in severity and brutality and in the degree of exhaustion of the loser. They are marked by technical and tactical advances, with major changes in the military art. Thucydides noted all these characteristics, and Caesar and Theodoric and Gustavus confirmed them. They are marked also by confusion about ends; announced strategic objectives turn out to be unimportant, and the mightiest efforts are spent for ends that are defined only afterward. The close is the complete defeat of the loser, with formal revolution imposed; that is, the removal and replacement of the government and the ruling class. As in the American Civil War, the victory of the North settled a question about the system of sovereignty, so did the defeat of Hitler, and so, had it occurred, would his victory have, also. Further, and again this accords with Thucydides, the absolute power exerted in the wars is astonishingly great. Athens and Sparta each put more power into the struggle with each other than all Greece together had displayed against Persia. The Roman system, in its last social wars, fought both sides in wars greater than the Punic Wars. The wars of religion in the revolution called the Reformation were civil wars of Europe, and were greater and more radical than any wars before them. In all of them the establishment, when peace returned at last, was something new, so different from the conscious purposes that those gave no hint of what had really happened.

It is almost commonplace today to affirm that we are in a world revolution, or that the world wars had the character of civil wars. The only large-scale theory for a world revolution, however, has been the Marxist one, and the rejection of that theory leaves the recognition of world revolution without articulate explanation. To relate it to a class of such occurrences at least invites a free intellectual run of analytic observation and analysis and opens the way to theory.

This world revolution of the present is the first in which all the world has been engaged. By implication of its politics it is bringing a new state system. By implication of technology, it must also bring a general peace. And a stable peace must mean giant changes in the capacity for change without war. The work has already gone far. The great actors on the scene were typical nation-states as late as 1914, and already they are cosmopolitan states of far larger scale, the U.S. and the U.S.S.R., with China looming as another, and the fourth beginning to coalesce out of the old system in Europe. These greater states do not promise peace of themselves; but that becomes a necessity, and a promise. The late John von Neuman offered as clear a version of this necessity and promise as has been seen in his article "Can We Survive Technology?" (*Fortune* magazine, June 1955).

MACRO-PROCESS AND REVOLUTION

The idea of a great political reaction (meant as in the term "chemical reaction," not as "reactionary") not understood by its participants is a strange one to modern rationalistic thought. Does it really demand a greater strain on the mind, however, than does the notion of vast economic changes not understood by their participants? Other large historical effects have occurred in the same fashion. A. L. Lowell pointed out (in a paper delivered at the Harvard Tercentenary) that many great movements, ranging from the settlement of the American West to the development of the British parliamentary system of government, have occurred without conscious design.

The role of organized political units in such a process is apt to be confused and obscure. But we can recall that even a national revolution draws factional lines to some extent in territorial terms. The one great civil war in a modern federal state has often been called "the war between the states." If a multistate system stood in enough need of change to bring on civil wars of the greater community, it would naturally take the form of a war between the states. And wars between states are frequently so ill-directed as to miss their points. So the First World War failed and its result was only a pretense at resumption of the status quo, so far as the state system was concerned. It was followed by the Second World War, in which Germany, under Hitler, undertook the role of revolutionist among the states, with deep miscomprehension by those who tried to explain it as a German revolution. This brought results that we see now in the dissolution of all the colonial empires, the Common Market in Europe, NATO, and an expanded American role in world affairs.

The idea of the blind process is not to be mistaken as a claim that history is inherently irrational. As with the other examples of such processes, they need not remain incomprehensible. Pareto chose this problem as the focus of his attention, as did Vico; and, if one considers it, Aristotle and Rousseau and others really did also. If we can understand and master, or moderate, the business cycle, we can understand and moderate other processes of complex change as well. Nor need this fall into a callow optimism. The interpretation of history would have been easy if all things done were done by men fully aware of and responsible for the consequences of their actions. It is not so easy as that. The difference is not an absolute one; it means enormously greater efforts and it means imperfect rather than perfect success. That may still be a plausible basis for strenuous effort and cautious hope.

The idea that man and society are in the relation of a microcosm to a macrocosm has become fairly familiar. Certain features of this relationship are different from that of any other however. This is the only case in nature, so far as we know, where the seat of awareness is in the micro-entity, and the orientation of attention is therefore a unique one. Essentially the sense perceptions are those of the individual, not of society, and the activity of ratiocination is in the individual, not in the mass. Man can observe and analyze society, not vice versa. And society is the only object of man's attention that directly comprises himself.

This requires the qualification that arises from Mannheim's pithy comment: "There is no such thing as purely individual thought." Man is social, or he would not have a society to watch and study. And his act of knowing, like that of the physicists, involves interaction between subject and object that can set a restraint on his reception of knowledge. (Heisenberg's principle.) But the obverse of that principle is present also, with ultimately positive effect. Perception can interfere with reality only because knowledge can and does

have a real link to reality, and this opens at least as many and as
wide vistas as it closes. We have always known in a vaguer sense that
man cannot study society without changing it through other chan-
nels than the immediate feedback from observer to observed; the
observer, as reporter, changes the thought and action of all who
hear.

Yet the acceptance of a macro-process that follows a logic of its
own that is not the logic in the minds of the men who are its
participants is one of the most resisted of concepts. Our economics
has accepted it, but our political thought is still written largely in a
rationalistic and idealistic idiom to which the notion is foreign.

To summarize: If the world depression of the 1930's was a
macro-process with an economic logic that was not understood well
in 1930, yet was accessible to study and analysis, then is it not sensible to consider the French Revolution also a macro-process, with
a political and social logic, also understandable only after the event?

The idea that justice and freedom are somehow inevitably served
by a great revolution is quite compatible with this. The situation of
other great mass phenomena that yield apparently good and logical
results is similar. The business cycle is an exception in that there
have been many of them, and most of them only discharged some
accumulated difficulties without a major improvement of structure.
Again the analogy holds. Any type of revolution that we can show
to be cyclical in nature may be said to have failed. Plato regarded
such a cyclical and recurrent mass action as having little merit. But
we have not regarded the great revolutions as cyclical. And the
business cycle and the cyclical revolutions do serve to illustrate the
epistemological relation, a mass social action conducted by men who
understand it, if ever, only after later study.

IMPLICATIONS FOR METHOD

This description of types and of mechanisms is not meant
to be taken as rigid or conclusive. Any classification system serves to
assist analysis and further study, and having done so it may always
prove open to correction or improvement. However, even the sim-
plest classification carries some implications for method on the one
hand, and for the analysis of causes and mechanism on the other.

If revolutions occur in the classes described, and somewhat in the
manner described, then the procedure to advance our understanding might include, among other things, the following:

The theoretical studies on revolution should be confronted with the historical studies, to see if the reactions described by the historians can be fitted to the models structured by the theorists.

Several good examples of the same class should be examined to see if one exhibits details not observed in the other, or if two or several afford a richer basis for analysis than one. Several might be used especially as a means of eliminating what might seem a key phenomenon in one but is absent, or unimportant, in another.

The theories of the nature of society and man, the vessel and the material of revolutions, should be confronted with the facts and theories of revolution. This will enable us to discover the contradictions or confirmations between the two sets of theories and, by coordinating them, clarify both.

From revolutions of one class we should look to revolutions of another class to see if the differences in the process support the distinction of classification. Discrepancies should be targets of attention.

The terminology should be redressed to reduce the obscuration of the essential by the peripheral concerns of those who selected older terms.

Each individual situation should be examined in as wide a range as possible in the study of any revolution, to permit the discovery of joint factors of causation among supposedly disparate elements.

In the study of revolution we should take what men say as evidence of what they think they are doing, but not as a true indicator of the forces at work, or of the causes and effects of the process.

THE MORE RECENT PICTURE

From the time of the American and French Revolutions to about 1940 it would seem fair to say that the general opinion in the West was that revolution is good when needed, and that the conditions in which it is needed can occur fairly often. There were voices to the contrary, of course, but they were at least seemingly outnumbered.

From about 1940 on, there has been slowly increasing doubt of this belief. (Cf. Hannah Arendt: *On Revolution*.) The supporters of revolution are now little heard in the advanced West. The great concern is with the countermeasures to revolution as an instrument of power politics, and with the means by which states and governments may be brought along most quickly and effectively to make revolution unnecessary. There is a strong emphasis on military strength as the immediate means of defending the existing regimes; and also considerable awareness that this may be overemphasis. But there is much agreement that revolution should be prevented or forestalled.

As discussed earlier, several great factors in the experience of the last few decades have contributed to this shift from pro- to anti-revolution in Western thinking.

The Communists, under Moscow's rigid control, have made the mechanics of revolution more and more a center of attention, and drifted toward forgetfulness of the end that was supposed to justify the means. So (with Vaihinger), the means became more and more predominant over the end.

Then came Hitler to exploit all of the tactics of revolutionary action in Germany, and later in the external crises of Austria and Czechoslovakia, and finally to bring against himself a coalition that could defeat him. In the meantime Nazism earned a place in universal anathema for its brutality, its ruthlessness, and its ever renewed breaches of trust.

After the defeat of Hitler there was a succession of Communist coups in many places. In Romania they took control and established themselves by the overwhelming power leverage of Russian dominance; in Czechoslovakia they resorted to a *coup d'état* of the most skillful and most cynical kind. If revolution occurs when its causes are too powerful to deny, and if it results in a fuller life and greater freedom, and therefore must be granted some justice, these were not revolutions. Obversely, if this is what revolution means today, then revolution must be opposed, for it is only the tactical means toward the world domination of Communism, and the one-party police state.

Another major phenomenon of our time is the great number of former colonial areas that have been made independent of their European rulers. This too has adversely affected the value set on revolution. These revolutions have brought a few countries into apparently capable constitutional and democratic political life; but many others have shown all of the characteristics of states that may need revolutions again, or may undergo a series of palace revolutions, or may fall into Communist dictatorships. Several have already had more than one major *coup d'état*.

What has emerged has not been what the West would regard as

mature political life. The implication is strong that there are several levels of political acumen or maturity that may be found in human societies. The three major levels are:

> The low level of political development at which a people can be conquered and ruled by an outside power,
> The level at which a people are able to expel foreign rule or able to make it a fruitless enterprise to try to bring them to order under such rule,
> The level at which they are capable of orderly democratic government within constitutional order and with effective progress in adaptation to problems of national development.

The United States stepped directly from colonial states into effective self-government; the former Spanish colonies were less successful; and the failures of some of the newer nations have pointed up the great need for political progress. The problem has a similarity to that posed by Rostow of the stages of economic development, and though we try to solve both problems, we have just begun to discover what it is we need to know.

The case of Vietnam is an especially anxious one for the United States at this time. The press has expressed the ambivalence of American feeling; the difficulty is extreme. As the military well know, a strongly directed guerrilla movement can make good its guerrilla being against forces that are much larger; something like ten to one is the ratio needed to crush it. Therefore, the persistent maintenance of a guerrilla operation is poor proof of the consensus of the feeling of the people. It is a part of the mechanical tactical system of aggressive subversive revolution, and its survival does not justify it. But to suppress it requires the exercise of the means of repression, and these in turn fail to prove the merit of the governmental system that successfully employs them. The mind of the man of good will has trouble with this dilemma, and consequently wishes for neutralization, or for other means of making the problem go away. Here once more we have a fundamental loss of faith that revolution is or can be a good thing in a world where no people can conduct a revolution unto itself, free of the concern and intervention of other powers.

Revolution is a fascinating subject of political thought, in part because it is rare compared to the bulk of political experience. It is also fascinating because it is significant of the nature of man, of communities of men, and of politics, in ways that are not otherwise

accessible to observation. The study of politics without the study of
revolution would be like the study of geology without that of volcanic action.

Even when it leads to the "right of revolution," the study comes
back to the search for political forms and methods that would make
revolution unnecessary and impossible. This is so even for the
Marxists, whose Communist dictatorship is justified in theory by the
fact that it will lead to the classless society, the elimination of injustice and social tensions, and a stable system.

The old answers have ceased to serve. Once it could be held that
democratic forms would be sufficient. We know now that it takes
far more than that. Copies or variations of the U.S. Constitution
or the British parliamentary system or other republican forms can
be set up quite easily in societies living in what was called above
the second of the three levels; and they can prove as subject to
recurring revolution as was the Greek city. Systems that follow the
advice of Plato and of Machiavelli, and seek a balance of monarchy,
aristocracy, and democracy in a more stable republic, can prove as
incapable of growth as the inert monarchy of France. The ability
to join a complexity of frequently conflicting interests into a unity
of aim, of need, and of action is something not implanted by a docu-
ment nor by agreement of a conference. It is in part what Elliott
calls "constitutional morality," and we do not yet know fully why
it is found in one state and not in another.

However, this new world in which we live, though strange, has
aspects of great promise. We can compare the record of serious
"reform" of the last fifteen years with any earlier time, and the
contrast is great. Once it was impossible to lower the American
tariff. Once it was impossible to make any change in the status of
Negroes. Where thirty years ago the nations of Europe were raising
ever higher tariff barriers, there is now the Common Market. Where
there were colonial administrations, there are self-governing communities, set free without war in most cases. Where socialists and
capital interests once opposed each other in rigid ideological postures, there is now a matter-of-fact consideration of which industries
should and which should not be nationalized, as in Britain. And even
in Russia, where Pasternak was not allowed to accept the Nobel
Prize, Yevtushenko and Solzhenitzin can now publish, and the Russian Communist Party has partially abdicated from the dictatorial
leadership of world communism. We live with one great problem

yet: Was the Second World War the last necessary war of the revolution in the world order in which we have lived since 1914, or only the penultimate one? The technology that has made such a revolution possible and necessary has gone so fast that it is making it equally necessary to finish the business by new rules, without the lazy convenience of a war. We will live for a while yet without knowing if the ending will be a happy success or a climactic tragedy. This, of course, is the dramatic condition, the condition that man has to live in.

3

REVOLUTION AS A PROBLEM
IN THE PHILOSOPHY OF HISTORY

PAUL SCHRECKER

Born in the field of astronomy, the term revolution first took on the historico-political meaning that we assign to it among the forerunners of the great French Revolution of 1789, which still stands as the true prototype of a political event deserving the name "revolution." Seventeenth-century writers called the conflict between King and Parliament which ended with Cromwell as Protector either a civil war or a rebellion: and what the English call their Glorious Revolution of 1688 hardly deserves the name. Montesquieu, Rousseau, and Mirabeau are responsible for the first appearance in modern times not only of the thing but also of the name, and this origin is by no means accidental. So long as religion was recognized as the

34

sphere which dominated all civilization and from which all others received their supreme laws, there could be no true revolution. No shock to the foundations of society, however radical, could be justified except through authorization by the divine law, which, in itself, was considered unshakable and unchangeable.

Even after 1789 the term revolution was, at first, restricted to certain political and social upheavals, and was scarcely ever applied to analogous changes produced in other branches of civilization. Only very gradually, *via facti* rather than through analysis of the analogy, and metaphorically rather than through recognition of a common structure, certain sudden and radical changes that were encountered in the histories of religion, of letters, of political economy, of the arts, of science, and of language began to be called revolutions or revolutionary. At first, the application of the same term to such diverse events as the posting of Luther's theses and the first performance of Victor Hugo's *Hernani,* the *Discourse on Method* and the *Declaration of Independence,* the so-called Industrial Revolution and the introduction of nonrepresentative painting seemed based only on a superficial impression. It needed a searching analysis using the critical method of philosophy of history to transform the analogy into a well-established theory. The problem is complex, and heretofore the philosophers, if they have not ignored it, have at least often treated it in a somewhat haughty and uneasy manner, more suggestive of professorial prudence than of philosophical boldness. However, since the philosophy of history claims to be the critical examination of universal history, it can hardly avoid an attempt to define "revolution." Any theory of history, indeed, which fails to recognize the striking fact that history has repeatedly received the strongest and the most decisive impulse from revolutionary exploits which stir the imagination and passions—any theory of history which fails to take this into account shows, by that very fact, its insufficiency. Alas, all too many reveal just this inadequacy.

The reason for this failure is probably the fact that the philosophy of history has based its ideas and concepts all too exclusively on the model of political events, using material that is poorly defined, worthy of little confidence, and almost always disfigured, consciously or not, by the irrational element of partisan passions. Philosophers of history have closed their eyes completely to the numerous examples of nonpolitical revolutions, which have changed and determined the destiny of humanity so radically and so profoundly that the torches of the most revolutionary political movements grow pale in their brilliant light.

Yet if, as seems clear, all the areas of civilization have experienced series of revolutions in their histories, it still is not easy to define the essential nature of the change which, in the history of religion, as in the arts, in politics, in the history of science, and so forth, conforms to the concept of revolution. At the outset there is a temptation to consider as revolutionary every profound change, in any sphere of civilization, which is produced suddenly, without sanction of law, and accompanied by outbursts of passion and violence. Yet none of these phenomena, nor all together, can suffice as a criterion. The *Principia* of Newton, for example, produced a radical change in physics, but is, nevertheless, hardly a revolutionary work in the same rank as the *Principles* of Descartes, which brought about a far less important change in that branch of science from the material standpoint. As to the element of a sudden break with the past, it is often only apparent and does not withstand historical analysis, the method of which requires that every event, however suddenly it appear, be conceived as a point in a continual flux. Jules Michelet, for example, affirmed that the Revolution of 1789 had begun with the *Discourse on Method,* and the historian of ideas, in his turn, traces the origin of the *Discourse* to certain currents in scholastic thought. Any stopping place in this limitless regression is, indeed, purely arbitrary. Thus revolution's quality of suddenness pertains only to its appearance as a phenomenon, just as the suddenness of an earthquake, a volcanic eruption, or an abrupt mutation is, from the standpoint of the natural sciences, by no means a break in continuity, but merely the macroscopic effect of an infinite number of infinitesimal changes. Nor is the illegality of revolutions a mark of adequate distinction. In the first place, it is not immediately clear what meaning that term would have in the field of science or of art, since it is not well defined except in the field where it originated, namely the juridico-political system. Secondly, even in that system, illegal actions, even those perpetrated with impunity and with increasing frequency, may well be merely an accumulation of crimes and not a revolution. Those who drank in the prohibition era were certainly not revolutionists. Finally, outbursts of passion and violence are certainly not a peculiar characteristic of revolutions; they may be totally wanting, and are often, even in the sphere of politics, rather the effects of a successful revolution than necessary features of the revolution itself. All of these phenomena are, then, merely secondary characteristics of revolution; the very essence of it must be sought elsewhere.

By analyzing this type of event in the political sphere, where it is more distinct than elsewhere, we can hope to arrive at a general theory to be tested in all spheres of civilization. Now, what political change is commonly and unanimously called a revolution? Two essential conditions are indispensable. The first is that the change shall affect the fundamental laws, written or unwritten, of a state or a nation; the second is that the change shall be illegal under the very law that it abolishes. These are two formal conditions, to which will be added later a material one. The fundamental law referred to is often called the constitution. A constitution is the system of the norms which establish the most general conditions and the generative principle of legality. Every constitution, however rudimentary, contains these elements. It may, for example, consist simply of the provision that the sole condition of legality shall be conformity to the will of a despot. On the other hand it may be detailed and elaborate, as is generally the case in "constitutional" regimes. Whatever form it may take, all the political life of a state, considered from the viewpoint of its structure, appears as the gradual and continuous specification by human action of the fundamental norms of the constitution. Every action, legislative, administrative, and judicial; every election, every international treaty, every declaration of war or conclusion of peace is legal, provided that it specifies or executes the conditions of legality established by the constitution. The normal political history of a nation is the development of these fundamental norms, which are gradually specified by the work of the public functionaries; and in democracies every citizen is a functionary, be it only in his capacity as an elector, a taxpaper, or a soldier. We may conceive of all the norms which determine the political life of a nation as arranged in a hierarchical order. At its summit, or rather, as will be seen, just below the summit, stands the constitution which is specified by the laws. These laws, in turn, are specified by decisions, administrative, judicial, or otherwise which are, in their turn, norms destined to determine lawful actions of men.

But the fundamental law, the constitution, is not unchangeable, and not every change that affects it is a revolution. Written or not, it can be transformed in a manner altogether legal. The majority of modern written constitutions provide for their own revision in a legal manner, containing provisions for such changes as integral parts of the constitution. And even a despotic regime can be transformed legally, without revolution, into a constitutional regime, if the despot grants a constitution by his own authority, as happened rather frequently in the nineteenth century. But when the constitution, whatever it may be, is changed by means other than those which it itself provides, we find ourselves faced by a true revolution.

In the realm of politics we can thus define revolution as an illegal change of the constitution, or indeed, since the constitution *is* the system of norms which establishes the conditions of legality, as *an illegal change of the conditions of legality.*

Undoubtedly, this definition raises a great number of problems which it is not necessary to discuss here, where only the philosophical problem is before us. However, it will not be useless to consider at least some important implications. What happens to the hierarchy of political norms when their fundamental law, their generative principle, is overthrown by a revolution which has attained its end? From a strictly formal viewpoint, all the laws, norms, decisions of every degree of specification, whose validity rested solely on the prerevolutionary constitution are automatically abolished along with the base from which they drew their validity. It is just as if, in a deductive system, the principles of deduction should be shown to be false; they would draw with them in their fall every proposition proved by means of them. That is why, in order to avoid a state of anarchy, the revolutionary constitutions often retain, although provisionally, the norms and other laws which were legally ratified under the old constitution. However, even while remaining unchanged in regard to their content, they rest thereafter on a new foundation; the source of their validity is no longer their conformity with the prerevolutionary conditions of legality, but their legitimation by the new constitution, which has explicitly or implicitly retained them. Expressed in another way, the hierarchy of norms invalidated by the revolution are revalidated by their incorporation in a new hierarchy with a new summit. Or rather, with a new hierarchical member intercalated between the summit, which retains its identity, and its specifications. Indeed, every political revolution is a break of continuity, at least when viewed from the angle of constitutional law, though not from the angle of the categories of history. But when a state has passed through a revolution, and all the more when it has passed through several—as is the case with

France since 1789—what is it, then, that preserves its identity throughout these breaks of continuity and radical changes? Neither the frontiers, nor the people, nor the laws are what they were more than a hundred fifty years ago; and no juridical continuity unifies the epochs between the revolutions. Yet we are used to speaking, and rightly so, of the modern history of France as having a relative unity. We could perhaps, for the purpose of resolving the question, call to mind the ancient paradox of the boat of Theseus, which was deemed the same boat through the centuries although every year a plank, a mast, an oar, or a sail had been replaced until, after a time, not a single one of its original atoms remained. But the "identical" idea of the boat, which was brought forward to resolve the paradox, will not prove quite effective here. For saying that all the successive constitutions of France are a part of the concept of France is simply veiling the problem under an expression more or less metaphorical, without solving it. For a constitution is a body of norms, and norms can variously specify or individualize other less specific norms; but it is not allowable, if logic is to be respected, to consider them as participating in the static entity of a concept. If, then, we claim to account for the identity of a state throughout the revolutionary changes in its constitutions, we must consider those successive constitutions as so many diverse specifications of one and the same constitutive norm. This constitutive norm is the veritable summit of the hierarchy whose evolution through the ages fills the history of this state. It is difficult to give a discursive and explicit expression to this constitutive and persistent norm, which is specified by the changing constitutions; which remains unchangeable in spite of all the vicissitudes of frontiers, of peoples, and of laws; and which, if it ever loses its force, if it ever ceases to determine the conduct of men, will draw with it in its ruin the entire political existence of the nation. Perhaps this unchangeable law can be approximately formulated by saying that this nation, this state, insists on the right of sovereign existence under any constitution whatsoever; that it claims to exist in history as an indivisible unity, and that it is the prosecution of this claim that is the very substance of its history and of the work of its citizens. If one really wishes to ask with sincerity, while looking only at the essential, what is the profound motive—and a motive is a norm which determines conduct—which has animated and will continue to animate the defenders of France, he will read in his own mind that it is this same primordial norm. He will read

there that the love of France, be it inborn or voluntary, aims first
at the very existence of France as a sovereign power, and only
secondarily at the constitution which specifies and actualizes that
supreme norm.

This hierarchical structure, and the concept of revolution as an
illegal change of the generative principle of legality, will become
clearer if we now turn our attention toward some other provinces
of civilization. Let us begin with science, and take as an example of
a revolution having taken place in its history, the work of Descartes.
What is the feature which obliges us to regard it as a veritable revolution in scientific thought? We may for the moment disregard
everything in positive knowledge which has been changed through
it. It will then be realized that the radical subversion of science
caused by the *Discourse on Method* is not a function of its immediate results, most of which might figure and do figure in some
precedent scholastic system. The original and genuinely revolutionary phenomenon is the introduction and use of a new *Method* whose
working has produced a new science. Now a method is nothing but
the generative principle of science; a system of norms which governs
scientific work and which demands obedience in the search for
truth. Method rules, if the expression be permitted, the conditions
of scientific legality just as the constitution establishes the conditions
of political legality. The results of scientific research are legitimized
by a valid method which has produced them (the control by experi-
ment evidently being only one of the possible methods), just as
political actions are legitimized by their conformity to the constitution, the generative principle of all political norms. In other
words, constitutions and methods have this in common, that they
are the principles, more or less variable in the course of time, of
the legitimate development of specific norms which, in the first case
are called laws or valid decisions, and in the second case, true propositions. It must not be forgotten, indeed, that every true scientific
proposition is, at the same time that it figures as a link in an objective system of knowledge, a norm which must be followed by our
thought, a model to which the mind must conform, if it desires to
reach the truth.

A thorough analysis of the change in method inaugurated by
Descartes shows clearly that it was truly a revolution, if there ever
was one, in the realm of science. Before his day, the prevailing, and
at the same time the most scholarly method, was guided by the prin-

ciple of conformity to a traditional authority, above all that of the Holy Scriptures, and secondarily that of Plato or Aristotle, Euclid or Archimedes, Hippocrates or Galen, Saint Augustine or Saint Thomas Aquinas. Nothing could be accepted as true unless it was compatible with the doctrines, or logical conclusions from the doctrines, sustained by recognized authority. Neither the heliocentric system, nor the sunspots, nor the circulation of the blood, nor negative numbers could then gain admission to the realm of scientific systems because this very admission would have violated that guiding principle. In all the collisions between tradition, on the one hand, and reason and experience on the other, tradition prevailed; it alone made a theory legitimate and any appeal to reason and experience was in vain. Against this principle of method, Descartes called for the autonomy and sovereignty of reason and evidence wherever scientific knowledge was at stake; it was with that freedom in view that he began his research in an attitude of universal doubt, striking deadly blows at all learning supported only by some authority or some tradition. This was, indeed, a revolution, exactly like a revolution which overthrows a throne and sets in its place the autonomy and the sovereignty of a free people. But just as political revolutions hardly affect, at least temporarily, the validity of specific laws, the Cartesian revolution left vast territories of the realm of science without apparent change; arithmetic, for example, or Euclidean geometry, or branches of metaphysics. But if the validity of the knowledge taught in those provinces had previously rested on the credence given to the authority of the ancients, it was to rest thereafter on the method of reason. It is not at all surprising to find that the differences in result are fewer, if we compare the system of Descartes with that of Saint Thomas, than if we compare it with that of Newton, although four centuries separate the first two and merely a half century the second. Yet the work of Newton is, as Ernst Cassirer has justly observed, itself a logical product of the Cartesian revolution in science, and cannot be understood in its historic setting, unless we recognize the new conditions of scientific "legality" established by Descartes. It was the same way with the new civilization in America, which certainly did not spring up immediately after the revolutionary Declaration of Independence, but much later; however, it is a fruit of that revolution, inconceivable without the new conditions of legality established in 1776.

If these considerations have shown that the scientific revolution, like a political revolution, is a change in the generative principle, a mutation of the conditions of legality, the parallelism is not yet entirely complete. It is still required to show in addition that, in the history of the sciences just as in political history, the event properly called revolutionary involves an illegal alteration of the conditions of legality. But what would constitute a *legal* change in method? Briefly defined, it would be a change sanctioned by a legitimate methodology, just as a legal change in a constitution is a change sanctioned by the legitimate constitution itself. Of course, the science of method need not be an elaborate and explicitly formulated system, although even the method of authority has had its theorists, as the method of reason had its Descartes. Constitutions are transformed insensibly, are adapted without a break in continuity to new situations created by changes taking place in other spheres of civilization, in the social economy, for example, or even in religion or scientific opinion. The possibility of their being adapted through evolution, thus avoiding the necessity of revolution, is a privilege of truly democratic regimes. Montesquieu has said that "all our histories are full of civil wars without revolutions; those of the despotic states, of revolutions without civil wars," anticipating with clear-sightedness worthy of all admiration a verdict of history, namely, that the *coups d'état,* followed most often by civil wars, usually overthrow constitutional regimes, while the veritable revolutions exterminate despotic regimes. The explanation of this phenomenon will be later found to lie in the very structure of revolution. But the same situation exists in the sphere of science. Methods are modified continually in the course of scientific work, and by this work itself. Explicitly or simply as a matter of practice, they adapt themselves to new situations, new problems, new ends. These adaptations are brought about by the process of evolution, by no means by revolutions, so long as the fundamental norm of method is not affected, so long as the specific methods employed only modify the general method, which they all specify. Whether, under the empire of authority, the Platonic norm replaces the Aristotelian tradition, or even whether under the empire of the method of reason, the logical formalism of Leibnitz takes the place of Cartesian evidence, these specifications of one and the same method are not separated, in time, by revolution, however radical the difference may be between the results produced by scientific work following the variations of specific methods. It is evident that here the method of reason offers the same advantages as a constitutional regime, namely the ease of adapting itself to new situations and new emergencies, while the rigid method of authority would be fatally exposed to a revolutionary overthrow.

Here again, just as in the political sphere, a question inevitably arises: What is it that authorizes the historian of the sciences to postulate the continuity of his subject, in spite of the many revolutions that occurred in its history? If it is true that those revolutions are breaks of continuity, what is it, then, which permits us to rank the systems born of the discontinuous series of methods within the unbroken series which represents the history of one and the same science? We cannot give a consistent and logically satisfying reply unless we consider all possible methods, however diverse and incompatible, as specifications and individuations of one and the same supreme norm, the veritable summit of the hierarchy of scientific norms, a norm which forms the very essence of the sphere of science. Analogously to the norm at the head of the political norms hierarchically organized, the constitutive norm of science would be the one which enjoins the search for truth, whatever that term may signify, and in whatever fashion the end may be pursued under the different principles of procedure. Thus all methods appear as roads starting from widely separated points, but converging toward the satisfaction of one of the primordial needs of civilized man, a need that Aristotle recognized: the need to know. The fact that all science is an effort toward the realization of this supreme norm, this and this alone creates the unity of the sphere of science through the ages and permits us to consider its history as a continuous evolution, in spite of the frequent revolutions which punctuate its progress.

It will be easier, after these considerations, to decide whether the definition here proposed of the type of events called revolutions —namely, illegal changes in the conditions of legality—is applicable to other spheres of civilization as well.

What is it, for instance, in the realm of the arts and of literature, which corresponds to the generative principle of norms, called constitution in the political system and method in the realm of the sciences? What is changed whenever the history of the visual arts, or music or of literature passes through a revolutionary turning point? We can hardly hesitate to attribute to style, in these spheres of culture, the same function which pertains to the constitution and to method in their respective spheres.[1] A style is a model of structure, a norm more or less general, unwritten, of course, and most frequently ineffable, which is specified, made effective and individuated by the work of the artist, which it helps to determine. The specification of one and the same norm by a multitude of works is exactly what we mean by saying that different works have the same style. Sometimes it is even possible to formulate the norm of a style in a discursive fashion; this, for example, was done in the Aristotelian rules of the three unities for certain styles of tragedy, or even in the painting of the Renaissance, with its specific rules of composition, parallelogram at Venice, isosceles triangle in Umbria, and it is done even more frequently with musical styles. We know, besides, that certain epochs, in which it was believed that art could be learned and taught, have, as it were, codified the norms of style regarded as legal. Every acceptable history of the arts bears witness to the fact that what changes with the passage of time is the generative principle which we call style. And the greater the period covered by such history, the more it becomes an account of the transformation of style, which the works of individuals merely specify variously.

To be consistent, we must, at this point, consider the individual work also as a norm, not altogether as an entirely determinate thing, which it is only in so far as it is a material object. In music a score is a norm which calls for performance by human skill; a poem asks to be read and understood; a painting, to be studied and assimilated. The ideal esthetic reaction is not merely a passive receptivity: it is an effort to conform consciousness to the norm incarnated in the perceived sensorial object.

Thus, esthetic apperception appears to be the ultimate actualization, the final individuation of the hierarchy of artistic norms, at the summit of which stands the constitutive norm that all styles specify, and which, by analogy to that of science, engages civilized mankind in the search for beauty. That the given concrete work is not yet the last specification, but that the esthetic reaction adds to it a degree of individuation, is shown by the fact that one and the same "material" work is differently "realized" in different epochs, by different persons, and even by the same person on different occasions; or it may not be "realized" at all. Incidentally, this applies to a scientific proposition as well, in so far as it is also a norm controlling human

[1] *Cf.* the author's *Phenomenological Considerations on Style* (Philosophy and Phenomenological Research, Vol. 8, 1948).

conduct: it may not be understood, it may be only partly understood, and it may be understood differently in different epochs and
by different persons. Which proves that it, too, receives its realization
and its ultimate interpretation by the act of human apperception.

Accordingly, in the realm of art also, revolution appears to be
a change in that system of conditions of legality that is called a
style. But how can this change be illegal? We may, at this point,
repeat, *mutatis mutandis,* the consideration we have just proposed
on the subject of an illegal change in method. What we generally
call the style of the Renaissance was specified in one way at the
beginning, in another at its apogee, and in yet another way in its
decline; moreover its development in Florence was not the same as
in Venice or Rome; in Italy it was not the same as in France or
Germany. The fact that all these special styles can be thought of
as subdivisions of a single type makes clear that there was no break
in continuity, no revolution between the various specifications of one
and the same style, that they are all "legal" modifications of a
single, fundamental, identical style. Just as the various methods that
specify the basic method of reason are all legitimate; just as the
different laws that follow one another, but are all based on the
authority of a single constitution, are all "legal," so the different
styles are variations that make up a basic style of art must be considered legitimate. The situation changes when we turn to the
passage from the Renaissance style to the baroque. The works
which specify the latter cannot any longer be regarded as specifications of the former. The norm which they follow is incompatible with that of the preceding style. If, then, we regard the style
of the Renaissance as the generative principle of the artistic works
of that epoch, we are justified in regarding the passing to the baroque style as an illegal change from that principle, in other words,
as a veritable revolution which fits the proposed definition.

The realm of religion presents so many structural analogies to
that of the state, on the one hand, and that of science, on the other,
and its normative character is so evident that we may be satisfied at
this point by calling attention to a few distinctive features. Every religion is the gradual specification of a particular revelation, on the
acceptance of which rests the validity of all the norms which constitute the religion in question. The demand for this acceptance is,
therefore, at the base of the entire hierarchy of norms which issue
from the particular revelation. No religion can recognize as legal a

change of this constitutive norm without abandoning its pretension
to existence. If, however, such a change takes place, we speak usually
of the birth of a new religion, not of a revolution in the old one. But
that is much more a matter of a terminological convention than of
an essential difference. Christianity may be considered as a new religion, since it emanated from a new revelation, or indeed as a revolution against the Mosaic law, which it claimed to fulfill. Analogies
to this special situation are not lacking in the realm of politics. It is
often very difficult to decide in history whether a state represents a
new creation or, rather, the revolutionary transformation of a predecessor. Revelation is specified by a system of fundamental dogmas, is-
suing directly from it, a system which, as the history of all religions
testifies, is subject to change, often despite its express claim to immu-
tability. But these changes can be of three different species. In the
first place, a religion, just like a constitution, may have provisions
concerning the legal modification of its norms. Thus, in the Roman
Church, the Pope and the Councils have, under certain conditions,
the power to develop the system of dogmas. On the other hand, the
fundamental norms of a religion may undergo modification, as an
effect of the actual process of their specification in religious work,
by adapting themselves to new conditions and to new problems;
just as constitutions are modified, *via facti,* by the normal operation
of political work. The fact that the Catholic Church long ago ceased
to persecute the partisans of the heliocentric system as heretics, and
the fact that it no longer regards lending money at interest as a
mortal sin are examples of this category of the *evolution* of dogmas.
But there are changes which affect not merely very special norms,
and which are produced neither by "constitutional" means nor by
custom, that is by the process of specification, but by a flagrant
rupture of the fundamental conditions of legality. These changes
abolish the generative principle itself, and replace it with another
one, incompatible with the principle of "legitimacy." The Reformation rejected the authority of the Pope and the Councils; it rejected
the majority of the sacraments; it placed the individual conscience
directly before its Creator and did not recognize any longer the in-
tercession of the Saints and of the entire ecclesiastical hierarchy.
Therefore we are, beyond question, dealing with a true religious
revolution whose structure corresponds exactly to the definition that
we have given of that type of historic event. We will not pursue the

analogy any further, although it might be tempting and instructive to show to what mass of details it could be extended.

There are still other provinces of civilization in which we ought to put our theory to the test, especially in the field of economic life. Here, we may begin the analysis by seeking the fundamental norm which is the essential feature of this realm, and which has the same logical function which the search for the truth has in the realm of science. We do not wish, however, to get mixed up in the often rather violent discussion of this subject which divides the authorities in the field of political economy. But one must admit that if there is a definite trend in economic history, if the historian of this province of civilization is free to choose, from the infinite number of movements and institutions of the past, certain facts to include in the series that he is studying, while excluding others, his principle of selection must be a norm that all economic movements and institutions specify and put into practice; just as the historian of science distinguishes from all the others the facts of history concerning his field, by their relation to the constitutive norm of science, which is the quest for knowledge. Perhaps the constitutive norm of economy may elude rational analysis and can be grasped only by intuition. However, if we consider the field of economy as including every activity whose dominant end is to satisfy needs with the minimum of expense, and as the constitutive norm of economy the demand for that type of activity, we shall have at hand an instrument necessary and sufficient for our purpose.

Evidently, this constitutive norm admits a great number of methods to be specified by the working of mankind. The principles which specify it immediately determine the various forms of economy, the "styles" of economic production, if we may apply this term here, such as free or planned, capitalist or communist, and so forth. All these forms of economic life should be understood as specifying, each in its fashion, the economic norm, which constitutes the realm as such, and as being specified in their turns by more special norms, leading to those which are highly individualized and which govern directly the economic work of man. But, just as, in the realm of art, revolution is the passage from one style to another, here it is the passage from one form of production and distribution to another which obeys a new fundamental norm. An example will make this assertion clearer. A liberal economy specifies the constitutive norm by maintaining, expressly or implicitly, that by granting to every one free economic activity, the greatest possible satisfaction of needs will be obtained with a minimum of expense. The norm which expresses this idea is in turn specified by more explicit norms, such as those demanding free trade, free enterprise in agriculture and industry, and so forth. But all those changes which occur in a free economy without affecting the fundamental norm on which it is based, are evolutions, not revolutions, however radical they may be. An economy may pass from agricultural preponderance to industrial preponderance, from extensive exploitation to intensive exploitation, from small business to monopoly; so long as it grants to everyone free economic activity, even if this liberty has become an onerous privilege, we will say that that economy has undergone an evolution, not a revolution. On the contrary, when the fundamental norm of liberalism is abolished, when the organization of the economy develops a plan which assigns to everyone his economic rights and duties, we will say that a revolution has taken place. The new norm of the economy specifies the constitutive economic norm in a new fashion, "illegal" under the economic norm that it has just replaced.

Evidently the structural analysis of the type of events that historians call revolutions still raises many problems for philosophy, methodology and history, which cannot be discussed here.[2] However, we may be allowed to propose a general consideration. It may seem as though the analysis and the definition to which our discussion has led so far established an unsurmountable difference between evolution and revolution, a difference which would be contrary to the principle that, like the natural world, history makes no abrupt leaps, but passes from one stage to the next by infinitesimally small and insensible changes. Yet up to this point we have studied only the macroscopic structure of revolutions. The apparent disparity will vanish as soon as we try to discover the microscopic elements of historic change, which are the same in evolution and revolution. We remarked earlier that the notion of style, conceived as a norm, applies as well to the common features of Venetian painting at a given moment as to those of all the works of art of the Renaissance. We may say, by analogy, that the idea of method embraces equally well the norm obeyed by a single act of research of a single scientist and the norm which has governed scientific research from Galileo

---

[2] For a more comprehensive treatment see the author's *Work and History. An Essay on the Structure of Civilization* (Princeton: 1948).

to Einstein. We may say, also, that the idea of a constitution applies just as well to the fundamental law of a single state and to that of the federation of the United States.

Briefly, in all the spheres of civilization there exists, interposed between the fundamental norm as the generative principle of legality and the norms which directly regulate man's work, a hierarchy of norms, more and more specified, the content of which changes constantly as time progresses. Now, whether an event is to be considered as a revolution or simply as a stage of evolution depends entirely on the scope of the sector of the hierarchy covered by our inquiry. The custom is well established, and not without reason, to consider as revolutionary only an illegal change which occurs at the level of the hierarchy that specifies directly the constitutive norm of each realm, and which we have called the generative principle of more specific norms. When our view embraces the totality of the hierarchy of the norms of science, no change will appear illegal to us because all the changes in method are legitimate, provided they are accomplished in order to fulfill the obligation imposed on civilized man by the constitutive norm of the realm. When, however, our view embraces only those branches of the hierarchy which derive from a single generative principle, for example, the method of reason, when we regard the field covered by the results obtained through this method as the whole of science, we pronounce revolutionary those changes of method which, in a vaster field, would appear to us merely as stages of an evolution. It is easy to discover analogous conditions in all the other spheres of civilization.

Thus the difference between evolution and revolution is reduced to a difference in degree: it depends on the extent of the field that we take in at a single view. Just as a material object may appear continuous and homogeneous to the naked eye, and yet its structure be found to be discontinuous under the microscope which uncovers only a minute portion of it; in the same way evolution, apparently continuous in history, is articulated into an infinity of revolutions, of illegal changes of the very conditions of legality, when the eye is looking only at an infinitesimally small section and is studying it in all its details. The storming of the Bastille was an illegal change under the fundamental law of the French monarchy; it was a legitimate and legal action under the fundamental law of France. And speaking generally, it may be said that what is an illegal change of the proximate higher norm of the hierarchy may well be legal and legitimate with reference to a still higher norm in the same hierarchy. There is, nevertheless, a good reason why the illegal transformation of the generative principle assumes in the history of every sphere of civilization a special importance which justifies reserving for it the customary name of revolution. The reason is that the extent and the depth of the change undergone in civilized life as the result of the replacement of one norm by another are, *caeteris paribus,* in direct proportion to the rank in the hierarchy of the replaced norm. And since the generative principles in those hierarchies rank just below the constitutive norm of each domain, which themselves are immutable, their alteration causes the maximum change which can occur in a sphere of civilization.

If our interpretation proves adequate, philosophy of history will have no reason to pronounce an absolute veto against the justice of revolutions. Incidentally, Immanuel Kant, the only great philosopher who devoted considerations worthy of the importance of that type of historical experience to the phenomenon of revolution, espoused the cause of American independence and that of the rights of men and citizens with an ardor enhanced by his rigid moralism. Indeed, every revolution may be found to be a legitimate change when considered in reference to the constitutive norm of the realm which it overturned. But on one condition only; and this remark will add to the definition of revolution the last essential element, which we have announced before. All the special spheres of civilization, religion, science, politics, economy, the arts, are also but specifications of a supreme imperative, which commands that civilization exist, that it be actualized with its provinces, diverse yet subject to one and the same law, which tends to give them unity. There is not, and there cannot be, a higher norm of mankind in the name of which this could be violated. Any philosophy, any doctrine, any action, which failed to specify and execute the supreme law of civilization, would be an irruption of a radically evil nature into the kingdom of civilization. And no movement of that kind could claim the sacred name of revolution. Indeed, rebellion against civilization itself would not modify the conditions of legality; it would exterminate every possibility of legality in every sphere whatsoever. It would not, therefore, be a revolution at all, it would be a monstrous crime, which, if crowned with lasting success, would bring about the end of all civilization. This is why the usurpation of the title of revolution, allegedly national or under any other name, by crimes against civilization, whose villainy is in proportion to the height of the norm which they dare to attack—this usurpation, however repulsive it may be, is, nevertheless, another "homage which vice renders to virtue."

It may seem, moreover, that by maintaining that every change occurring in a sphere of civilization may be considered as revolution, however minute, we are making of history an infinite series of illegal actions, thereby degrading it to the rank of a collection of petty crimes. It would be easy to reply to this objection by recalling our thesis, according to which whatever appears illegal under one norm, may well be legal under a norm closer to the summit of the hierarchy. But we do not mean to fall back on that exception. If there is one certain lesson to be drawn from history, it is that civilization does not advance by the action of orthodox conformists. May we be allowed, in closing, to illustrate this assertion by an example drawn from a hitherto neglected field, namely the history of language? Every language is a body of norms called grammar, vocabulary, and so on, which govern the relations between signs and meanings, and which are specified and obeyed in every act of speaking, writing, or understanding what is said or written. These norms, too, undergo changes in the course of their history; it would be possible to show that some of these changes correspond to our concept of revolution. But how does language change? It changes through a series of innumerable acts of speaking or writing, among which those that adhere scrupulously and meticulously to the traditional or conventional norms of grammar, vocabulary, and pronunciation make no contribution to the process of mutation of the norms. Only those which infringe on the laws of correct language, in other words creative offenses against those laws, the linguistic "illegalities," can eventually contribute to the introduction of a new "legality" in this sphere. This fact in no wise implies a general absolution accorded to grammatical errors; for not every neglect or ignorance of the rules of grammar is a creative act, just as not every heresy causes a change in religion, although all the changes in the norms of that sphere were heresies when they first appeared. The Declaration of Independence was a crime under English law, but not every political crime creates a great nation.

And yet there is something shocking in having to admit that, in all its spheres, the progress of civilization is often brought about by *illegal* changes in the conditions of legality, to revolutions, to a type of event, therefore, the idea of which almost inevitably evokes images of disorder, atrocities, insecurity and destruction. Hence it is incontestable that we can and should take all measures to transform revolutionary energy into forces of evolution; historically, the most efficacious of these measures have been liberty, equality, and fraternity. But we cannot eliminate the necessity of radical change, which has surged and always will surge in the course of history, and against which human inertia has erected and will continue to erect Bastilles. The laws and norms, the traditions and conventions of every kind, which claim the respect of civilized man, are always manifestations of a given state of civilization. Yet, as long as civilization has not finished its course, that is until the constitutive norms of civilization are completely realized by the existing state of things, civilization will continue to be a mixture of perfections and imperfections, but it will always remain perfectible. For in all the provinces of civilization, the very idea of man's work implies the perfectibility of the object of that work by work. All the norms and systems of norms that history sees rise and fall are consequently specifications, incomplete and imperfect, of the constitutive norms of civilization. All the political and economic organizations, all the religions, all the sciences, all the works of art, all the languages, fulfill but inadequately the tasks imposed upon them; and their generative principles must therefore be violated in order to make civilization advance in a desirable direction; although it may not be true, we repeat, that every violation will mean progress. Only those which are undertaken, not from hedonistic and egoistic motives, but from disinterested and responsible love of God or of justice, of truth or of beauty, in short, of a more perfect civilization, have a chance of succeeding in bringing about a better "legality."

4

COUP D'ETAT: THE VIEW OF THE MEN FIRING PISTOLS[1]

DAVID C. RAPOPORT

The purpose of this essay is to suggest a useful way of looking at the *coup d'état*. Contemporary discussions rarely try to distinguish its unique characteristics. Sometimes the *coup d'état* is treated as analogous to a constitutionally prescribed way of expressing public opinion; other times it is classified as a type of revolution; in either instance a distorted image emerges. Furthermore, most academics seem unaware that their discussions are at variance with ordinary language usages. By ignoring ordinary language we not only create unnecessary confusion, but willy-nilly we also cut ourselves off from a potentially rich source of insight.

The view offered below leans heavily on standard dictionary

[1] I am most grateful to the Institute of War and Peace Studies, Columbia University, for making the completion of this article possible.

definitions which emphasize that the *coup d'état* is an "unpredict-able" or "unexpected" act, deriving its primary political meaning from its "extra-legal" qualities. To develop the argument as far as possible in the short space allotted, I have decided to rely heavily on Gabriel Naudé's seventeenth-century *Considerations politiques sur les coups d'état*[2]—the first systematic analysis of the subject, an analysis which I believe to be still unsurpassed.

"I don't know what you mean by 'glory,' " Alice said. Humpty Dumpty smiled contemptuously, "Of course you don't—till I tell you. I meant 'there's a nice knock-down argument for you!' " "But 'glory' doesn't mean 'a nice knock-down argument,' " Alice objected. "When I use a word," Humpty Dumpty said in a rather scornful tone, "it means just what I choose it to mean—neither more nor less." "The question is," said Alice, "whether you *can* make words mean so many things." "The question is," said Humpty Dumpty, "which is to be master—that's all."

In a recent George Lichty cartoon two fat American tourists appear seated in a Latin-American café obviously distressed by the sight of several men outside firing pistols at one another. An unperturbed waiter calms his customers by telling them that it is an election, not a revolution they are witnessing. Perhaps the scene is meant to appeal to our sense of the ridiculous since the ordinary cartoon reader may think it impossible to equate firing bullets with casting ballots.

Whatever the reaction of cartoon readers, some scholars would not think the waiter's remark entirely absurd. William Stokes, an authority on Latin-American politics, believes that our ingenious neighbors may have "developed procedures for measuring and representing opinion different from, but as valid as the techniques of election, initiative, referendum, and plebiscite of the Anglo-American and Western European states." "Violence seems to be *insti-*

[2] The book was first published privately in Paris in 1639. I have used the Paris 1667 edition primarily but my references are to Dr. King's more accessible translation, *Political Considerations upon Refined Politicks and the Master-Strokes of State as Practised by the Ancients and Moderns* (London: 1711), 200 pp. Spelling and grammar are modernized.

Naudé cites as predecessors in the study of *coup d'état* Machiavelli, Clapmar, Balzac, Lipsius, and "most of all Montaigne and Charron." But none of these writers discussed the concept in an exhaustive and systematic manner. His primary classical sources were Seneca, Plutarch, and Tacitus. I am familiar with only two discussions of Naudé in English: F. Meinecke, *Machiavellism*, tr. W. Stark (New Haven: 1962), pp. 196–204; and James V. Rice, *Gabriel Naudé* (Baltimore: 1939), 134 pp.

tutionalized in the organization, maintenance, and changing of government in Latin America. The methodology of force is found . . . whenever and wherever Hispanic culture is. . . ."[3]

Samuel Huntington is more specific; he calls the typical Latin American revolution a *coup d'état* and likens it to an election. Distinguishing two types of *coups d'état,* the first, primarily a nineteenth-century phenomenon, aiming merely at patronage distribution, and the second at social reform as well, he concludes in a striking passage, "Frequent reform *coups d'état* should not be viewed as a pathological but rather as a healthy mechanism of gradual change, the non-constitutional *equivalent* of periodic changes in party control through the electoral process."[4]

Huntington does not comment on the differences between election and *coup d'état.* However, it is obvious that one act is legal and the other is not; and we commonly assume that an act's legal status influences the manner of its initiation, how it will be justified, who participates, the kinds of problems they face, and whether or not the initial accomplishments will be secure. The breach in law which the *coup d'état* implies creates *at least* five separate but logically related *political* problems. To my knowledge, no contemporary student of politics has seriously attempted to solve them all.

To be sure, we are all aware of the act's extra-legal quality, and most grant some credence to Lichty's tourists' fear. George Pettee, for instance, states that a *coup d'état is* a revolution and must be analyzed with revolution study categories, but he insists that it is only a "minor revolution."[5] Inasmuch as he neither elaborates this remark nor explains why a revolutionary typology must embody quantitative distinctions, his view raises at least as many questions as it solves.

Henry Spencer (*"Coup d'état," Encyclopedia of the Social Sciences*) is more subtle, arguing that a *coup d'état* is a revolution in law but not in politics—a view which Alfred Meusal[6] and Hannah

[3] William Stokes, "Violence as a Power Factor in Latin-American Politics," *Western Political Quarterly,* V (September 1952), p. 468 (my emphasis) and p. 445.

[4] Samuel P. Huntington, "Patterns of Violence in World Politics," in his *Changing Patterns of Military Politics* (New York: 1962), p. 40 (my emphasis).

[5] George Pettee, *The Process of Revolution* (New York: 1938), pp. xi–xii.

[6] "Revolution and Counter-Revolution," *Encyclopedia of the Social Sciences,* XIII (London: 1931), pp. 367–376.

Arendt[7] endorse. They go on to point out that the two events have antithetical political meanings. A *coup d'état* preserves a political system while initiating minor changes, but a revolution creates an entirely new order. This position, however, is no more satisfying than Pettee's.

In the first place, not all events we call *coups d'état* in ordinary language initiate minor political changes. The Communist capture of government in Petrograd 1917 and in Prague 1948 have been called both *coups d'état* and revolutions; the first term refers to the manner in which government was seized and the second to the ultimate consequences. Secondly, to suggest that *coup d'état* and revolution are synonyms in law but antonyms in politics does violence to the common assumption that law and politics are intimately related fields. This curious way of looking at the phenomena may ultimately be correct, but our three authors merely assert their conclusion with only a phrase to justify it.

Does the legal commentator *have* to consider all *coups d'état* as revolutions merely because they violate the law? Hans Kelsen offers the best affirmative argument available in English.[8] He notes that the practicing constitutional lawyer must make a fundamental distinction between legal and illegal successions. When a government comes into authority legitimately, foreign states automatically accord it recognition, but in the case of a *coup d'état,* they have opportunities to delay and sometimes to refuse recognition. With regard to municipal law, a legal succession leaves unaffected all laws previously made, because the reason for their validity—the constitution—is still itself valid. A *coup d'état,* by rupturing the constitution, invalidates all existing law. Judges and lawyers, to say the least, find the election analogy bizarre. In effect, Kelsen argues that Lichty's tourists would be right to refuse the waiter's sophisticated assurances, and to trust their common-sense impression that a revolution was being consummated since it has precisely the same legal consequence as a *coup d'état.*

Kelsen's argument obviously has implications for the student of politics. Major D. G. Goodspeed's brilliant book, *The Conspirators,* studies six twentieth-century *coups d'état* and shows convincingly that the reaction of foreign powers was an important and sometimes

---

[7] H. Arendt, *On Revolution* (New York: 1963), p. 27.
[8] Hans Kelsen, *General Theory of Law and State* (Cambridge, Mass.: 1946), pp. 117, 219ff., 368ff., and 372.

crucial problem the conspirators had to face.[9] In municipal affairs, the case of West Germany since 1945 also illustrates the political importance of Kelsen's argument. Successive governments have had to make "political" decisions to determine which acts of the Nazi government they would consider binding—a fact one cannot understand without referring to the consequences of legal discontinuity.

Nevertheless, Kelsen's view has limited utility, because his distinctions simply do not exhaust the concept of illegality associated with the *coup d'état*. There were many *coups d'état* in nineteenth-century Spain but the usurpers did not always have to seek recognition. A recognition problem emerges only when the office traditionally accredited to receive foreign representatives is unoccupied or when a new body claims that right. Thus, when Queen Isabella fled Spain in 1868, the British did not recognize the new government for nearly a year.[10] They did not have the opportunity to consider the question in many previous *coups d'état* because the latter concerned the Cortez and not the monarch, who alone received foreign representatives. Mussolini's rise to power is generally termed a *coup d'état*, but because he left the monarchy intact, he did not have to seek recognition. Furthermore, since the Italian courts refused to recognize his act as a breach of legal continuity, Mussolini did not have to face the political questions which plague contemporary West German governments. In short, if we follow conventional designations of the *coup d'état*, we shall find that the act is not always a revolution as the lawyer understands the term, and the very limited justification for equating *coup d'état* and revolution becomes untenable.

To recapitulate the argument so far. Without considering the political significance of the extralegal qualities of *coup d'état*, it is impossible to assess analogical arguments. The lawyer, however, provides only limited help, for the legal problem comes from a conception embodied in ordinary language usage. Does that image imply meanings which justify treating the phenomenon as *sui generis?* It is worth remembering in this regard that not everyone in Lichty's cartoon has been consulted. The participants, the men in the streets firing pistols, also have a point of view, and we can-

[9] D. G. Goodspeed, *The Conspirators, A Study of the Coup d'état* (New York: 1961), 252 pp.

[10] H. Lauterpacht, *Recognition in International Law* (Cambridge, England: 1947), p. 120.

not assume that they would agree with either the waiter or the tourists.

> In these states great events are not necessarily preceded by great causes; on the contrary, the least accident produces a great revolution, often as unforeseen by those who cause it, as by those who suffer from it.
>
> When Osman, Emperor of the Turks, was deposed, none of those who committed the crime had ever dreamed of committing it; they merely asked as suppliants that a wrong done them should be rectified. A voice which was unknown to everybody issued from the crowd by chance; the name of Mustapha was pronounced, and suddenly Mustapha was emperor.
>
> —Montesquieu, *The Persian Letters*

What *do* we mean by the terms coup and *coup d'état?* The words are common in English, French, Spanish (*golpe, golpe d'estado*) and Italian (*colpo di stato*); in all languages the set of meanings is similar.

There are two coups in English, but the one moderns know best was introduced from French in the eighteenth century.[11] It has two primary meanings: "a blow or stroke," and "a blow that is sudden, unexpected, and successful." In French *coup* is habitually linked with other nouns to constitute a single term, and this term is used to describe a large variety of different actions. But it always suggests a sudden change from a previous condition, invariably sharp, unexpected, and more often than not violent. A *coup de grâce* is a death blow; *coup de tête,* an inspiration; *coup de main,* an unexpected attack; *coup de théâtre,* a sudden change of scenery; anyone who has taken a nap at the beach will know why a sunburn is *coup de soleil,* as will anyone trying to finish an article recognize a telephone ring as *coup de téléphone.*

In both English and French the term seems especially appropriate in conflict situations where the parties cannot fully anticipate each other's moves, and where their purposes are mutually exclusive. It designates a special move in many games (i.e., billiards, bridge, dueling and roulette) and is found in our political and military vocabularies. (Bardin's military dictionary *L'Armée de Terre* uses

---

11 The definitions which students of politics use suggest that revolutions have favorable and *coups d'état* unfavorable connotations. There is much truth in Mario Cattaneo's remark that the term we use depends on whether we regard the event as "good" or not. See his *Concetto di rivoluzione nella scienza del diritto* (Milan: 1960), p. 67.

eight pages to list terms using *coup*.)[12] In each context, coup is a decisive but not necessarily successful stroke, giving one party an advantage often great enough to bring the struggle to a rapid conclusion. The executor of a coup in billiards has made a decisive, disastrous move, for his play has been so unskillful that he is obliged to forfeit the game regardless of previous scores. Applied to North American Indian military practices, a coup was a surprise attack which captured the enemy's horses or weapons, and was thus a crippling blow. When American newspapers called Senator Dirksen's decision to nominate Senator Goldwater at the 1964 Republican convention a coup, they were suggesting that the conflict over civil rights between the two men made it totally unexpected for Dirksen to make this move, and that it would have a decisive effect on the convention's nominating decision.

A *coup d'état* is an *act of state*. According to the Oxford Dictionary, it is "A sudden stroke of *state* policy: especially a great change *in* government carried out violently and illegally by the *ruling power*" (my emphasis). The Webster's Third International reverses the definitional order, and probably reflects contemporary usage more closely thus, "a sudden decisive exercise of localized or concentrated force unseating the *personnel* of government" (my emphasis) and "violently and unexpectedly reformulating state policy," "an unexpected or sudden measure of state often involving force or the threat of force."

Larousse's definition of *coup d'état* fails to emphasize the sudden unexpected qualities always implicit in coup, but the latter is so commonly employed in French that these matters may be understood. At any rate a *coup d'état* is a *"violation délibérée des formes constitutionelles par un gouvernement, une assemblée, ou un groupe de personnes qui détiennent l'autorité."*[13]

It is interesting to speculate why eighteenth-century Englishmen took the French word *coup* to describe state affairs. The native English coup (pronounced kōp)[14] which shared a common root with the French word was available and also signified "blow or shock."

---

[12] My colleague, Neal Wood, made me aware of this point.

[13] *Le Grand Larousse Encyclopédique* (Paris: 1960). *Littré* defines it as a *"mésure violente à laquelle un gouvernement a recours."*

[14] The noun is a cognate of the two verbs, to cope. The origin of the word is not certain, but most authorities believe it derives from the Latin word *colaphus* meaning blow or cuff which in turn came from the Greek word *kolaphos.*

But Dr. W. King, Naudé's translator, apparently felt that when Frenchmen spoke of coup in politics, it had overtones that transcended mere sudden physical contact. The key term (*coup d'état*) is translated not as "coups (kōps) of state," but as "master strokes of state." King, according to the Oxford Dictionary, found the last term used in art criticism, and was the first to employ it in politics where it signifies "a masterly execution of skill; a surpassingly skillful act (of cunning, diplomacy, policy, *etc.*): one's cleverest move or device." A half century later, King's "master stroke" was supplanted by *coup d'état*.

In sum, the *coup d'état* is an unexpected, sudden, decisive, potentially violent, illegal act, dangerous for plotter as well as for intended victim, and needing great skill for execution. Its professed purpose is to alter *state* policies. The Oxford Dictionary and Larousse specify that the act must be undertaken by public officials and that it often causes the removal of other officers who presumably would or have opposed the conspirators. Webster visualizes the possibility of a *coup d'état* by private parties, but in this case the minimum requirement involves government personnel changes.

Needless to say the definition is still incomplete. We have rejected the lawyers' legality criterion but have not specified a substitute standard. Nor is the proposed definition precise enough to exclude certain acts never called *coups d'état*—such as the assassination of a high official by a private person, an act which, in effect, may alter public policy. Both shortcomings are important, and they are intimately, though not obviously, related, but we shall attend to them later.

I want now merely to emphasize the way in which the dictionary definition differs from the one most academics employ. The former specifies *means* and allows a wide range of ultimate objectives. Most academic definitions, on the other hand, are comparatively elastic about means, providing they are illegal, and stress a single objective —the overthrow of government. If definitions were simply arbitrary matters as Humpty Dumpty told Alice they must be, the advantage of convenience would make the familiar always preferable. But definitions do serve heuristic purposes; a good one calls attention to important, previously obscured considerations which, when seen, enable us to relate seemingly unconnected phenomena and help distinguish events from others that appear similar but actually are not. I think that the dictionary emphasis on means does ultimately imply the perspective we seek; but as we shall have to pass first rather quickly through unfamiliar country, I propose that we hire as a guide one who, starting from ordinary language premises, has made the journey before and knows the terrain well—Gabriel Naudé.

Throughout his essay Naudé dwells on the importance of means in shaping the response of others to one's conduct. In particular, he contrasts the making of public policy according to a customary rule or law (ordinary prudence), with acting outside or in defiance of law or custom (extraordinary prudence).[15] Clearly defined and accepted rules increase the possibility that men would act toward each other according to *expectation*. Rules provide a justification for action; they enable one to predict the specific chain of actions and reactions most likely to occur in given circumstances, and their strength gives guarantees that those endowed with temporary advantages cannot press their superiorities beyond known prescribed limits. Where law or custom prevails men necessarily act in public —or in full view of interested parties—for specific and defined objectives.

To act in defiance of law[16] and to avoid punishment at the same time requires one or both of two conditions: "special justification" and concealment. But the lawbreaker knows that his justification will probably not be accepted, and his effort to conceal may fail. To the detector, because the act has been withdrawn from public scrutiny, the only thing of which he can be reasonably certain is that the offender wants to avoid punishment. If the offender surmises that this is all his apprehender understands of him, a potentially dangerous situation results. A burglar suddenly surprised in his work may try to explain, give himself up, run, wrestle with his apprehender, or use a lethal weapon. At any rate, neither man can

---

[15] The development of meanings associated with the transitive verb, to cope, seems to be reflected in Naudé's discussion of coup and *coup d'état*. To cope originally meant "to strike a blow" and "to repay," then "to meet or encounter," and now it means "to struggle or contend on equal terms usually with some success." As Naudé points out, one does not normally create healthy social relations by violence, but occasionally unusual problems require extraordinary means. Invariably he justifies the act on defensive grounds and emphasizes that the outcome can never be guaranteed in advance.

[16] For the sake of convenience, the term "law" will be used from this point—though clearly Naudé has in mind the more inclusive term "legitimate rule."

be certain of the other's reaction because the incident takes place outside the law. In affairs of state, Naudé contended, the lawbreaker or the man who resorts to extraordinary prudence must be concerned with *both* justification and concealment; and he may involve many others in the ensuing unstable and hazardous circumstances.

Since mutual predictability is a condition of confidence and justice (the strength of all sound states), behavior in accordance with public rules must be encouraged as much as possible. But a state cannot be governed solely through law. The very fact that law is made *by men for men* implies that it possesses inherent limitations. The most gifted and public-spirited lawmaker cannot imagine how every future circumstance affects the operation of his rules. Besides, rules, to be useful as guides, cannot be infinitely complex; they are made to fit *most* circumstances, and by that token are inapplicable in some. A rule may have worked well in the past and we may have good reason to think it will work well in the future; yet, although it is certain that disastrous consequences would occur if the rule were eliminated as a prescription for action, despite all, there might still be an excellent, urgent case for a single violation to serve the public good. We may even be impelled to violate a rule in particular to secure the rule's general purpose and indeed to preserve the rule itself.

There are two types of extraordinary prudence: *maximes d'état* and *coups d'état*. An official operating according to the *maximes* does something he knows is illegal, but can be made to appear legal, because he has a superficially plausible case, and sufficient control of the administrative apparatus to get away with it. When the consequences of failure are not disastrous, when time and other circumstances permit, acting in this quasi-legal fashion is most desirable.

The problem of the *coup d'état* is different. The objective is so manifestly improper that the mere announcement of an intention to consider pursuing it would encourage resistance and might stimulate a violent counterreaction. To accomplish a *coup d'état,* the public must be presented with a *fait accompli* and its approval solicited through a special extralegal justification.

> When anything is done by Maxims, all causes, reasons, manifestos, declarations, forms and methods to prove an action unlawful precede the effects and operations of them, whereas in these *coups d'état,* the thunderbolt falls before the noise of it is heard in the skies. Prayers are said before the bell is rung for them, the execution precedes

the sentence, he suffers the blow that thinks he himself is giving it, he suffers who never expected it, and he dies that looks upon himself as most secure, all is done in the night and obscurity amongst storms and confusions, the Goddess Laverna (the patroness of thieves) presiding and the first grace requested of her is this: "Make me a saint and just to human sight, but away my cheat in clouds and crimes in night."[17]

It should be emphasized that academics often use *coup d'état* in ways which cut across Naudé's distinction between *maximes d'état* and *coups d'état*. When a Latin-American president extends his tenure by using his "influence" to induce a legislature to amend an unamendable constitution, Spencer says that a *coup d'état* has occurred. This usage is at variance with dictionary prescriptions, and Latin Americans themselves, according to Fitzgibbon,[18] would call our example an instance of *continuismo* whose meaning resembles *maximes d'état*. At any rate Naudé's use of *coup d'état* must be kept in mind if we are to understand his description of the unique dangers and problems it presupposes.

Naudé discusses four types of *coups d'état*.[19] The first is common among "newly established" states where the law-abiding habit and the constitution are not fully formed. The "lawgiver" (i.e., Moses, Romulus, and Mohammed) employs spectacular deceits or magic to create an extralegal justification for appropriate foundations. Fully established states are generally subject to three other types: the first, to eliminate allegedly corrupt or inept leadership, is clearly the most common variety, as in Pepin's murder of the last Merovingian king; the second, to destroy the political strength of parties claiming outmoded constitutional privileges, as in the attack of Philip II on the Aragonese nobles; the third, to eliminate a person or persons who

---

[17] *Political Considerations . . . , op. cit.*, pp. 79ff. I have substituted *coups d'état* for King's "master-strokes."

[18] Russell H. Fitzgibbon, "*Continuismo* in Central America and the Caribbean," *The Inter-American Quarterly*, II (July 1940), pp. 56–74. Fitzgibbon says that the term is common among Latin Americans although it is absent from Spanish dictionaries. He defines it as "the practice of continuing the administration in power . . . by a . . . (constitutional) provision . . . exempting the president . . . from the historic prohibition . . . against two terms." Stokes, *op. cit.*, also distinguishes between *coup d'état* and *continuismo*.

[19] *Political Considerations . . . , op. cit.*, pp. 73ff. Naudé lists seven types of *coup d'état*, and I have reduced them to four. His classification rationale is confusing; the categories overlap, and he seems occasionally to confound legally authorized "crisis" powers with *coup d'état*. The discussion is clearly the weakest portion of the essay.

want to depose the legitimate holders of power (i.e., the St. Bartholomew Massacre).

In all instances the planner of the *coup d'état* has no legal warrant for his action, but is not held responsible in law. The most important obvious change is political, for the personal relationships in the public arena are drastically altered. The charismatic leader destroys the appeal of potential rivals, reconciles malcontents, and tightens his grip on the "devoted." Pepin, the "Mayor of the Palace," becomes king; many Huguenots forfeit their lives; and the Aragonese nobles, because they were foolish enough to let Philip's agents provoke them into attacking their sovereign, have lost their allies and made themselves vulnerable to legal sanctions. The resulting legal changes occur *after* the *coup d'état* is completed, and *as a consequence* of the altered strength of the affected parties. Mohammed, by demonstrating that he is Allah's agent, has an extralegal justification for making his recommendations law. The Aragonese nobles have no political strength to resist Philip's desire to "amend the constitution." When Pepin succeeds to the throne, no court declares that the succession is illegitimate. The office remains the same; a new man occupies it, a man who actually uses its powers.

Naudé, in effect, is disputing both Kelsen's contention that revolution and *coup d'état* are necessarily identical for the practicing lawyer, and the commonplace notion that *coup d'état* is a legal but not a political change. His meaning is best illustrated with a hypothetical instance free from the particular historical questions associated with his own examples. Suppose a constitutional monarch believes that the "public safety" requires new parliamentary leadership. But there is no emergency rule to cover the case, and he executes a *coup d'état*. How can a court respond if someone challenges the validity of acts which the new ministers perform?

The court has two alternatives: it may take or refuse to take the case. In taking the case, the court is obliged to "find" an applicable rule and therefore its decisions bind future courts. The court then will be increasing or restricting the monarch's power indefinitely; otherwise it makes no sense to talk about decisions according to rule. If it refuses the case, the court declares itself unqualified to handle the question, because no legal rule covers the instance or no evidence is available that can be properly assessed in a court of law. Consequently, the monarch's act is unchallenged, but he has no clear legal authority for similar deeds in the future. The court and the monarch himself may have reason to think that this is the most prudent solution. A real contemporary court, confronted by the same problem, may declare, as many Latin-American courts have learned to do, that it lacks competence to judge political questions, or that it will not examine the credential of a particular questionable government providing the latter agrees to abide by the existing constitution.[20] Parenthetically, Naudé's image of extraordinary prudence, as action not subject to scrutiny by legal rule, is similar to Locke's concept of prerogative "as the power to act according to discretion for the public good without the prescription of law and sometimes even against it."[21]

Neither alternative confronting our hypothetical court applies to revolution. In fact, if the court refuses to act, less change occurs for the lawyer than would be the case if the legislature frames ordinary legislation. *If* a legal system is an arrangement of *rules* and not a relationship of men, as most contemporary legal theorists argue, then the *coup d'état here, at least, is the exact antithesis of* revolution. Paradoxically, the conventional notion that *coup d'état* represents a legal but not a political change must, in many instances, be completely reversed. In altering personal relationships it effects a political change, not a legal one. This last conclusion, which I must confess startled me, is clearly reflected in contemporary dictionary definitions, which state that rules are violated but not that they are changed; that officers are removed but not that their offices are abolished. *Le Petit Larousse,* however, most clearly describes this result as political, *"conquête du pouvoir politique par moyens illegaux."*

Naudé's discussion provides material to fill in the gaps I previously noted in the dictionary definitions. What makes the *coup d'état* unlawful is not a judicial decision—the lawyers' authoritative guide—but the initiator's belief that his action cannot be legally

---

[20] William W. Pierson and F. G. Gil, *Governments of Latin America* (New York: 1957), pp. 155ff. It may be argued that, when a court accepts evidence from usurpers that they are willing to abide by the constitution as "proof" of their legitimacy, a rule for judging validity has been developed. But at best we have only a quasi-legal rule because a government has to be overturned before the law is "enforced."

[21] John Locke, *The Second Treatise of Government,* XIV, par. 160. Or, "prerogative is nothing but the power of doing public good without a rule." *Ibid.,* XIV, par. 166. In English and in international law the conception lying behind the "acts of state" doctrine seems to embody similar reasoning.

justified and his fear that others may try to use the law against him. His triumph is complete when the courts surrender jurisdiction. An assassin, therefore, who has no reason to think that the court will give up its right is not committing a *coup d'état*.

Naudé's argument does have one deficiency. If we stress that the means are the primary distinguishing characteristic and that the victims will not receive legal redress, then it is conceivable that instead of simply using his power to gain immunity, the usurper may go much further and attempt to establish a new fundamental law. Thus Kelsen's position is not always indefensible. It should be amended to read that most acts political observers call *coups d'état* lawyers must recognize as the antithesis of revolution, but a few *coups d'état* may be revolutions, depending upon ultimate accomplishments.

The actual circumstances which give rise to particular *coups d'état* vary greatly. A plot may issue from a decision to take advantage of fortuitous events, as the convening of the Huguenots in Paris to celebrate the marriage of their leader provided the opportunity for the St. Bartholomew Massacre. Or it may emerge from years of careful planning, as in the case of Philip's move against the Aragonese nobles. But in either instance, the object is to *surprise* potential resistance and thus, with minimum effort, achieve maximum results.

> There is no necessity of overturning the whole world to occasion the changes of the greatest empires. As Archimedes could move the greatest weights by three or four pieces of timber joined together according to art, so one may ruin, or bring about the greatest of affairs by means that seem almost of no consideration.[22]

Coups d'état obviously attract men willing to gamble to change their personal circumstances in a single act. But unlike the gamester who wages a fixed amount for a given sum, the player in this more dangerous sport may lose everything, including his life, through miscalculation. So much depends upon surprise, and the effect of surprise can be lost by unforeseeable circumstances. The initiator, like Gideon, must limit his forces to gain the full advantage of surprise, and if surprise is thwarted, he has necessarily become vulnerable to a decisive counterstroke.

---

[22] *Political Considerations* . . . , *op. cit.*, p. 129. The fulcrum image is common in *coup d'état* literature. *Cf.* Goodspeed, *op. cit.*, p. xi.

These *coups d'état* are like a sword that may be managed well or ill, as the lance of Telephus that can kill or cure; or like Diana at Ephesus that had two faces one sad and the other pleasant; in short, like the metal invented by the heretics, which represented the devil and the Pope under the same features and lineaments, or the pictures that show life and death according to the different sides that you stand to look upon them.[23]

At the very minimum, a *coup d'état* which has misfired in the process has exposed the initiator's hand, revealing him to be the antithesis of what he once seemed to be. He gains new enemies, and the ensuing consequences are not always clear. What would have happened to Moses and Mohammed if reputable witnesses had disputed their claims concerning the origin of the sacred writings? Pepin could have lost his life; Philip II or Charles IX might well have lost their thrones. In each instance, unpredictable elements of great contingent danger accompany the *coup d'état*; deceit provokes anger, intensifies the will to resist and the desire to destroy.

The invariable alteration of personal relationships, expressed in the loss or gain of personal authority, the sudden transformation of identities, the liquidation of important officials, and so forth, throws the body politic into momentary confusion, and the master of the situation is in an extraordinarily favorable position to frame new laws, eliminate old ones, and alter the constitution.

In the *immediate* aftermath of a *coup d'état*, the masses *can* assume great importance. The act must not antagonize the population. For the moment, the unity of the governing class may be broken and habits of obedience may be shaken, providing opportunities for the normally unimportant but discontented classes to throw their weight into the political scale. No one knows the real strength of the plotters, or how far they intend to go; the first must be demonstrated and the second explained. After the first blow, "twelve eloquent orators" may be more valuable than "two powerful armies."[24] Fickle masses or those easily persuaded to transfer their affections and dissolve their prejudices for established procedures both make a *coup d'état* possible and provide the incentive for those who want one.

---

[23] *Political Considerations,* . . . , *op. cit.,* p. 68. The passage, originally penned by Pierre Charron, illustrates well the reason for King's decision to translate *coup d'état* as master stroke. *Cf.* P. Charron, *Of Wisdom,* tr. George Stanhope (London: 1697), III, 2, p. 18.

[24] *Political Considerations* . . . , *op. cit.,* p. 153.

If popular fickleness made it possible to complete a *coup d'état,*
only men dressed in public authority, Naudé believes, could initiate
one. His view resembles that of the Oxford Dictionary more than
that of Webster's, the latter saying that *coups d'état,* like revolutions,
can be launched by private persons. Yet there are very few empirical
instances to fit the Webster's definition. There are many reasons
why this is so, and it is worth our while to dwell on some of them
in a paragraph or two.

All creatures are vulnerable to unexpected attack; "There is
nothing but what is endangered by that which is weaker than itself."[25] Most powerful animals understand each other's strength and
will attack only for good reason. Their mutual apprehension provides security but simultaneously prevents more than rudimentary
cooperation. Men, on the other hand, though equal to lions in their
capacity to hurt each other, are able to put aside their fears, stimulate mutual trust, and cooperate. But if apprehension provides
security and trust dissolves apprehension, we unwittingly make ourselves more liable to unexpected assaults than ever before. No matter
how well a man knows his neighbor, trust can never be fully war-
ranted. For we are essentially isolated beings, never able to penetrate
each other's minds completely; the signs we depend upon to reveal
meaning can be fabricated to deceive.

In a primitive society the mutual confidence of the participants
is sustained by personal experience. Each has many opportunities to
observe the other *directly,* and a sound assessment of the appro-
priateness of particular actions is strengthened by the fact that
nearly all critics can perform, or have had some direct experience
with, the activity. The private sphere here (the world from which
the coup originates) is limited to its barest physical and psychological minimum.

In a social body involving large numbers performing specialized
tasks, a different set of possibilities necessarily emerges. Everyone has
less contact with other members of the public, and standards of
competence are not easily accessible to all who want to judge. Efficiency requires that some be granted a trust to make decisions for
others, and since direct knowledge of persons and circumstances has
become extremely limited for most persons, confidence in public officials is an act of faith.

The head of state must delegate authority to make and enforce

25 *Ibid.,* p. 133.

decisions to assistants whom he cannot observe directly and continuously. The larger the size of his administration the more indirect
his knowledge of its members becomes. To the extent that he can,
he will surround himself with those who seem reliable, but the action
has unwished for consequences. It makes him vulnerable to the in-
trigues of his assistants, for they cannot be effective in their public
responsibilities unless they have the right to have access to him, to
move freely in critical areas, to meet with colleagues to discuss
common or overlapping jurisdiction, and to have subordinates
trained to follow orders without question. All of these rights give
one invaluable advantages in executing *coups d'état*. And needless
to say, the same reasons which make our administrative head a possible victim of a few of his officials apply with much stronger force
to his own ability to conspire to deprive them of their constitutional
powers.

But for members of the public at large, no badge of trust allows
them access to relevant information and strategic positions, to evade
detection and deceive potential opposition at the crucial moment.
To compensate for the lack of protective camouflage, they must as-
semble a much larger striking force to achieve a *coup d'état*, and
accordingly there is the greater possibility of detection before the
decisive blow is launched.

> Where men are to one another objects of affection and of confidence,
> where they are generally disposed not to offend, government may be
> remiss; and every person treated as innocent until found guilty. . . .
> But where the manners of a people are considerably changed for the
> worse, every subject must stand on his guard, and government itself
> must act on suitable maxims of fear and distrust. The individual,
> no longer fit to be indulged in his pretension to personal consider-
> ation, independence, or freedom, each of which he would turn to
> abuses, must be taught by external forces and from motives of fear
> to counterfeit those effects of innocence and of duty to which he
> is not disposed.
> —Adam Ferguson, *An Essay on the History of Civil Society*

Naudé notes that the final accomplishments of a single *coup
d'état* depend on how extraordinary or unusual the event seems to
be. When citizens believe that the safety of the state has been
jeopardized by unique circumstances, a *coup d'état* will be fully
accepted, but when *coups d'état* occur so often that they seem commonplace in the political world, men suspect the explanations offered, and are tempted to go outside the law themselves to secure

their private purposes. A truly successful *coup d'état*—one that produces a lasting important change—must re-establish a law-abiding habit it has momentarily broken.

In this respect, it is worth noting the difference between Goodspeed's assessment of *coup d'état* and the one conventional among specialists in underdeveloped area studies. To the latter, the individual *coup d'état* rarely alters a body politic much; but to Goodspeed, whose examples come from twentieth-century Europe, a *coup d'état* is clearly the most economical way to achieve a revolution. The reasons for these two very different estimates are obvious. In Europe, where veneration for constituted authority is deeply embodied, only a profound crisis provides opportunity for *coup d'état*. Those who capture government, therefore, have captured an institution which commands respect. They are in a position to make laws which will be obeyed. In Latin America, where a comparatively insignificant incident can topple a government, an illegitimate regime will find it carries its predecessor's albatross.

Perhaps Naudé's major omission is his failure to speculate much about the effects of frequent *coup d'état* on a political system. Had he done so, we would have had some ready-made leverage for a fair assessment of the view that in some countries the act is truly analogous to a constitutionally prescribed procedure—more specifically an election. The contention raises numerous questions and I lack the space to examine them in detail here, but several considerations are pertinent. First, the writer who uses an analogy has a responsibility to demonstrate that the obvious differences between the two phenomena are superficial. Until the obligation has been accepted, the presumption should lie with common-sense distinctions. Second, before any discussion of "constitutional equivalents" is completed, we need an analysis of the consequences of the compared acts on the capacities of the effected states to create agreement and carry on normal administrative functions. States experiencing frequent *coups d'état* notoriously have a low capacity in these respects, and the logical links between the practices and consequences are easy to grasp.

The major argument for the *coup d'état* as an "institutionalized" way of expressing public opinion rests on the undeniable fact that in some states they are common, and the more questionable assertion that they follow a regular, hence predictable pattern with reference to how many lives are lost, who will lose which office, etc. I cannot argue the statistics of the case, for they have not yet been published,[26] but if the events alluded to do not involve the potential dangers, surprises, and suspense associated with *coups d'état* in our language, we ought to use more adequate descriptive terms. However, when Stokes tells us that a well-executed Latin-American *coup d'état* sheds little blood, while a badly bungled one may cost several thousand lives, Naudé's elaborations do not seem to be beside the point. At least, it is difficult to believe that Stokes is talking about procedures with clearly defined and well-understood rules.

Finally, even if regularity is demonstrated, institutionalization is not thereby established. Accidents and robberies can be treated statistically, but we do not then call them institutions. The distinction suggested is similar to the one the lawyer makes beween practice and convention. To say that a convention exists is to imply that the parties to a transaction willingly accept it as the right way to manage affairs even though one party may suffer disadvantages. But there are practices no one considers binding. A government which has the sanction of convention in this sense possesses a right or mandate to rule or represent the citizenry within prescribed limits. A government which lacks a right to rule, whether it attains power through election or *coup d'état,* depends almost entirely on its ability to coerce. Its dilemma is poignantly illustrated by a recent *New York Times* photograph. The picture showed the Venezuelan President Betancourt embracing the Argentine President, and in Betancourt's hip pocket was a pistol! During his five-year administration, he frustrated fifty-six attempted revolts. His right to rule depended partly on his personal willingness to use that pistol, since many of the uprisings were led by men hired to protect his person and office. It takes unusual courage to keep a level head, and, indeed, to survive in such an atmosphere, and the pressures are bound, in time, to engulf the whole state.

No matter how we regard the *coup d'état,* to get a complete picture we must explore the subjective element—the mutual anticipations of those most intimately affected—Lichty's participants. Members of a regime where *coups d'état* are commonplace know that they are likely to be deposed by violence; but before the actual

---

[26] I have been working on a study of the specific immediate consequences of *coups d'état* in selected underdeveloped states. My preliminary research indicates that the presumption of "predictable patterns" is based on very erroneous impressions.

event they do not know who the usurpers are, when they will strike, or what will be the consequences for the members' separate lives and fortunes. The implications of this uncertainty cannot be overestimated. The political world becomes the Hobbesian state of nature where one might be well advised to "shoot first and ask questions later." A prudent government will understand that those most likely to threaten it are posing as loyal supporters occupying positions of trust and protected by the strength of the regime. Its anxiety must obviously influence those who have no desire to overturn the status quo but have reason to think they are peculiarly vulnerable to an "unsteady trigger finger." In a state prone to *coup d'état* there can be little mutual confidence among officials, and since individual initiative, according to law, will breed suspicion, it cannot be permitted much scope. Can government in these circumstances face crises calmly when it does not know who its true supporters are, and when it does know that those who command its separate administrative tools may be able to save themselves by throwing their support to enemies whom the crisis has spawned?

The mutual uncertainty of government officials must invariably affect the government's relationship with the public. In Naudé's view, after the limited objective of the *coup d'état* has been achieved, the logic of the situation compels the usurpers to seek public confirmation of their deed—a confirmation which no one can assume will be forthcoming automatically. But if popular approval is indicated, the value of this apparent approval must always be suspect. Members of the public will always have reason to hide their true feeling; the real strength and purposes of the usurpers are unknown; the examples of how the usurpers treated other officials— especially their confederates—and how the latter, in their time, handled their opposition are still fresh. By the same token, the knowledge that the public has reason to dissemble must sap the new officials' confidence in popular demonstrations. They cannot fail to understand that the public's favorite can become the public's villain in a matter of moments. "The Romans in the morning adored Sejanus and before night . . . he is dragged about the city like a traitor."[27]

The more often *coup d'état* occurs, the more widespread lawlessness must become. A successful *coup d'état* illustrates how profitable it is to evade the law, and that those entrusted with its enforcement

---

[27] *Political Considerations* . . . , *op. cit.*, p. 139.

cannot be expected to treat their responsibilities seriously. The dilemma of an official wishing to abide by the law in such situations is readily imaginable. If he does his duty and attempts to put down subversion, stamp out corruption, and administer justice, that may be the very reason for his elimination when the government he serves is broken—a consideration he can never forget in a country like Venezuela, where there have been eighty illegitimate successions in a century and probably four hundred and eighty unsuccessful attempts.[28] On the other hand, the official who uses his position for private purposes is not easily detected in the great confusion and ineffective supervision implicit in perpetual instability.

In countries where governments succeed one another legitimately, and where the scope of the act vis-à-vis specific officeholders is defined ahead of time, successions may not breed much innovation; but what is more fundamental, though not so obvious, is that each government will receive its predecessors' powers—powers that have not been withered by disrespect, and powers ample enough to accomplish the state's purposes. Where there has been a long tradition of peaceful succession, we can learn much about the distribution of power simply by analyzing constitutions, but in states where *coup d'état* prevails we have learned to use the curious phrase "paper constitutions," which indicates fundamentally that we cannot specify rights and obligations.

When one cannot reckon on the authority of offices or institutions for protection, one will risk "loyalty" only because there seems to be a reason to think the intentions and ability of particular men are different from the type most men display, or because interest compels men to behave in a particular way. Where *coup d'état* is common, so are personal and corrupt regimes. But neither interest nor extraordinary personalities can afford stability and continuity. Interest devoid of the certainty of law varies with circumstance; when a regime is unchallenged, an official's interest is one thing; when it shows signs of crumbling, interest dictates another course.

---

[28] There are many reasons why it is virtually impossible for an American relying on newspaper reports published in this country to know the correct ratio of unsuccessful to successful *coup d'état* attempts. My six-to-one estimate, based entirely on information since 1945, is very conservative. In fact an eight- or nine-to-one ratio is probably more accurate. I have also assumed that the ratio remained constant throughout the nineteenth century, but I believe in that period the percentage of unsuccessful ones was even larger.

And the same conditions that make extraordinary personalities necessary in a "lawless" state make it immensely difficult for them to create something which will outlive them.

Everything an impersonal law nourishes is threatened by continuous *coups d'état*. The moral fiber disintegrates; injustice is widespread in all states with a tradition of *coups d'état*. The material world is also grossly affected. Rich men buried their gold in ancient despotisms plagued by *coups d'état*, and they send it to Swiss banks from modern underdeveloped countries, where it is almost impossible to find three consecutive legitimate successions. In both cases the fear of arbitrary administrative events prevents a socially beneficial employment of capital.

This essay can be summarized quickly. The *coup d'état* has been misunderstood because we have paid insufficient attention to its distinguishing characteristics. In ordinary language, the ideas of uncertainty, danger, surprise, and illegality are integral parts of the concept. But the political meaning of these terms cannot be fully grasped without remembering that they are most readily felt by the protagonist and victim. Naudé's analysis rests on these assumptions; and although he left an incomplete account, it remains our most appropriate starting point.

5

TOCQUEVILLE'S CONTRIBUTIONS TO THE THEORY OF REVOLUTION

MELVIN RICHTER

THE PLACE OF REVOLUTION IN TOCQUEVILLE'S OWN METHOD AND THOUGHT

Perhaps more than any other thinker since Aristotle, Tocqueville gave the phenomenon of revolution a central place in his political theory. For his principal concerns were to determine the preconditions of a free, stable, and constitutional regime and to explain why and how revolutions occur. Seen from his perspective, these issues were inseparable and would henceforth have to be taken into account by any serious political theorist. For the Western world, along with the areas it dominated, could not escape what Tocqueville came to recognize as a permanent revolution. The trend toward greater equality in the structure of societies constituted on the European model, the decline in the importance of distinctions based upon birth alone—these trends would increasingly define the central issues of politics. The events of 1848 convinced Tocqueville that the next phase would involve the application of the principle of equality to private property and economic arrangements.

Tocqueville's concern with revolution was lifelong. His great study of the United States was not least a consideration of how a democratic society, after a purely political revolution, was able to reconcile equality with liberty. The further contrast he was to draw between American and French experiences of revolution were developed, not only in the work he never finished, *L'Ancien Régime et la Révolution,* but in the youthful essay translated by John Stuart Mill as "The Political and Social Condition of France" twenty years before in 1836.[1] Nor did Tocqueville ignore English revolutions and their effect upon free political institutions. Indeed, as Mr. Drescher has recently demonstrated, Tocqueville, fascinated by the skill displayed in handling threats to political stability by the English governing class, sought an explanation in the realism and lack of self-deception developed by practicing politicians in a setting distinguished by a high degree of liberty.[2] What happened between the outbreak of the Revolution of 1848 and the *coup d'état* of Louis Napoleon in 1851 provoked much speculation on Tocqueville's part as to the causes and costs of revolution. The central theme of his *Souvenirs,* and perhaps of all his later work, was that "if one great revolution can lead to the establishment of liberty in a country, a number of successive revolutions makes all regular liberty impossible for a very long time."[3]

Despite his sustained preoccupation with revolution, Tocqueville's contribution to its theory has seldom been treated in isolation from the individual events and societies he analyzed. That Tocqueville's views on this subject should be regarded as of interest principally to historians is a comprehensive, but ultimately unsatisfactory, state of affairs. For historians are apt to limit their concern to what

[1] Alexis de Tocqueville, *Oeuvres complètes. Edition définitive publiée sous la direction de J. P. Mayer,* Tome II, volume I (1951–). Hereafter cited as *Oeuvres* (M), II, i. This same volume contains *"Etat social et politique de la France avant et depuis 1789,"* translated in the *London and Westminster Review* (1836) by Mill. I have used the reprint in *Memoir, Letters, and Remains of Alexis de Tocqueville,* tr. by the translator of *Napoleon's Correspondence with King Joseph* (2 volumes, Boston: 1862), I, pp. 202–252.

[2] Seymour Drescher, *Tocqueville and England* (Cambridge: 1964).

[3] Alexis de Tocqueville, *Souvenirs,* Luc Monnier, ed. (Paris: 1942), p. 74.

Tocqueville has contributed to the present status of their specialty, and although it is most valuable to have his work assessed from this point of view by men of the quality of Georges Lefebvre and Marcel Reinhard, they do not attempt to extricate the hypotheses or theoretical frame of reference that would be applicable to revolutions other than those of 1789 or 1848. It is true, as they emphasize, that Tocqueville tended to generalize by first immersing himself in particular cases.[4] As he himself wrote, "I shall do nothing of value by reasoning *a priori*; but perhaps from a consideration of details, general hypotheses will emerge."[5] Yet the fact remains that, whatever the genesis of his ideas, Tocqueville did produce ultimately an extraordinary number of abstract explanations of how and why revolutions originate and develop. In their quality, suggestiveness, and applicability to situations far removed from situations he studied, they rank high by any standard.

Perhaps the most basic cause of revolution, in Tocqueville's mind, is contradiction between key aspects of the social and political systems of a given country. Such major discrepancies may be corrected either piecemeal or by wholesale change, it may be by force. If this is the case, then it is all-important whether such a frontal attack on the old order is partial, limited—that is, to the political, social, or ideological spheres—or total, involving all of them. Tocqueville placed much stress on analyzing ideas that have served as the intellectual basis for revolutionary movements, as well as the conditions that produce them and the practical effects that result from acting upon such doctrines. He inquired into the basis of their appeal to the audiences attentive to their message, and he insisted that this could not be done adequately except by reference to classes, whether active participants in prerevolutionary society, or alienated from it. Tocqueville clearly perceived the significance of that phenomenon later called "the desertion of the intellectuals," and did so in a way that Raymond Aron still found useful in dealing with the politics of French men of letters a century later. Tocqueville posed the issue of why it is that the original intentions of revolution-

---

[4] Georges Lefebvre, *"Introduction,"* in *Oeuvres* (M), II, i, 9–30; Marcel Reinhard, *"Tocqueville historien de la Révolution,"* in *Alexis de Tocqueville: Livre du centenaire, 1859–1959, Editions du Centre National de la Recherche Scientifique* (1960), pp. 171–180. Another work directed almost entirely to historical questions is Richard Herr, *Tocqueville and the Old Régime* (Princeton: 1962).

[5] Tocqueville, *Oeuvres* (M), II, ii, 173.

aries characteristically produce unanticipated and undesired consequences. Nor did he pass over the issue of leadership. Mosca and
Pareto owed much to Tocqueville, who contrasted elites at the beginning and end of revolutions in terms of their social composition
and psychological make-up; their relative accessibility to new talent:
the protection they afforded to those privileged, but lacking individual merit: and, most important of all in his eyes, their performance of functions defined as essential by the society. In this connection he isolated a phenomenon he identified as new to history:
the proscription of an entire social class and the denial to them
not only of a legitimate claim to participate in government but of
any right to have their interests taken into account.

That standards of legitimacy may themselves be transformed by
changes in the structure of society; in the system of property or inheritance; the pattern of trade, industry, or urbanization; and the
formal arguments of intellectuals—these were matters he regarded
as essential to the theory of revolution. Tocqueville was quick to note
new human types; he was among the first to identify and stress the
importance of the professional revolutionary. As for the times and
places when revolutions are most likely to occur, he tested by comparative analysis the propositions of common sense and found them
of no merit. For he denied that revolutions are made because of
intolerable suffering on the part of the general populace. Rather,
he suggested, that they most often occur when economic hardship is
less than it has been in the recent past and when an oppressive
regime is attempting to reform itself by mitigating its severities.

If Tocqueville thus anticipated many subsequent hypotheses, can
it be said that his method excluded any of the major explanations
of why revolution occurs? Such a question casts much light both on
Tocqueville as a theorist and on his relationship to the interests and
modes of thought characteristic of the aristocracy into which he was
born. Particularly noteworthy is the fact that he specifically rejected all conspiracy hypotheses of the sort so dear to members of
his class.[6] Instead of attributing the French Revolution to a well-
organized conspiracy of Freemasons, or, for that matter, of irre-
ligious and anarchical elements, he asserted that the fault lay rather
in the aristocracy of the old regime, which was on the whole
decadent and in default of its plain duties, the fulfillment of which
had once justified their privileges. It was an essential part of his
notion of what is entailed in an adequate explanation that revolu-

[6] A notable disavowal occurs in Tocqueville, *Souvenirs*, p. 49.

tions, like all events of comparable magnitude, must be seen as the result of long-range trends impersonal in nature, just as they are touched off by accidents unforeseen by those considered by themselves and others as the leaders of the movement. For his failure to perceive these aspects of the French Revolution, Burke was severely censured by Tocqueville, who shared neither the Englishman's contempt for the men of 1789 nor his simplistic notion of why these momentous situations had come into being.[7]

Yet it cannot be said that Tocqueville transcended political partisanship. His admiration for the first phase of the French Revolution stemmed from his belief that its slogans should be applied only to politics and not at all to economic arrangements. It is difficult to deny the truth of M. Maxime Leroy's observation that Tocqueville's contempt for the Socialists of 1848 was based on an almost complete ignorance of the conditions they sought to rectify. More serious are certain congenital defects that consistently marred his books: the inability to define key terms and to persist in their use in a single sense; the intrusive moralism that led him to confuse judgments of value with those of fact; and the occasional tendency to push conclusions beyond the evidence available for them. Nevertheless Tocqueville is read, and deserves to be read, for the fertility of his hypotheses and the subtlety of his method of dealing with the phenomenon of revolution.

Precision in defining terms was not among Tocqueville's virtues. His equivocations about the use of *démocratie,* are notorious, for sometimes he used this word in referring to political form, a regime in which the majority holds ultimate power, but more often he meant a society characterized by a high degree of equality in the conditions common to its members. Toward the end of his life he wished to reserve the term for a political system in which the inhabitants take a large part in government and enjoy liberty.[8] Much the same range of variation is to be found in his use of *révolution,* which varied from the notion of any large-scale qualitative change in a society to that of a sudden and convulsive transformation by

---

[7] "For Burke the Revolution was due, not to the natural emergence of emotions long-felt, but to the artful work of a conspiracy." Tocqueville, *Oeuvres* (M), II, ii, 341. "Burke failed to see what was taking place before his eyes, that it was to be the achievement of the Revolution to abolish 'the ancient common law of Europe.' " *Ibid.,* II, i, 96.

[8] Cf. George Wilson Pierson, *Tocqueville and Beaumont in America* (New York: 1938), pp. 158n–159n, 757–758; Tocqueville, *Oeuvres* (M), II, ii, 199.

force of its political arrangements, and possibly its social system and religious beliefs as well. In the first sense, he wrote of *"une grande révloution démocratique"* and *"la révolution industrielle,"* but, as will soon appear, he also could make the use of force into the critical element in his definition.[9]

Change in the Essential Principle of a Society

Tocqueville is increasingly acknowledged as one of the founders of political sociology. Determined to penetrate beneath surface appearances, he insisted that the quality of a nation's political life depends not primarily upon its geographical position, nor even upon its legal codes or constitutional structure, but upon its *moeurs,* "what the ancients called *mores."*[10] This concept, fundamental to all of Tocqueville's work and derived from Montesquieu, is heavily used in what he wrote on revolution. He tended to think of *moeurs* as involving the totality of a society's operative ideas and attitudes, those cultural patterns of behavior that depend upon habit and social sanctions rather than cerebration and legal punishments. The *moeurs* of a society always have a high degree of internal coherence, what Montesquieu called *l'esprit général,* and Tocqueville in various places called *la cause génératrice, le principe d'action,* or *le principe régulateur.*[11] Equality or inequality of conditions are among the regulative principles most often stressed by Tocqueville. Any given society must be dominated by one and only one such principle. What Tocqueville wished to emphasize is the type of strain, the critical instability that is produced by a contradiction between the structure of civil society and the make-up of the political regime. When this occurs, either the society will fall apart or it will undergo a revolution. Hence Tocqueville's insistence that, given the conditions existing in France toward the end of the eighteenth century, the old order was doomed, although not necessarily by violent overthrow.[12]

[9] *Ibid.,* I, i, 1, and *Souvenirs,* p. 72.
[10] *Oeuvres* (M), I, i, 300, 319n *et seq.*
[11] *Ibid.,* I, i, 5, 262–63; II, i, 51; V, ii, 36.
[12] "Whoever wished to penetrate beneath external aspects . . . could not help concluding that France, as it was then, for all its nobility, state religion, its aristocratic laws and usages, was already the most democratic nation in Europe . . . because of its social condition, its civic condition, its ideas and its *moeurs." Ibid.,* II, i, 53. This passage was translated by J. S. Mill in *Memoir, Letters . . . of Tocqueville, op. cit.,* pp. 232–233. I have made some changes.

Resort to Violence

In thus dealing with revolution, Tocqueville called attention to the problems of transition from a society of ascribed status to a new order based upon achievement and legal equality. This was predominantly a European problem, for the full realization of the new order there was obstructed by what was left of feudal institutions. These had to be replaced by "a social and political order more uniform and simple and based upon equality of conditions." Tocqueville never doubted that the old regime had to fall; its disintegration had been in process for ten generations before 1789. But everything depended upon the means used to secure its passage from the scene. Had the Revolution not occurred, the ancient social fabric would have crumbled all the same, but piecemeal and unevenly, instead of being destroyed at a single blow. "The revolution achieved suddenly, by a convulsive and painful process, without transition, without precaution, without prior calculation, what, in the long run, would have taken place gradually by itself. Such was its work."[13] Violence, then, rather than degree of change was the distinctive quality of the French Revolution.

This was the conclusion of Tocqueville's last word on the subject in his *L'Ancien Régime et la Révolution*. Earlier he had wavered in his choice of the decisive element in revolution. Tocqueville visited England for the first time in 1833, after his return to France from the United States, but before he completed the first part of his *Démocratie*. Arriving with the conviction that England was on the verge of revolution, he, by the end of his visit, decided that he had been wrong. His reflections reveal how inventive his mind was, and how he could not bring himself to give simply one meaning to the term "revolution."

> If "revolution" means all fundamental changes in the law, all transformations of society, all substitutions of one regulative principle for another, then England is certainly in a revolutionary condition. For every day the aristocratic principle, which was the vital part of her constitution, loses in strength; and it is probable that within a given time, the democratic principle will take its place. But if by "revolution" is meant a sudden and abrupt change, then England does not seem to me to be ready for such an eventuality.[14]

[13] Tocqueville, *Oeuvres* (M), II, i, 96.
[14] *Ibid.*, V, ii, 36.

Adoption of a General Theory Prescribing
Subversion of the Existing Order

Tocqueville, therefore, did not believe that the change from one type of social system to another necessarily involved the use of force. But instead of giving his reasons for so thinking, or specifying just what it is that enables one country to manage such a transformation without domestic convulsion, he leaped to a new hypothesis, that the crucial consideration is the presence or absence of revolutionary theories:

> The English have, then, embarked on a dangerous road, but they are proceeding detail by detail, without having yet embraced any of those great, general ideas that announce the total subversion of the existing order.
>
> To sum up, England appears to me to be in a critical situation in that certain contingencies could in a minute throw her into a state of violent revolution. But if things follow their natural course, I do not believe that this will happen. Rather I see a good chance that the English will succeed in modifying their political and social order, passing through a period of considerable unrest, but without the ultimate convulsion of civil war.[15]

When Tocqueville defined what he meant by a genuinely revolutionary theory, he left it unclear whether he considered such ideas symptom or cause. And he was no more definite about whether such ideas necessarily oblige their adherents to take up arms. "Those theories that are revolutionary in character are so by the fact that they cannot be realized except by a complete, and it may be sudden, change in the order of property and persons. . . ."[16] Thus a third strand has been added to the definition of revolution by Tocqueville; revolutionary theories join fundamental change and the resort to violence as elements to be taken into account.

Application to One or More Sectors of Society

Many, perhaps most, revolutions never go beyond changing the political arrangements of their society; rather fewer are social as well; and only one, as of the time Tocqueville wrote, had been simultaneously political, social, and religious. No doubt the Russian Revolution would qualify as a second example, and indeed it is striking to see how many of Tocqueville's generalizations about the

15 *Ibid.*, V, ii, 39, 42.
16 *Ibid.*, I, ii, 262.

significance of the French Revolution facilitate understanding of what happened later in the Soviet Union.

Tocqueville seems to have considered the American Revolution as the paradigm of a political revolution that left quite unaltered the social structure, the system of property, and the religious beliefs of the country.[17] The English Revolution, in his eyes, was political and religious; the changes brought by the Reformation and the introduction by force of Islam were religious only. A political revolution, then, involves a change in the nature of the regime, and is distinguished from rebellions aimed at nothing more than substituting some persons for others in power.[18] To the extent that Tocqueville was ready to sanction revolution at all, he favored those of the purely political variety. His praise for the French Revolution was restricted to its first phase, and he thought that because the American Revolution had never gone beyond its initial and limited objectives, its leaders had been able to succeed and to consolidate their victory.

What did Tocqueville mean by his reference to the social dimension of revolution? As was common in his time, he included economic phenomena, such as the system of ownership, production, and distribution in the category of the "social question." But perhaps of equal or greater importance in his mind was what he regarded as one of the great and pernicious innovations of the French Revolution—the declassification by law and the banishment from the national territory of an entire category of persons whose position had previously been conceded. Nor was the issue simply that of dislodging the aristocracy from a position of privilege. Its members were allowed no place in the reconstituted body politic, their interests were not regarded as even worthy of consideration. Tocqueville here was criticizing the substitution of revolutionary justice for what he considered the essence of politics, "the *political* or *republican* way where it is attempted to conciliate these differing interests by in some manner letting them share in the business of government."[19] Even before the Revolution began, its theorists left no place

---

[17] Mr. R. R. Palmer has argued that the American Revolution produced social changes of a magnitude comparable to those wrought by the French Revolution. He uses two criteria, the number of refugees and the amount of property they lost. R. R. Palmer, *The Age of the Democratic Revolution* (Princeton: 1959), p. 188.

[18] Tocqueville, *Souvenirs*, p. 52.

[19] I use here the language of a recent writer, who identifies politics with

for compromise or bargaining with the interests of the *noblesse:*
"The very idea of a *transaction* is not to be found—the idea that
there be an accommodation between different interests, the old and
the new. The only thing that mattered was to attain a certain ideal
of the constitution. Any obstacle to it, whether in antecedent institutions or the men who represented them, was declared illegitimate and deprived of the right to defend itself and its interests."[20]
Tocqueville made no attempt to represent his class as guiltless, even
in this matter, but he thought that a dangerous precedent had been
set, and that grave political damage had been done to future stability and to the human resources of the country. "Certainly the
noblesse deserves to be condemned for having emigrated. But it
also ought to be recognized that no other people had ever declared
an entire class of citizens to be outside the protection of the laws,
thus in effect driving them out of their own country."[21] The way
was open for the new regime to subject all Frenchmen without
distinction to its laws; it did not do so. The result was that after the
noblesse returned, it became permanently hostile to any government
associated with the revolutionary tradition. And in addition to this
permanent alienation, the country lost the use of a class that was
not without its qualities.

These remarks do not exhaust what Tocqueville had to say
about the social aspect of revolution. The replacement of one elite
by another drawn from a different class; the leadership of previously
disadvantaged groups by disgruntled members of the ruling class—
these were matters Tocqueville thought to be of the greatest importance. They will be discussed in the section devoted to Tocqueville's application of class analysis to the sociology of revolution.

There remains what Tocqueville thought to be the most extraordinary quality of the French Revolution, its religious character.
Just what did he mean by this? Although he took pains to make
himself clear, his point is still confounded with views he explicitly
rejected. He denied firmly that the Revolution had been directed
against the Church because of its doctrine of pastoral function.
Rather, he argued, the evidence strongly indicated that it had been

---

the processes of a free and constitutional order, as did Tocqueville. Bernard
Crick, *In Defence of Politics,* revised Pelican edition (Baltimore: 1964), p.
163.
    [20] Tocqueville, *Oeuvres* (M), II, ii, 163.
    [21] *Ibid.,* II, ii, 140.

the Church's involvement in the political and economic order that had created animosity against it. Nor was Tocqueville any more friendly to the view that everything lamentable about the Revolution could be attributed to its embracing a false secular religion. Quite to the contrary, he contrasted the acquiescence of the devout in the dictatorship of Louis Napoleon to the "moral grandeur unparalleled in history" of the revolutionaries in 1789.[22]

Among the distinctively religious aspects of the French Revolution were its international character and its intensive use everywhere of propaganda and proselytism. The French Revolution resembled the Thirty Years' War in that all international disputes took on something of the character of civil wars, while every actual civil war fought at that time was marked by the active intervention of foreigners. All at once the habitual calculation of interest by rulers was superseded by their preoccupation with abstract principles. International politics became a very different thing when statesmen thought of themselves as fighting a holy war, or defending their way of life against satanic adversaries. This occurred because the French Revolution spread so far from the country of its origin and did so by an ideological offensive intended to make conversions in mass among the subjects of its enemies.[23]

The revolutionary doctrine further resembled that of religious movements in that it discovered what is most distinctively human and valuable in qualities easily divorced from a man's membership in any given society. Its message was cosmopolitan, and, indeed, its appeal was far more to those who hoped to regenerate the entire human species than to those who would have been content to engage in a piecemeal reform of their own country. The high idealism, the generosity of revolutionary ideals aroused passions not ordinarily involved in politics. Thus it was that the Revolution covered the world with its soldiers, its apostles, and its martyrs.

No part of Tocqueville's method meant more to him than the use of the comparative method. Thus he felt obliged to specify the differences between the French and English Revolutions, particularly in terms of the levels on which they had operated. As for the English Revolution, it had barely touched the country's administrative and legal systems, let alone its customs and usages. In England the people as a whole had participated to only a small extent, com-

[22] *Ibid.*, II, ii, 131n.
[23] *Ibid.*, II, i, 87–90; II, ii, 190, 220.

pared to the French Revolution. And the English had been more interested in liberty than equality, which was not the case with the French, although both revolutions were part of the same historical movement. Yet all these contrasts counted for less than the fact that, although the government underwent violent change, the English revolution was less political than religious and the society remained unshaken. Despite attacks on the summit, the social base remained firm. Thus in England not every aspect of national life was recast simultaneously.[24]

Characteristics and Consequences of Total Revolution

The French Revolution had been unique in all history because the antecedent system of belief was officially abandoned at the very time that the political and social orders were being transformed. This had two effects: it removed simultaneously all the forces usually restraining men's wills and imaginations—religion, social custom, and legal sanction; and it thereby made it difficult, if not impossible for political actors to engage in rational calculation of the consequences likely to follow from one or another course of action. In such a revolution, there must be great discrepancies between intention and actual effect. This is one explanation of why from a movement based upon generous and benign maxims, there had ensued acts of violence on an unprecedented scale. In the absence of all fixed points, it became impossible to settle upon appropriate means; to know what ought to be retained, and what discarded; which innovations might succeed, and which were doomed to failure. Above all, there was no way to determine at what point the Revolution ought to stop.[25]

To this lack of orientation, the religious dimension of the Revolution contributed much. Tocqueville's point here should not be confused with the conventional pietism of conservatives. He rejected their assertion that lack of faith inevitably produces political anarchy.[26] While he was doing his study of the Revolution, the

[24] *Ibid.*, II, i, 242; II, ii, 334–35.
[25] *Ibid.*, II, i, 85, 87–90, 202–208, 245.
[26] Cf. Doris Goldstein, "Alexis de Tocqueville's Concept of Citizenship," *Proceedings of the American Philosophical Society*, 108 (February 1964), 39–53. My interpretation of Tocqueville's position differs in some respects from Dr. Goldstein's comments (p. 51) on the passage in *Oeuvres* (M), II, i, 207–08.

Church, acquiescing in the dictatorship of Louis Napoleon, identified political virtue with unquestioning obedience to the forces of order. Speaking as a liberal who detested this repressive regime, Tocqueville found a good deal to praise in the men of the Enlightenment who put their stamp on the Revolution's first phase; speaking as a sociological historian, he nevertheless had to conclude that the chief effect of irreligion had been further to unsettle men's minds in a situation already chaotic because of political and social upheaval.

Respect for law and obedience to authority had long been taught to the mass of men by their Church; to a significant extent the legitimacy of the regime and the sense of political obligation rested upon religious sanctions. Yet the loss of faith does not immediately create a spiritual vacuum. The place of religion is filled for a time by other emotions and ideas that serve the same function. These were supplied for the French Revolution by some of the Enlightenment thinkers. Their initial effects were to create a set of qualities Tocqueville wished were still alive in his time: a virile confidence in man's capacity to perfect himself; an idealism that led its devotees to acts of heroism and disinterestedness far removed from the egoistic individualism of a bourgeois society that professes piety so as to safeguard property. Although they did not believe in God, men of that time still believed in themselves. This did not make monsters of them; it did not even corrupt their *moeurs*. The effects of irreligion were far more "to confuse men's minds than to debase their hearts, or even to lower their principles of conduct."[27] Tocqueville's use of the term *déréglant* resembles Durkheim's concept of *anomie* in that it emphasizes the drastic effects upon men of living in a disorganized setting where they lack recognized standards of conduct. It was for this reason that irreligion contributed to the immense damage wrought by the Revolution. Because it occurred as part of a total upheaval, it produced consequences that were undesired and unanticipated.

Among them was the rise of a new human type, formed by total revolution and destined to play a prominent role in the politics of

---

[27] "Quand je cherche à démêler les differents effets que l'irréligion produisit alors en France, je trouve que ce fut bien plus en déréglant les esprits qu'en dégradant les coeurs, ou même en corrompant les moeurs, qu'elle disposa les hommes de ce temps-là à se porter à des extrémités si singulières." *Ibid.*, II, i, 207.

the nineteenth and twentieth centuries. The professional revolutionary promises to realize the doctrine of the movement in all its
purity. The price he exacts is the absolute obedience of his followers
and the exclusive right to speak in their name without consulting
them. Once installed in power it is not the people who direct revolutionary governments, but those who know what is best for the
people, "a happy distinction, which permits them to act in the
name of nations without consulting them and to claim their grati-
tude while trampling them underfoot. . . . Until our day it had
been thought that tyranny was odious in all its forms. Now it has
been discovered that there are legitimate tyrannies and sacred injustices, provided that they are exercised in the name of the people."[28] This variety of "democratic despotism" Tocqueville identified
with the "race of revolutionaries" or the "esprit révolutionnaire."[29]
The applicability of this concept to subsequent revolutionary regimes
is so obvious as to need no emphasis. The same is true of what
Tocqueville had to say about the position of individual or minority
rights under a government dominated by revolutionaries subscribing
to such a view:

> There emerged from the French Revolution and there survives a
> race of revolutionaries, a new phenomenon, it would seem, in his-
> tory . . . which not only practices violence, the scorn for individual
> rights, and the oppression of minorities, but also, and this is al-
> together novel, teaches that all such things ought to be done as a
> matter of right; which has as its doctrine that there are no individual
> rights and, so to speak, that individuals have no reality, a quality
> reserved for the mass to which everything is permitted to attain its
> ends.[30]

It goes without saying that the carriers of this tradition had an
interest in making the revolution permanent, in perpetuating symbols
and modes of thought justifying violence in the name of right.

[28] *Ibid.*, I, i, 413.
[29] Cf. *Souvenirs*, p. 163, written toward the end of his life, and in a
letter of his youth: "I do not believe that there is a man in France who is
less revolutionary than I, or who has a more profound hatred for what is
called the *esprit révolutionnaire* (which, parenthetically, is very easily joined
with love for absolute government)." *Oeuvres complètes d'Alexis de Tocqueville*, Gustave de Beaumont, ed., 9 volumes (Paris: 1864–66), V, 436. Hereafter cited as *Oeuvres* (B).
[30] *Oeuvres* (M), II, ii, 337. This passage is an extended comment on
Tocqueville's own passage closing out his chapter explaining why, because
of a total revolution, irreligion contributed to the creation of this new human
type.

Summary of and Comment Upon Tocqueville's
Definitions of "Revolution"

Tocqueville's conception of revolution included a number of elements. Although each of them may be understood without difficulty within the context given them by their author, they do not form a single and coherent conceptual scheme.

When Tocqueville speaks of the single principle or spirit that animates the *moeurs* of a society, he is using an organic concept that assumes the necessity for internal congruence among all the aspects of a society.[31] Presumably it is for this reason that he denies the possibility of an enduring system in which more than one operative principle is at work. Contradictions must be resolved, or else the society will be rent in two by revolution or by the spontaneous decomposition of institutions and *moeurs*. Clearly Tocqueville was dealing with the same problem that preoccupied Hegel and Marx when they dealt with contradictions by their respective formulations of dialectic. Hegel, like Tocqueville, accepted Montesquieu's method as the appropriate means for his own investigations.[32]

When viewed in the perspective of subsequent theorizing about society, Tocqueville can now be understood to have combined an ideal-type analysis with what Professor Popper has called "essentialism."[33] That is, Tocqueville attempted, again following Montesquieu, to establish categories, referring at once to types of regime and society, and to place certain nations of his time within these categories. While later theorists who made use of this method of ideal-types, notably Max Weber, stressed the fact that no actual

---

[31] "It might be said of human institutions, as of the human body, that there is a central and invisible force, which is the very principle of life, independent of the organs that fulfill functions necessary for continued existence. When this life-giving flame is extinguished, the organs cannot act as before, and they all languish and then die." Tocqueville, *Oeuvres* (M), II, i, 144.

[32] ". . . Montesquieu proclaimed the true historical view, the genuinely philosophical position, namely, that legislation both in general and in its particular provisions is to be treated not as something isolated and abstract but rather as a subordinate moment in a whole, interconnected with all the other features which make up the character of a nation and an epoch." *Hegel's Philosophy of Right*, T. M. Knox, tr. (Oxford: 1942), p. 16. Although Tocqueville referred to Cuvier and the vitalism of the Montpellier School, his real model was Montesquieu.

[33] Karl Popper, *The Open Society and Its Enemies* (New York: 1963), II, 9–21, 37.

society would ever be found to embody all the characteristics of the
type to which the analyst assigned it, Tocqueville was committed to
the belief that it is possible to discover just what is the single, uni-
fying principle of integration in any social and political system.
Thus he passed over the possibility that a society may embody several disparate characteristics. He failed to see that his terms of analysis permitted such a conclusion, that he was in no way obliged to
decide whether England was essentially democratic or aristocratic.
By using the method of ideal-types, he could have maintained that
England was, and would long continue to be, a baffling combination
of both. Instead, his conviction that a society can be dominated
only by one principle led him to believe that he had to assign England to one or the other category. Had Tocqueville renounced "essentialism," his conceptual scheme would have been a better tool
for the analysis of revolutionary situations.

Nor is the assumption of a *principe régulateur* really compatible
with his proposal that revolutions be studied in terms of the three
possible levels on which revolution may occur. For if every important aspect of society is organically related to every other in a
system, how is it possible to isolate one level, such as politics, from
social and economic arrangements? Presumably what occurs in one
must vitally affect any other part of the same system. It is characteristic of Tocqueville's unsystematic way of proceeding both that such
an inconsistency should exist and that each scheme of anaylsis
should be so adequate to the particular range of problems for which
he used it. As a theorist he was highly pragmatic, but also capable
of devising a scheme of middle-range abstraction to cope with the
considerations that have to be taken into account by anyone dealing
with revolution in the modern world.

To sum up what has been said thus far about his definitions, a
political revolution is, according to him, a change in the quality of
a regime; a social revolution is a drastic declassification from membership in a society of certain categories of persons, the replacement
in leadership of one class by another, or the substitution of one system of property for another. Finally, a religious revolution is the
abandonment of one set of principles involving belief in the nature
and destiny of man, and it may be, man's relation to God, and the
acceptance of an alternative set of beliefs. This term would also apply to general systems of beliefs which include theories of legitimacy
and political obligation. Tocqueville argued that any revolution at-

tempting to transform all three spheres simultaneously will most likely go out of control because the results of major decisions cannot be rationally anticipated or calculated. To terminate such a revolution is difficult, if not impossible, for it breeds ideological dynamism of a sort that will tolerate no barriers to the achievement of the movement's ill-defined goals, and bestows leadership upon professional revolutionaries. A total revolution, therefore, is apt to produce a sequence of successive resorts to violence. Once this happens, there grows up throughout that society a low estimate of legal procedures and constitutional forms; there tends to be an acceptance, although different groups will interpret this according to their own interests, of the theory of social utility—i.e., that individuals and minorities have no claim against the overriding purpose of society. In terms of centralization, both conservatives and revolutionaries tend to believe that there should be such an omnipotent sovereign, for both think in terms of using that power against their enemies. Even if a stable government should be established in the wake of a total revolution, its violent origins tend to be perpetuated in its patterns of administration and in the *moeurs* of the ruling class, particularly its intolerance of opposition or of groups not under its direct control. These are the costs of a revolution such as began in 1789.

ROLE OF IDEAS AND INTELLECTUALS IN REVOLUTION

It has already been noted that Tocqueville identified as a condition of revolution the presence of general theories about the nature of a good society, theories that could not be realized except by changing completely, and possibly violently, the status of persons and property under the existing order. This hypothesis, along with Tocqueville's treatment of eighteenth-century *philosophes* and *physiocrates* has led some of his readers to represent him as an implacable enemy of the Enlightenment and, indeed, of all general, abstract statements of political ideals.[34] For it is thought that, like Burke and Taine, Tocqueville believed that the world would be spared great convulsions if only there were no radical intellectuals or men of letters subverting society by their impractical speculations.

---

[34] Peter Gay, *Voltaire's Politics* (Princeton: 1959), pp. 7–8, 8n; and the same author's *The Party of Humanity* (New York: 1964), pp. 166–167, 266–267.

In fact Tocqueville held a number of theories on this subject at various times of his life. In his most mature and sophisticated treatments of this persistent theme, he offered a more complex set of explanations of the origins and functions of abstract ideas, and made a more balanced philosophical assessment of the Enlightenment, and of theories of legitimacy in particular. At the end of his life, he wrote in a note unprinted until recently, "I find the absolute and systematic denigration in our time of what is called eighteenth-century philosophy to be as blind and foolish as the infatuation it once produced among its admirers."[35]

Ideas, Interests, and Passions

In stressing the relation between ideas and revolution, Tocqueville made use of an explanation as old as Plato and Aristotle. Ever since the latter found the root of revolution in discrepant theories within the same society, of what is justice, there have followed a number of other hypotheses emphasizing the role of ideas and those who formulate and disseminate them. Such analyses tend to fix upon one or more of the following assertions about the ideas that are prominent in revolutionary movements: men are moved to take extreme political action when and only when they hold a rigid set of beliefs that lead them to judge and condemn the existing order; alternatively, it is held that all ideologies or political formulas are in fact rationalizations of personal or group interests, whether consciously calculated or unconsciously imposed; finally there are champions of the view that revolutionaries, like all other men, are capable neither of the rationalism that is implied by considering them to be simply translating their principles into action nor of that required for men to devise arguments they themselves do not believe. This third type emphasizes nonrational or irrational forces within men, and discounts all intellectual constructions as derivative from such forces. Which of these positions did Tocqueville hold?

The truth is that there was no one of them to which he adhered throughout his life. In the second part of the *Démocratie,* he maintained that it is essentially strong emotions that produce revolutions. On that basis he argued that, since the citizens of democracy become so involved in enriching themselves, there is little likelihood that they can be interested in revolution. "It is enthusiasm that

[35] Tocqueville, *Oeuvres* (M), II, ii, 348.

drives men's minds off the beaten tracks and produces the great revolutions both in thought and in politics."[36] Tocqueville distinguished between the United States and France and asserted that in the American republic there were to be found only democratic ideas and passions, while in France, revolutionary ideas and passions still rang strong. Although in this passage Tocqueville made ideas subordinate to emotion, he reversed himself within a few years when he delivered an address on the occasion of his entry into the Académie Française in 1842. Here and in a number of other texts preceding his *L'Ancien Régime,* Tocqueville espoused a theory resembling that of the philosophical idealists who found history to be the working out of the implications immanent in ideas. But by the time Tocqueville came to write his last major work, he subscribed to a far more sophisticated conceptual framework that included ideas, passions, and interests in his account of revolutionaries' motives. Now he came to adopt a political sociology that was almost incompatible with his previous idealist stand, and wrote of ideas as the product of social structure and political organization. The principal function of ideas was described as providing a definition of the situation for those acting in politics.

When at the height of his idealist position, Tocqueville found it easy to fit ideas into the organic metaphor he used so often. Ideas are the vital principle of the body politic; a society's philosophy is its *principe régulateur.* Thus when the thinkers of the eighteenth century replaced what had been believed by new concepts of good and evil, truth and falsity, justice and injustice, "the vital principle of the old monarchy was fatally wounded, and the great social revolution of 1789 began."[37] Philosophy was turning gradually into actual revolution, illustrating once more that great intellectual upheavals produce inexorably similar results in politics and society. Ten years later in another discourse given in his capacity as President of the Academy of Moral and Political Science, Tocqueville once again attributed the Revolution not to the *hommes politiques* of the old regime but to those thinkers who had put into the minds of men the seeds of those novelties that were to become the institutions of the new order. From general ideas "come the facts statesmen deal with and the laws they devise. Such ideas are to be found at work in every society, for they form a kind of intellectual

---

[36] *Ibid.,* I, ii, 267.
[37] Tocqueville, *Oeuvres* (B), IX, 6.

atmosphere, in which the minds of governors and governed breathe, and, often without knowing it, draw the principles of their conduct."[38] And what were the motives of eighteenth-century thinkers? Tocqueville first attempted to explain them by the psychology of resentment. Men of letters, once admitted to noble houses, were angered by the benefits of birth. Hence the desertion of the old regime by intellectuals.

These earlier treatments of writers and their part in revolution were almost completely discarded in Tocqueville's *L'Ancien Régime* and the notes he compiled for its sequel. Although scarcely better disposed than before to the *philosophes* and *physiocrates,* he now considered their thought a result of the structure of society and the patterns of political life established by the monarchy, rather than their envy. At the same time, Tocqueville took up once again the question of the relation among ideas, interests, and passions. In a remarkable passage, he identified man's need for general ideas to justify himself and his causes with what he called one of the noblest aspects of human nature, the inability to regard individual or group benefit as sufficient warrant for conduct. Without adopting the easy but unconvincing view that interests count for nothing, without representing human action as more rational than observation could confirm, he underlined what are the functions of legitimacy as a political force:

> Usually men become committed with all the ardor, energy, and staying power of which they are capable, to only those causes that have aroused passions connected to their own self-interest. But however intense these passions, their effect will be limited unless the cause is made legitimate by joining it to some cause that serves all mankind.
>
> It is an honor to human nature that we need such a stimulant. Do you wish to see what man can achieve? Then join to the passions originating in personal interest the goals of changing the face of the world and regenerating the human species.
>
> This is the history of the French Revolution.[39]

Tocqueville thought that there is always a gulf between ideas, as conceived by theorists, and their practical application. Political philosophers accept logic as their norm; the mass of men who act upon their maxims are actually dominated by their passions. This an-

---

[38] *Ibid.,* IX, 122.
[39] Tocqueville, *Oeuvres* (M), II, ii, 349–350; *Oeuvres* (B), IX, 118.

tinomy between ideas and passions, as well as that between the original form and intention of upper-class theorists and the uses to which they are put by the classes beneath them were prominent in Tocqueville's *L'Ancien Régime*. He used these points to complete his explanation of why the Revolution made in the name of the most benign ideals became so cruel. Thus he did not hold the thinkers of the eighteenth century responsible for what he deplored in the Revolution. Their most permanent and pernicious contribution to French politics was their habit of judging it by standards derived from literature, but altogether inapplicable to the affairs of a free society. This approach, so far from being part of the French national character, was quite unknown prior to the eighteenth century. It contributed, although it was far from being the exclusive cause, to the Revolutions of 1789 and 1848, and became thereafter an unhappy characteristic of politics:

> . . . seeking what is novel and ingenious, rather than what is true; preferring what is showy to what is useful; showing more interest in the acting and speaking of the performers than in the outcome of the play; and finally deciding on the basis of mere impressions rather than by solid reasons. . . . To tell the truth, the entire nation rather tends to act in this way, and the French people, taken as a whole, very often make political judgments characterized by *l'esprit littéraire*.[40]

Readers of M. Aron's *The Opium of the Intellectuals* will note that Tocqueville's observations were not altogether outmoded after the Second World War.

Even with such hypotheses about the political style of men formed as writers, we have not arrived at the heart of Tocqueville's analysis. For in the *L'Ancien Régime* he carefully refrained from making the assertion that it had been ideas that had caused the Revolution. If he attributed great importance to the style of "abstract, literary politics," which he claimed to discover in everything from the weightiest treatise to popular songs, he did not hold men of letters uniquely or directly responsible.[41] His analysis was more complex, and can best be understood in the light of later theorists who developed more systematically the method Tocqueville practiced but never codified. One of these was Karl Mannheim, who explicitly acknowledged Tocqueville's contribution to the sociology of knowl-

---

[40] Tocqueville, *Souvenirs*, p. 76.
[41] Tocqueville, *Oeuvres* (M), II, i, 194.

edge;[42] another was Max Weber, the author of a sociology of religion, which in its formulation of the role played by ideas in social action closely resembled Tocqueville's mature position; and the third was Karl Marx, whose theory in this respect, as in so many others, converged with Tocqueville's attribution of "false consciousness" to a class.

Why Revolutionary Ideas Developed Within a Given Milieu and Assumed Their Characteristic Form

Mannheim believed that styles of thought could be understood only in terms of the functions they performed for the social group to which thinkers belonged. Their insights into reality and their deformations of it are both due to a perspective derived not from an individual's characteristics but from the location in society of his group.[43] Tocqueville's treatment of political thinkers in the old regime is phrased in very much the same set of terms. He asserted that these men of letters, although differing in the details of their respective systems, all had the same point of departure—they believed that nothing was more important than to base society upon simple, uncomplicated rules drawn from reason and the natural law, principles which would replace the existing tangle of tradition and obsolete law.[44] This mode of thought, so revolutionary in its implications for eighteenth-century France, was in fact not new. It had been a recognized strand of Western thought for two thousand years. Why, then, instead of remaining confined to the milieu of philosophers and theologians, as in the past, did it in this instance spread from these limited circles to every level of society in such a way as to become a political passion?

Tocqueville's first hypothesis was not unlike Hegel's theory of dialectic, with its suggestion that out of the inherent contradictions of a stituation, there necessarily emerges its antithesis:

> It was not by accident that the *philosophes* generally held notions so opposed to those that served as the basis of their society. These notions were naturally suggested to them by that society itself. In it there existed so many ridiculous privileges, so many abuses,

---

[42] Karl Mannheim, "Conservative Thought," in *Essays on Sociology and Social Psychology* (London: 1953), p. 83n.

[43] In addition to the essay, "Conservative Thought," already cited, Mannheim's fullest statement of his position is to be found in *Ideology and Utopia* (London: 1936), Louis Wirth and Edward Shils, trans.

[44] *Oeuvres* (M), II, i, 194.

the weight of which were increasingly felt at the very time that their rationale became mysterious, that everyone was pushed, or rather precipitated, towards the idea that all men should be equal in status.[45]

Like everyone else living in this disordered society, men of letters had a false consciousness, or an incomplete awareness of what consequences were apt to result from acting upon their principles. In this they were no different from the agents of the monarchy, the nobility, the Church, the *bourgeoisie,* and the people. All suffered from the absence of empirical wisdom, willingness to compromise interests, and capacity to cooperate in achieving shared purposes, qualities developed by participation in a free political system. In addition to contrasting France under the old regime to the United States and England, Tocqueville further developed this point in a number of ways. The absence of communication among classes accentuated their ignorance of each other, for "free institutions are no less necessary to those most highly placed, so that they may know what menaces them, than to those of a lower status, who need friends to help secure their rights."[46] Both the monarchy and the nobility lacked that minimum of practicality that would have led them to avoid their more flagrant errors. The officials of the crown, like liberal aristocrats, denounced the injustice of the existing system and acknowledged the sufferings of the people in a way which suggests that it never occurred to anyone that such pronouncements could be heard by those who would one day revolt against these abuses. Similarly, a large part of the *noblesse* accepted political theories and attacks upon the Church that in the first instance divested them of any claim to legitimacy, and, in the second, of the protection against subversion offered by an established Church sharing the same privileges. No one in the society, whatever their grievances, had any inkling that revolution could come. Of this peculiar lack of understanding, Tocqueville wrote: "Most of all, I am struck, not by the genius of those who served the Revolution's cause, but by the stupidity of those, who, without in the least wishing it, caused it to occur."[47] Even stupidity, a phenomenon nowhere foreign to men, had, because of its prominence in the public affairs of this society, to be explained by reference to political sociology.

[45] *Ibid.,* pp. 194–195.
[46] *Ibid.,* p. 197.
[47] *Ibid.,* II, ii, 115.

As for the men of letters, the political inexperience due to their virtual exclusion from public life, which, in any case, was not that of a free society, concealed from them what dangers are involved in the complete reconstruction of society on new principles. Had the French been allowed freedom to change their ancient institutions gradually, their thinkers would have been less inclined to insist upon the value of untried principles. But their predilections were those of a generous inexperience, a deficiency that was ultimately the fault of the monarchy's traditional policy of concentrating as much power as it could in its own hands. Generalities were further encouraged by a censorship that permitted philosophical speculation about the origin and nature of society, the rights of man, and the proper principles of government, so long as no specific persons or institutions were named. Thus every political passion repressed by the regime made its way into political philosophy. Politics became merged with literature and philosophy; writers assumed the leadership of public opinion exercised in free countries by the heads of parties. The *noblesse* had long abdicated this role. In England those who wrote about politics usually had participated in them; in any case, new ideas were applied by statesmen aware of the practical situation. And the existence of regular arrangements to make changes peacefully did not make it appear, as in France, that the only real choice was between total approval or total condemnation of the system as a whole.[48]

Tocqueville argued that none of the major groups with a stake in the existing order behaved in a rational manner, even in the minimal sense of choosing means appropriate to its own material interest. For there was no perception of the potential consequences of the slogans used or positions taken. As he had done in the *Démocratie,* Tocqueville asserted in *L'Ancien Régime* that revolutions are less apt to occur in free societies than in despotisms. Where freedom exists, communication among groups is better, and a major subversive movement is usually detected. By contrast, up to the last moment, no person or group suspected that the old regime was tottering. Its administrators felt strong enough to request statements of grievances from the entire population, which responded fully to this unprecedented and rash request. Tocqueville told of how, while reading through the massive responses in these *cahiers,* he carefully noted the request for the abolition of a custom here,

48 *Ibid.,* II, i, 193–201.

an ordinance there, the ending of this or that privilege or abuse. When he looked at his notes, he realized "with a sort of terror" that the sum of these demands amounted to nothing less than the systematic annulment of every law and usage then in force. What was in prospect was the most complete revolution yet known. Of this, those who were to be its first victims had no inkling. This was just as true of the royal bureaucracy as of anyone else. Although in possession of all that was to be learned from the study of public administration as then practiced, they were ill equipped by their experience in an absolutist system to judge what was going on in the minds of the various classes, to gauge the major trends at work, and to foresee the consequences of the reforms being contemplated. Thus, even when proposals were specific, they were assessed and applied by men who did not see their implications.

To clarify Tocqueville's point, it should be compared to Max Weber's theory of the role played in human action by ideas. Weber contended that interests, material and ideal, such as that in salvation, are the dynamic forces that move men to act. But ideas nevertheless perform an important function. By defining the meaning of potential courses of action, ideas influence their choice and direction. Images of the world, through which ideas are created, have acted as switchmen, determining the tracks along which the dynamic of interest moves. In short, ideas define situations so that an alternative may be perceived or blocked by a person's or group's view of the world, or by the categories in which he or it thinks.[49]

Revolutionary Ideas as Definitions of the Situation

The resemblances of Weber's theories to Tocqueville's statement about the interrelation of ideas, interests, and passions are patent. When he applied this theory to the analysis of the old regime, Tocqueville asserted that the terms in which Frenchmen had learned to think about politics had created a fatal contradiction between the ideal of equality and political liberty. A number of ideas that could have obviated disagreements and contradictions of a major and persisting kind were either ignored or never thought of because other notions held the field. The passion for equality first dominated the political thinking of men in the old regime. Later the passion for liberty made its appearance. But by this time the French had al-

---

[49] Max Weber, *Gesammelte Aufsätze zur Religionssoziologie*, 3 vols. (Tübingen: 1947), I, p. 252.

ready come to think in terms of ideas that not only put obstacles
in the way of free institutions, but were virtually incompatible with
them:

> They had taken as their ideal, a society in which the citizens would
> have no aristocracy but that of public officials, a single and om-
> nipotent administration to direct the state and prescribe the details
> of individuals' lives. Thus, when they came to desire freedom as
> well, they never considered abandoning this ideal of administration,
> but wished only to fit their new value into it.
>   What they attempted to combine was an unchecked administra-
> tive centralization with a legislature that was to be predominant; an
> administration that was to be in the hands of the bureaucracy, while
> the government was to be in the hands of the voters. The nation, as
> a body, was to hold all rights of sovereignty, although each in-
> dividual citizen was to be even more confined by the administration.
> Thus from the nation was expected the experience and qualities of
> a free people; from the citizens, those of good servants.[50]

To this failure to understand the patent contradictions between
liberty and the unexamined prior values of equality and centralization, Tocqueville attributed the single most tragic aspect of French
history—the alternations between the nation's attempts at achieving freedom by revolution and its subsequent exhaustion and acceptance of the dictatorial rule of a single person who restored order
but did so by establishing an equality of servitude under an omnipotent administration. Thus it was Tocqueville's position that these
consequences should be attributed to the political ideas developed
by Frenchmen under the old regime. "Ideas being what they were,
it was almost impossible that events, as they in fact occurred, could
have turned out any differently."[51] Even the passions aroused by
class warfare were less important than ideas in determining the
final result of the Revolution. This was true in both a positive and a
negative sense; existing ideas accentuated the incompatibility between the passions for liberty and equality; and all the possible solutions were not so much as considered.

What was missing could be summed up, Tocqueville thought, in
three concepts: that of a mode of government which, although
recognizing what was just in the claims for equality, nevertheless

[50] Tocqueville, *Oeuvres* (M), II, i, 216.

[51] Tocqueville wrote this as a note to himself: "Pénétrer dans cette idée
et montrer que la Révolution a été là plus encore que dans les faits: qu'il
était comme impossible que les idées étant telles, les faits ne fussent pas à
peu près ce qu'on a vu." Tocqueville, *Oeuvres* (M), II, ii, 117n.b.

could be reconciled with liberty; that of politics as a process for the peaceful adjustment of interests; and that of the separation of Church and state.

> The very idea of a moderate and balanced government . . . in which the classes that make up society, the interests that divide it also limit one another, where men are represented, not only in terms of number, but also in those of property, interests, and contribution to the general welfare—not one of these notions was to be found even among the most moderate (or could be said to be prominent in the thinking of the most privileged). All these ideas were supplanted by that of a homogenous mass (*foule*), made up of identical elements represented by deputies elected on the basis of population rather than interest or person.[52]

Similarly it never occurred to anyone inside or outside the Church that its religious functions might be separated from its social and political aspects. Because of this the Church had put itself in a position where it had to be attacked along with every other hated part of the old order. In fact such animosity as existed against it was due to its land holdings and its participation in highly resented privileges. Had the hierarchy perceived this, it might have been able to maintain the Church's religious function relatively unimpaired at a time when its stabilizing influence would have been beneficial. In the *Démocratie*, Tocqueville recorded his own amazement at how in America the Roman Catholic Church had prospered in a system of separation from the state. There was no reason why the Church should regard itself, or be regarded as, incompatible with a democratic polity. Separation was a notion, however, that failed to appear, just as was the case with the conception of politics as the conciliation of interests by allowing them a part in government.

The absence of these ideas was, in Tocqueville's view, decisive. With the stock of ideas actually available to them, the men of the eighteenth century could not have behaved otherwise than they did. Both their ends and means thus phrased implied the overthrow of the existing order. But of course, Tocqueville's way of making this point raises an important comparative question: Why do certain concepts develop in some societies and not in others? The answer he gave in his *L'Ancien Régime* was that the politics of a free society generate those notions that make possible the peaceful compromise of conflicting interests and the resolution of basic problems without

[52] *Ibid.*, II, ii, p. 117.

resort to violence. The monarchy and its administration at a number of crucial points acted in accordance with its traditional policy of attempting to isolate classes and to turn them against each other. Patterns of cooperation, mutual trust, willingness to defer demands for benefit—these might be developed in a once absolutist political system by a regime attempting a transition to greater freedom and participation, but there would have to be far more creative thinking and capacity to break with the past than was exhibited by a mediocre king and his staff.

Tocqueville's treatment of the contribution of intellectuals and ideas to revolution was sophisticated and suggestive. But he did not see the incompatibility between his theories in the forms in which he held them at various times. Nor did he ever take a clear-cut stand on the issue of whether ideas are determined by the social, economic, or political setting of the men who hold them; or whether ideas may be created by exceptional individuals or generated by the contradictions or immanent logic of already existing systems of thought. Yet it is to his credit that he was able to relate the style of eighteenth-century French thought to the conditions that shaped its principal theorists; that he specified how such intellectual definitions of the political situation have profound consequences for revolutionary and peaceful movements alike; and that at the end of his life he refused to settle for any explanatory scheme that did not take into account ideas, interests, and passions. This concern with the subjective behavior of historical agents did not imply that their milieu had nothing to do with the occurrence or prevention of revolution. For in Tocqueville's view, it was impossible to make sense of that subject without reference to social class.

CLASS AND REVOLUTION

"Class" Defined

In a well-known passage, Tocqueville wrote that "No doubt individuals may be produced as evidence against my generalization, but I am discussing classes, which alone ought to concern the historian."[53] In addition to this assertion that classes are the unit of

---

[53] *Ibid.*, II, i, 179. In his public speeches Tocqueville often assumed an edifying tone and spoke rather differently about the use of the term: "I dislike this word, 'class' . . . Instead of speaking about the middle, upper, or lower classes . . . I prefer to speak of the general interests of France."

reference that ought to be used in historical explanation, Tocqueville insisted that a healthy political society relatively immune to revolution is characterized by one kind of relationship among its classes, while quite another is to be found wherever revolution is likely. "There is no government that will not fall when subjected to the violent shock of class struggle, once the combat is joined."[54] Tocqueville also claimed that every society must be dominated by one or another type of elite, and that revolution comes because that elite fulfills or neglects its functions, or because it will or will not admit to its ranks those outside it who have demonstrated their superiority to others of their class. He saw as a salient feature of European history the fact that one class had declined, while another rose, only to see its own claims to leadership declared to be illegitimate by a third. These were of course the aristocracy, *bourgeoisie,* and working class. In addition to holding a broad view of history stated in class terms, Tocqueville often interpreted particular events by reference to the passions and interests of the classes involved. Thus he explained the support for Napoleon I by the generalization that so many members of the middle class and peasants had gained materially from the Revolution, that, although they did not wish it to continue, they also could not risk supporting any movement that might restore the old order. France, which had ceased to love the Republic, remained attached to the Revolution.[55] This was true not only because of interest but because of passion as well.

At this point, it becomes necessary to ask whether Tocqueville intended to establish a technical meaning for "class" or whether he used it as would an essayist addressing himself to a general audience. Certainly his use of this term varied considerably from one context to another. Nor did he ever acknowledge such changes. It is for this reason that each of his pronouncements on class must be identified by the work in which it appeared. Apparently he thought himself to be using language precisely within a carefully prepared framework.

In the first part of the *Démocratie,* Tocqueville asserted that all societies are composed of elements which, although their propor-

---

Le Moniteur Universel, February 7, 1840, p. 263, cited in Drescher, *op. cit.,* p. 14. Cf. also *Souvenirs,* p. 54, "The safest method for our government . . . is to govern in the interest of everyone."

[54] Tocqueville, *Oeuvres* (M), II, ii, 114, 114 note b.
[55] *Ibid.,* pp. 282–292.

tions may vary, are always and everywhere present. Every society contains the rich; the middle classes, who without being wealthy, are well off; and the poor, who have little or no property and must live by the work they do for the members of the other two categories. The number of persons in each of the classes varies with the level (*état*) of society. But it is impossible to abolish classes altogether.[56]

The application of this scheme to revolution was extended in the second part of the *Démocratie,* where it became even more reminiscent of Aristotle. Almost all major revolutions have been made either to confirm or to reject the principle of equality. In the first case, the poor wish to despoil the rich of their wealth; in the second, the rich have attempted to fix the poor permanently in their status. Tocqueville, concerned to establish that democratic societies are relatively immune to revolution, based his argument on the assertion that in a society of this type, there exists an overwhelming majority of persons, who, without being precisely rich or poor, have enough property to desire order, but not enough to excite envy. Since all revolutions menace in one or another way the security of property, this middle class is fully conscious of what it could lose by wholesale violence. By contrast, the poor are susceptible to appeals they might gain by using force, while the rich are apt to be careless, taking for granted the pleasures they have long enjoyed.[57]

This scheme of class analysis was narrowly, almost crudely, economic. It was by no means altogether compatible with his division of societies into aristocracies and democracies. Nor did it preclude him, as it should have done, from using the ordinary names for classes prior to and during the Revolution: *noblesse, tiers-état,* and *peuple.* For these were all more or less homogenous groups, united within themselves by common interests, historical experiences, and *esprit de corps.* Their sense of corporate identity was a key element, creating as it did a high degree of class consciousness. Tocqueville, however, like later elitist thinkers who followed him in this regard, divided society into classes on the basis of objective criteria specified by himself, the analyst. But classes so defined have little or nothing to do with the aggregations that identify themselves with, or are identified by, the labels in use within a society. To confuse these two ways of defining social class is a procedure not uncommon

[56] Tocqueville, *Oeuvres* (M), I, i, 216.
[57] *Ibid.,* I, ii, 258–260.

among theorists who contend that every society is dominated by a ruling class. Yet it by no means follows that because in every sphere of society there are pre-eminent persons, all of them do in fact communicate, share a sense of common identity and interest, and thus are enabled to act together.

All the definitions of class to be given by Tocqueville in his *Démocratie* were unmentioned by him when he wrote his articles, "The Political and Social Condition of France." For his purposes in 1837, Tocqueville developed still another theory of the elite.

Aristocracy and Caste, Open and Closed Elites; Community of Interest Among Members of the Natural Aristocracy; How Legitimacy Depends Upon a Ruling Class's Performance of Its Functions

Again Tocqueville asserted that there exist sociological laws that determine the nature of political systems.[58] His purpose was to demonstrate by comparing their respective ruling classes, just why the French had undergone a revolution, and the English had not. They had both begun with approximately the same feudal institutions. Yet, like all continental aristocracies, by the end of the eighteenth century, the French was far more exclusive than the English. Indeed even being ennobled did not make a family part of the French *noblesse*, a word that had no precise English equivalent. For the French word was to the English term "aristocracy" what the *species* is to the *genus*. Tocqueville contended that France had had a caste system, rather than an aristocracy properly so-called, as existed in England. There new persons were admitted because of ability or achievement, claims which in French eyes had no bearing upon qualifications for the *noblesse*. Tocqueville's point was only partially that every elite must renew itself by recruitment from other classes. He also attempted to redefine the notion of aristocracy so as to make it applicable to all societies—in short, to identify it with leadership.[59]

---

[58] The first sign of Tocqueville's retreat from this position appeared in his 1843 sketch of a study on the British conquest of India. He wrote: "The time has come to penetrate the haze that still conceals the circumstances under which the English empire was established in India and to connect this event to the general causes of all human affairs." In the margin of his manuscript, he wrote, "Too ambitious." *Oeuvres* (M), III, i, 445, 445 note b.

[59] Tocqueville, *Oeuvres* (M), II, i, 37; *Memoir, Letters . . .* , I, p. 220.

Aristocracy as such cannot be eliminated. Every society, however egalitarian, must make distinctions about the worth of its members on the basis of one or another criterion:

> There exists among mankind, in whatsoever form of society they live, and independently of the laws which they have made for their own government, a certain amount of real or conventional advantages, which, from their nature, can only be possessed by a small number. At the head of these may be placed birth, wealth, and knowledge. It would be impossible to conceive of any social state, in which all the citizens, without exception, should be noble, highly intellectual, or rich. These three advantages differ considerably from one another, but they agree in this, that they are always the lot of a few, and give, consequently to those who possess them, tastes and ideas of a more or less peculiar or exclusive kind. They therefore form so many aristocratic elements, which, whether separated or united in the same hands, are to be found amongst every people and at every period of history.
>
> When the governing power is shared by all those who possess any of these exclusive advantages, the result is a stable and powerful aristocracy.
>
> During the eighteenth century the French *noblesse* possessed within itself a portion only of the natural elements of an aristocracy. Some of those elements remained with the classes beyond their pale.
>
> In isolating themselves from the aristocracy of wealth and from that of intellect, the nobles believed that they were remaining faithful to the example of their fathers. They did not remark that in imitating the conduct they were missing the aim of their ancestors. In the Middle Ages, it is true, birth was the principal source of all social advantages; but in the Middle Ages the nobles were also the rich, and had called into alliance with them the priests, who were the instructed. Society yielded, and could not but yield to these two classes of men a complete obedience.[60]

Two assertions dominate this remarkable passage: that it is essential that a ruling class be open to new talent, whatever its origin, and that it include all these groups in possession of those advantages making up power (objectively considered). Tocqueville was saying that it is not inequality as such that creates resentment of the sort that leads to revolution, but inequality of a particular kind. If everyone in a society may hope to gain great privileges in open competition, then the very extravagance of the prerogatives of the ruling class may enhance its attractions to those outside it. "In a country

[60] Tocqueville, *Oeuvres* (M), II, 45–46; *Memoir, Letters* . . . , I, pp. 219–20.

where it is not impossible that a poor man may come to the highest offices of the State, it is much easier to continue excluding the poor from any share in government, than in those countries where all hope of rising to a higher rank is denied them."[61] The existence of social mobility has striking political consequences, "it is a game of chance, where the enormous possible gain lays hold of the mind in spite of the almost certainty of loss."[62]

This redefinition of aristocracy had other implications as well. It insisted upon the existence of a natural aristocracy in every society and the real community of interest among all its members, whether or not they realize it. In applying this analysis to France, Tocqueville revived one of the oldest theories of revolution, Plato's observation that it always begins in divisions among members of the ruling class. Tocqueville had defined this class as it ought to be, based on the objective criteria he had set out. Thus he could argue that the most distinguished members of the *tiers-état* should have been recognized by the *noblesse* as members of the natural aristocracy and allowed to share in power and privilege. Instead they were rejected because of their birth. This left them with nothing to do but to adopt principles, which, although efficacious as weapons against the *noblesse*, were ultimately to be turned against themselves. The most significant of these ideological principles was that of equality. In time it would be utilized by another disadvantaged class to attack the very principle of private property, the source of the wealth and claim to power of the *tiers-état* itself.

In fact there are but two ways for an aristocracy to maintain its influence over the people—it may govern them, or it may unite with them to check the government. At the end of the eighteenth century, the French *noblesse* did neither. By its exclusive concern for the highest offices of the administration and army, it proved that it cared more for the outward appearance of power than for its reality. An aristocracy builds its true strength by its direct services to the population, which appreciates local administration far more than foreign affairs, bureaucratic eminence, or military distinction. To the active participation of the English aristocracy in local government, Tocqueville attributed much of their popular support. And they had perceived the importance of making themselves appear as the virtual representatives of the people against the Crown.

---

[61] Tocqueville, *Oeuvres* (M), II, i, 46; *Memoirs, Letters* . . . , I, p. 221.
[62] *Ibid.*

Already implicit in this youthful essay was one of the major hypotheses of *L'Ancien Régime,* which appeared twenty years later. There Tocqueville used comparative analysis to test the common-sense notion that popular revolts against aristocracies should be ascribed to the latter's excessive privileges. Why did the Revolution occur in France rather than elsewhere? Was it because the French *noblesse* still possessed and exercised onerous feudal dues? Tocqueville, who learned German at an advanced age so that he could carry through a sustained comparison, concluded that in France peasants were more emancipated in this regard than anywhere else in Europe, including the Rhineland, which bordered on the motherland of revolution. The key point, he argued, was not the severity of feudal dues, but the fact that the French *noblesse* at the end of the eighteenth century enjoyed a special tax-exempt status, monopolized the most prestigious places in the army and administration, and possessed the right to impose annoying charges or demand services. Yet for the most part, its members did not live on the land or perform any of the functions that had justified the far greater privileges of its ancestors in the remote past:

> When the *noblesse* possessed not only privileges, but power; when it governed and administered, its special rights could be at once greater and less apparent. In the age of feudalism, the *noblesse* was considered in much the same way as the government today— its demands are met because of the guarantees it furnishes. The nobles had irritating privileges; they possessed onerous rights, but they assured public order, dispensed justice, executed the law, came to the aid of the weak, and managed enterprises of common interest. To the extent that the *noblesse* ceased to do such things, the weight of its privileges seemed heavier, and in the long run, incomprehensible.[63]

Tocqueville also claimed that where the nobility continued to live on the land, there it was capable of leading an armed struggle against the Revolution. It was in the Vendée that feudal dues were most strictly enforced, and yet because the nobles stayed in the country, they led the resistance that so troubled the Revolutionary government.[64]

[63] Tocqueville, *Oeuvres,* II, i, 105.
[64] For a recent study very much in the spirit of Tocqueville, but reaching more complex conclusions based on exhaustive research and modern sociological method, cf. Charles Tilly, *The Vendée* (Cambridge: 1964).

Political Consequences of Class Relations:
Solidarity, Alienation, Class Warfare

In his writing on revolution, Tocqueville invariably approached the subject of class relations by a prior consideration of how solidarity is attained in aristocratic and democratic societies respectively. Thus when alienation or class warfare are found, they are interpreted as symptoms of internal contradiction within the social system. Tocqueville came close here to Aristotle's and Montesquieu's classification of states as being healthy or vitiated in terms of their particular type. In short, every system has a particular kind of social relations appropriate to it. When such ties do in fact exist, there is no danger of revolution.

In a functioning aristocracy, as opposed to a regime of caste, the services performed for the classes low in the social scale by the governing class produce a close contact, an intimate set of relations rather than isolation. This assertion Tocqueville attempted to substantiate by a sustained comparison, this time between France in the Middle Ages and as it was in the eighteenth century:

> Many centuries ago inequality was actually greater than in the eighteenth century. That is, there were more significant differences between the nobility and other classes in regard to political power, wealth, and cultivation. But in the eighteenth century, the noble and bourgeois were equal in political rights (neither possessed such rights properly speaking), and often were on the same level in wealth, and even more often, in culture. Yet there was a degree of isolation of one class from another that was unknown in the remote past. Then the various classes had much to do with one another; they found that their functions brought them together, although they remained separate in status. Together they concerned themselves with common business, they made mutual efforts and coordinated courses of action; together they met the cost of government and shared the right to participate in ruling. . . . In a word, if inequality existed, isolation did not.[65]

Revolution may come to an aristocratic society because of the isolation of its ruling class. What are the normal or healthy relations among classes in a democracy? How liable are democracies to revolution? Tocqueville's principal answer was given in the second part of the *Démocratie*, where he argued the thesis that equality of con-

---

[65] Tocqueville, *Oeuvres* (M), II, ii, 360–361.

ditions does not promote revolution, but rather presents grave obstacles to it. Central to his reasoning is the assumption that a democratic society is classless, that its essential quality is the presence of
isolated individuals preoccupied with the well-being of themselves,
their families, and immediate friends. Although very rich and poor
persons are to be found, neither group is as large proportionately
as in aristocratic societies. Most significant of all is the fact that no
one in the society is attached by law to an inherited position. Mobility upward and, just as important, mobility downward, are thus
assured, as is the possibility of accession to the ruling class. In
democratic societies, there is little danger that revolution will occur
because of barriers to the able. Even the presence of wealth is less
likely to have a dangerous effect because rich individuals are less
conspicuous in a democratic society than aristocrats in their own
type. This invisibility derives in part from the fact that the rich do
not typically have their wealth in land or exercise political power,
as did the territorial nobility, and in part from the additional point
that there is no easy way of distinguishing their interests from those
of the numerous other persons who own property, though less of it.
This middle class is the natural enemy of all violent movements, and
by their own immobility keep those above and beneath them in
order. Their passions are involved in making money, and hence do
not usually become political, let alone revolutionary. And it is obvious to them that although the interests of those engaged in com-
merce and industry may ultimately be served by a revolution, its
immediate effect is to ruin them by upsetting the balance between
supply and demand.[66]

These generalizations about egalitarian, commercial societies were
not meant to demonstrate the impossibility of subverting such an
order. Two things may lead to revolution in an egalitarian society:
excessive apathy on the part of its citizens and military *coup d'état*.
These forces may be simultaneously operative. Essential to both of
them is Tocqueville's distinction between revolutions made by ac-
tivating whole classes through appeals to their passions and those
made by small, activist minorities that take advantage of general
apathy. When a society is characterized by relatively equal conditions, its members tend to become self-centered and to forget the
public good. If legislators in democratic societies do not succeed in
combating this tendency, or if preoccupied with the danger to them

<hr />

[66] Tocqueville, *Oeuvres* (M), I, ii, 258–269.

of revolution, they encourage this retreat from politics, then the possibility arises that they may very well bring about the evil they seek to avoid. A few individuals, inflamed by ambition, may be able to capitalize upon the egoistic individualism and lack of civic courage of the majority.[67] This argument may be regarded as Tocqueville's rephrasing of Montesquieu's insistence upon civic virtue as the essential principle of a democracy. Tocqueville was taking into account the phenomenon of revolution, a subject that had assumed an altogether new importance after Montesquieu's death. And looking to the future, Tocqueville foresaw the possibility of a novel kind of revolution based on general apathy and executed by an exceptional minority of activists.

The other potentially revolutionary force in a democratic society, Tocqueville contended, is its army. "Although democratic peoples, by their interests and instincts, are naturally inclined towards peace, nevertheless their armies push them in the direction of war and revolution."[68] Revolutions by the military, which are almost never a danger in aristocratic societies, are to be feared at all times in democratic ones. In the first, officers already hold a high social rank; in the second, they have no income except their pay, and no other claim to consideration than their military rank. The professional soldier can flourish only by practicing violence; his real loyalty is to military, rather than civilian society. And since his prestige is low, he wishes war, which makes him indispensable rather than supernumerary, or revolution, which, by the use of the violence that is his stock in trade, gives him the opportunity to seize power and compel the respect otherwise denied him.[69]

Although Tocqueville designated the particular dangers of revolution in an egalitarian society, he nevertheless concluded that it is relatively immune to this contagion. Of the United States he wrote in this connection: "If America ever undergoes great revolutions, they will be produced by the presence of Negroes on its soil, that is to say, not because of equality of conditions, but its opposite."[70]

In both parts of the *Démocratie,* Tocqueville's approach was sociological, stressing the egalitarian or aristocratic aspects of society rather more than its form of government. But after the seizure of

[67] *Ibid.,* p. 263.
[68] *Ibid.,* p. 273.
[69] *Ibid.,* p. 273.
[70] *Ibid.,* p. 263.

power by Louis Napoleon, Tocqueville's emphasis changed to the effects of political liberty upon solidarity among classes. In his comparison between France nad England on this score, he wrote, "political liberty . . . has this admirable capacity to create among all citizens, close relations and ties of mutual interdependence. Yet this does not make them identical in every other way as well. It is the government of a single man, that in the long run, has the invariable effect of making them indifferent to one another's fate."[71] A free government teaches men to work together; it gives them a sense of realism that has its origin in their responsibility for managing their own affairs. In such an atmosphere, the English aristocracy was capable of seeing that to maintain its power it was necessary to assume the burden of taxation. Not so in France, where the *noblesse* allowed itself to profit from its privileged exemption from taxes, accepting this consolation for their loss of a place in government. Thus they fell into the trap of the monarchy, which used taxation as one way of setting social classes against one another. This ancient strategy succeeded all too well. When the moment came for the monarchy to seek to reform itself, the isolation of classes, their mutual distrust, and incapacity to cooperate was to help produce the downfall of the entire structure.

Nowhere were the effects of class isolation felt more than in the case of the *peuple,* by which Tocqueville meant the peasants, rather than inhabitants of cities. Peasants were made to bear the brunt of royal taxation, they were denied the leniency extended to others in the application of the laws. But worst of all, they were left in a state of ignorance that gave them no way of entering into the material or cultural advantages of their age. The peasant's style of life gave him an outlook that was unknown and incomprehensible to the *noblesse* and *tiers-état*. The people had supported the weight of misgovernment for so many generations that they had developed in silence their own prejudices and hatreds against those set by society above them; they had become so toughened by their rigors that they could endure great suffering, and, for that matter, had no hesitations about inflicting the same treatment upon others when the situation arose. Of this, the other classes and the government had no inkling. This was the consequence of absolutist political arrangements, just as the gap between the noble and bourgeois was due to social arrangements based on caste. In the absence of elections, local

[71] Tocqueville, *Oeuvres* (M), II, i, 146.

government bodies including all classes, and political institutions set between the national administration and the *peuple,* no means existed for the upper classes to make contact with the lower. The result was an ignorance of one another as complete as if they had been separated by the diameter of the globe.[72] As the result of such isolation of the classes from one another, they all had a false consciousness of the actual situation.

Yet it was not so much these practical consequences of class isolation that Tocqueville emphasized, as their moral implications. To describe the condition of his own class under the old regime, he coined a phrase rather more expressive than what Hegelians and Marxists call "alienation" but with much the same meaning. He wrote of *l'absentisme du coeur* (absenteeism of the heart), the *noblesse* no longer were capable of feeling sympathy for the peasants' misery or the injustices which weighed upon them. Since nobles no longer ruled, they had no tie of interest; since they were exempt from taxation, they did not share the emotions of those who were taxed. The *peuple* were no longer their subjects; they were not yet their fellow citizens.[73]

The same absence of fellow feeling, of involvement with others outside one's class, or even with many inside it, existed among the members of the *tiers-état.* Its members could not rise above devotion to their class to concern for the general interest, a fact that was to be critical once the Revolution began. In this they were no different from any other class in the society, political ties and moral solidarity were no longer to be found. But there still existed social ties within classes. These were of a peculiar sort. Within each class there were a number of groups formed by raising barriers of an insignificant kind, which nevertheless sufficed to make its members think of themselves as being united by bonds of interest and feeling, thus creating loyalty to this group rather than to any larger unit. Even so these groups, for all their particularism, were refractory to the organized power of the state. The Revolution was to destroy even these social ties, for the barriers established by these groups were strong enough to separate them from one another but not sufficient to protect them against the great tide that swept all before it. From this society, fragmented and lacking social solidarity so that its members could not act in concert and come to each other's aid, there emerged an-

[72] Tocqueville, *Oeuvres* (M), II, ii, 415.
[73] *Ibid.*, II, i, 178–179.

other, more homogenous and tightly knit than any other previously known to history. The old regime, therefore, paved the way for the formation of a mass society particularly prone to a new despotism based on egalitarian and revolutionary slogans.[74]

As for class warfare, Tocqueville considered this not as a phenomenon characteristic of all societies, as did Marx and Engels, but rather as abnormal, the product of prolonged and bitter revolutions or as the chronic condition of an old and exhausted people. The struggle among classes that developed in the French Revolution Tocqueville attributed not to the intrinsic principles of its philosophy but to the antecedent political and social arrangements and to the incapaciy of the monarchy to resolve its problems without violence. "Which man or class has ever seen just when the moment has come to descend from a dominating position, so as to avoid being thrown off it?"[75] The King, by treating the constitution of France as he did, made it inevitable that the class struggle would take a violent form. This struggle among classes would have broken out in one or another form, but had it been carried out by an established procedure, such as that of the Estates-General, and focused on specific problems, class feeling might have been held within bounds. Instead the King opened the field to general discussions that stimulated each class to imagine a future dominated by it and its interests.[76] This same incapacity to know when and how to yield power also explained why the French *noblesse* was to be excluded from any constructive role in politics during the transition to an egalitarian society, in contrast to the English aristocracy. For the animosity inspired by a class that has once ruled is determined not by its former abuses of privilege, but by the way in which its power has been modified or destroyed. Even if such a class has been extremely oppressive, feeling against it will not be strong, provided that it yield power gradually, or that it be deplaced by the intrusion of a foreign aggressor, rather than by a long civil war.[77]

In the long run, it was not only the *noblesse* that was to suffer from the class warfare that had erupted during the Revolution. Thereafter it was unlikely that any government could be established that would, at the same time, be constitutional, strong, and free. It

---

[74] *Ibid.,* II, i, 143, 301, 302; II, ii, 416–417.
[75] *Ibid.,* II, ii, 113.
[76] *Ibid.,* II, ii, 105–106.
[77] *Ibid.,* II, ii, 336.

was not that France would be doomed to an unending series of revolutions made on a class basis; there might be long intervals of order, tranquillity, prosperity, but the achievement of a satisfactory social and political order was not likely.[78] Violent class struggle cannot produce a free and constitutional political system.

THE CAUSES OF REVOLUTION

Primary and Secondary Causes

The time has come to put together the component parts of Tocqueville's analysis of revolution and to fit them into the scheme of historical causation he arrived at toward the end of his life. For in his final decade he treated all of the revolutions between 1789 and 1848 in much the same set of terms.

Tocqueville's theory of causation was not particularly technical or philosophical. He divided causes into categories, called, respectively, primary and secondary; he asked not only why certain events had occurred, but the reasons for their having done so at a particular time and place. Thus comparative method was an essential element of his analysis of revolution. Finally he combined in his account of causes the functions performed by social classes, the structure of the society itself, and the nature of the political system (all of which he regarded as exerting a direct effect upon the revolutionary situation); and in addition, the way in which the situation was defined for the contemporary actors by their ideas and style of thought.

This scheme was rationalistic without being deterministic. That is, Tocqueville believed that most, although not all, of the causes of major events are accessible to rational analysis. However, "chance or the tangle of secondary causes we call chance, for lack of knowledge of how to unravel them," plays a great part in revolutions.[79] Tocqueville went on to enumerate their primary and secondary causes, but denied that there is any single cause, which, unmediated by human agency or by chance, produces all the events usually grouped together as constituting the events of a revolution. Many of these are due to accidental circumstances; others are altogether inexplicable. Tocqueville's formulation, although striking, is far from being clear,

---

[78] Tocqueville, *Oeuvres* (B), VI, 457–458. Letter to Eugène Stoffels, July 21, 1848.
[79] Tocqueville, *Souvenirs*, p. 72.

for he added that chance does nothing that has not been prepared beforehand.[80] In general, it is easier to understand what sort of explanation he is disposed to reject than the implications of his own statement.

Where are the primary causes of revolution to be sought? Tocqueville identified the areas he thought worth investigating: antecedent facts, the nature of institutions, the cast of minds, and the state of *moeurs*.[81] The first of these appears vague at first glance, for of course any historian will seek causes in some prior condition or set of conditions. But Tocqueville illustrated what he meant in the last chapter of *L'Ancien Régime,* where he stated that, given the facts he had set out about the old order, the revolution had to occur. What he meant was that some sort of qualitative change had to come, although not necessarily by force. In his reference to the nature of institutions, Tocqueville meant that men characteristically make decisions within the framework of structures, political and social, which they find rather than create. Hence their volitions and ideas are far from being the only data that must be taken into account if their actions are to be explained. Yet the intellectual categories used in human action, as well as the dominating habits and passions of the society as a whole, play a critical part in the way men perceive their environment and take steps to preserve or transform it.

In a justly celebrated passage, Tocqueville applied his scheme to the Revolution of February 1848. Like other great events, it was due to primary causes, impregnated by accidents. Both the general causes and immediate occasions of the Revolution were responsible for its principal characteristics. What were these? It is worth noting not only what types of causes Tocqueville cited, but also whether they were among the inventory of propositions he drew up to explain the Revolution of 1789. He explicitly stated that in 1848 Paris was a manufacturing city with an altogether new population of workmen. These, along with more casual laborers attracted from rural areas by the construction of fortifications, constituted a fertile field for certain ideas and passions. Among them was the taste for material luxury that the July Monarchy had encouraged as a way of distracting the population from interest in politics; the leveling disposition peculiar to egalitarian societies, in short, the democratic

80 *Ibid.*
81 *Ibid.*

disease of envy; and the new socialist theories that claimed society could remake its foundation and thus banish poverty from the human condition. All these explanations centered upon what was felt and thought by working-class persons. Only one of these elements had played an equal part in the Revolution of 1789, the passion for equality that made everything aristocratic appear intolerable. Then Tocqueville referred to the loss of legitimacy suffered by a government no longer regarded as performing its proper functions: ". . . the contempt into which the governing class, and especially its leaders, had fallen, a contempt so general and so profound that it paralyzed the resistance to the revolution of those who had the greatest interest in maintaining the status quo."[82]

Tocqueville was asserting that interest does not always dominate human action: either it may not be perceived, or it may be subordinated to other values designated as superior by custom or ideology. And he was pressing his point that the business of government is to govern, to carry through the affairs assigned to it. When a government fails to do so, it must sooner or later lose power. This phenomenon had occurred during the Directory and prepared the way for Napoleon. "Without revolting, everyone ceased to obey. The situation resembled that of an army falling apart. . . . France refused to obey its government."[83] As M. Aron has remarked, Tocqueville's comments apply equally well to the fall of the Fourth Republic in 1958.[84] Then, too, commands were issued by the government and simply disregarded by its citizens; even those who had most to lose by a change in the regime displayed no inclination to fight for its preservation. Perhaps this is a persistent phenomenon in revolutions, although Tocqueville might just as well have considered this a sympton as a cause. He thought that one aspect of 1789 which had never been satisfactorily diagnosed was how it had happened that a class, ostensibly at the head of society for a thousand years, had become an officer corps without soldiers, and thus could be overthrown in a single night.

Finally, Tocqueville summed up the other primary causes of the February Revolution. The centralization of administration that had made it possible for revolutionaries in Paris to succeed simply by seizing the machinery of government was crucial in 1848, as it had

[82] Tocqueville, *Souvenirs, loc. cit.*
[83] Tocqueville, *Oeuvres* (M), II, ii, 272, 274.
[84] Aron, *Les Grandes Doctrines,* I, p. 211.

been in 1789. Indeed the seven major revolutions that had taken place since that time had produced an infinitely unsettled state of affairs, in which institutions, ideas, *moeurs,* and men were alike mobile in the extreme.[85]

So much for primary or general causes, without which the February Revolution would have been impossible. The immediate occasions or accidents that precipitated it were the passions of the opposition, who, although beginning by desiring no more than reform, finished by producing a revolution. As for the government, it first reacted by excessively severe measures, and then suddenly abandoned its efforts altogether. When the ministry fell, its successor was unable to re-establish command over the machinery of state. Confronted by such a crisis, the generals proved irresolute, while the sons of Louis Philippe, themselves experienced field commanders, were absent from Paris. Their father, stunned by the failure of the strategy he had worked out to avoid the errors of his predecessors, turned out to be unaccountably weak in the face of this emergency.[86]

Summary and Critique

In his treatment of 1848, Tocqueville displayed many of the strengths and some of the weaknesses of his method. Although he made much of class antagonisms and the effects of socialist theories on the working class, he did not investigate what had been the actual effects of the economic system upon the society as a whole. It is curious that, although condemning determinisms and their pseudo laws of society and history, he for the most part accepted the theories of laissez-faire economists like his friend, Nassau Senior. Poverty was alleged to be the work of providence, not man, and only those ignorant of these iron laws could conceive of a government attempting to change them. It is true that, in a characteristic turn upon himself, Tocqueville asked whether these laws, said to govern modern society, and particularly the laws of private property, might not be nothing more than those to which we have become accustomed.[87] But for the most part he contented himself with received opinions on the state of the Parisian working class. His failure to concern himself systematically with economic phe-

[85] Tocqueville, *Souvenirs,* p. 72.
[86] *Ibid.,* p. 73.
[87] *Souvenirs,* p. 84.

nomena was also responsible for some of the *lacunae* in his account of the old regime. As Lefebvre pointed out, Tocqueville centered his analysis upon the decadence of the *noblesse*. Yet the Revolution was for the most part directed by the *bourgeoisie,* which also was its principal beneficiary. Tocqueville never directed his attention to the sources of bourgeois wealth, nor did he, when dealing with liberty, ever ask what the concept meant when applied to production and distribution.[88] Finally, it might be said that, useful as is Tocqueville's distinction among the religious, social, and political aspects of revolution, it would be even more useful if it included a consideration of economic arrangements before and after the resort to violence.

On the other hand, it is much to Tocqueville's credit that, when discussing the relation between economics and revolution, he recognized that it was precisely the most prosperous parts of France that had most enthusiastically supported the Revolution. Few passages in all that has been written on the subject have been as revelatory as Tocqueville's summary of his comparative analysis:

> To the extent that there developed in France the prosperity just described, the general temper became more unsettled and discontent; the sense of grievance grew, as did hatred of all vestiges of the old order. The nation was visibly moving towards revolution.
> . . . Revolution does not always come when things are going from bad to worse. It occurs most often when a nation that has accepted, and indeed, has given no sign of even having noticed the most crushing laws, rejects them at the very moment when their weight is being lightened. The regime that is destroyed by a revolution is almost always better than the one preceding it, and experience teaches us that usually the most dangerous time for a bad government is when it attempts to reform itself.[89]

Economic development, particularly when uneven, may make more prosperous regions of a country revolutionary, while those least touched by the change brought along with the new prosperity are most willing to defend things as they are. These contrasting dispositions and expectations, when combined with a government which, because of the demands of the developing regions, attempts to reform itself, may produce the conditions for revolution, and, as Mr. Charles Tilly has demonstrated, counterrevolution. In such regions as the Vendée, increased governmental activity was sharply

---

[88] Tocqueville, in his introduction to the *Oeuvres* (M), II, i, 21–22.
[89] *Ibid.,* II, i, 222–223.

resented by the least urbanized areas. Tocqueville was a pioneer in treating the interrelation of the economic and political aspects of revolution. He did so with great theoretical originality as well as close attention to determining the actual facts of the case. Nor was this accidental. His general scheme of analysis had prepared him to look for everything that affects the integration of different parts of a society. Drastic incompatibilities can cause revolution.

Not all of Tocqueville's theorizing about revolution was so detached and so firmly based on objective study. Tocqueville, like the classical political philosophers, never separated judgments of value from those of fact. He believed that institutions must be judged, as well as described. If this procedure had certain undeniable advantages as employed by Tocqueville, it also led him on occasion to adopt a moralizing tone and edifying conclusions. When he condemned the July Monarchy and diagnosed its failure, he concluded that it was due to the fact that this regime had ruled exclusively in the interest of the middle class, whereas it should have had as its goal the welfare of all. This is singularly unimpressive because Tocqueville never indicated how, given his own estimate of democracy in general and French society in particular, such disinterested public virtue could have been achieved. However, his diagnosis was firmly based on a mode of argument basic to his thought: "the real reason that causes men to lose political power is that they no longer are worthy to hold it."[90] This was of course among his principal arguments in *L'Ancien Régime,* where he made his point sociologically in the way already noted: a ruling class falls not because of its privileges but because it no longer fulfills the functions that once legitimatized its place. This assertion was explicitly criticized by Pareto in terms that could just as well have been used by Max Weber: Tocqueville was committed to a theodicy. He believed, or at least publicly asserted, that from good comes only good, and that only evil can produce evil. Quite apart from the unverifiable quality of such a theological assertion, Pareto remarked, it is also a patent ethical derivation of a sort that has no place in generalizations about revolution. What exactly did it mean when Tocqueville argued that a class which does good is invariably rewarded? Surely this is inconsistent, because of its simplistic monism, with Tocqueville's own emphasis upon the complexity of historical causation.

To criticize Tocqueville's theory of revolution on this score, as on

[90] Speech of January 29, 1848, reprinted in *Souvenirs,* p. 33.

that of loose and discrepant definition of terms essential to his analysis, does not necessarily lead to the conclusion that his work was thereby vitiated. For his writing still must be considered to possess substantial merits: a remarkable fertility of general hypotheses; the frequent, although not invariable capacity to challenge successfully common sense and received opinion; and a set of analytical tools designed to reveal the interdependence of political institutions and social forces. In his treatment of revolution Tocqueville applied the comparative method to historical materials, and thus was able to suggest what trends were at work on Western society as a whole. Yet this did not keep him from giving detailed attention to national character, by which means he pointed up the distinctive aspects revolution takes on within a given political culture. Tocqueville's standards for an adequate theory of revolution were high. Although he himself did not always meet them, the sum of his achievement will long stand as a challenge and stimulus to all those investigating this subject.

6

THE CONCEPT OF A POLITICAL REVOLUTION

EUGENE KAMENKA

The twentieth century is and is not the era of revolutions. In the past six decades we have witnessed one upheaval after another; the momentous revolution in Russia and two or three revolutions in China, the rise of Kemal Pasha Atatürk, the collapse of the Austro-Hungarian Empire, the abortive attempts at revolution in Germany and Hungary, the seizure of power by Nazis and Fascists, the "revolution from above" in most of Eastern Europe, the collapse of the old regime in Egypt followed by revolutionary impulses throughout the Arab world, and finally, the revolution in Cuba. In Latin America, the almost institutionalized cycle of revolutions

Based on a paper delivered in the Institute of Advanced Studies, Australian National University, on June 3, 1963 as part of a series of seminar papers on "Problems for Social Theory in the Twentieth Century."

and *coups d'état* remains unbreached; in the old colonial and neo-colonial territories of Asia, Africa, and the Pacific there have been momentous transfers of power, some peaceful, some more violent. The twentieth century, at first sight, seems the century of revolutions and instability *par excellence.*

Yet to many of us whose attitudes are shaped by conditions in the highly industrialized countries of the West, these revolutions and upheavals now seem to be *in* the twentieth century, but not *of* it. We write, as I myself have written, that the revolution in Russia was successful precisely because Russia under the Czar was not like modern England, or Norway, or Australia, or the United States; we tend to agree with Karl Kautsky in treating the Austro-Hungarian Empire as a grotesque survival from the past, notable not for its fall, but for its astonishing ability to totter on into the twentieth century. Consciously or unconsciously, sweepingly or cautiously, we liken the social struggles in Asia, Africa, and Latin America to the social struggles of eighteenth- and nineteenth-century Europe and not to the problems confronting advanced industrial societies in the modern age of technology. Communism, *the* revolutionary movement of our time, smacks to us of 1848; we see it and the revolutionary ideology in general, as the understandable, whether regrettable or commendable, ideology of backward nations. The aim of all this fuss is not really to change the course of development in the twentieth century, but to catch up with it.

The revolutions that seem to us in some sense not "of" the twentieth century are, of course, *political* revolutions—the only kind of revolutions I am concerned with in this paper. One can also speak of the industrial revolution, the scientific revolution, the computer revolution, the Freudian revolution, or, perhaps, of the annual revolution in female fashions. These revolutions are very much *of* the twentieth century: indeed, the more men see such revolutions as part of the regular life of their country, the less prone they seem to be to turn to political revolutions for salvation. Viewed in terms of the historical development of Western society, which we see as now setting the fundamental economic objectives and values pursued in contemporary history, the twentieth century is notable not as the era that gave the world political revolutions, but as the era that successfully institutionalized society's passage from one nonpolitical, social or economic revolution to another.

What is a political revolution? When Aristotle spoke of revolutions, he used the term *metabole,* change, and where appropriate, *metabole kai stasis,* change and uprising. But what sort of change, and how important is the element of uprising or violence? Aristotle thought the change had to be one in the *type* of political organization, e.g., from monarchy to oligarchy, from oligarchy to democracy, and so on. Today, we are perhaps somewhat less confident than Aristotle was that the political changes that amount to a change in type, or in the *essence* of the social order, can so readily be detected among other changes; at the same time, we tend to pay even greater attention than he does to the ideology, the beliefs and habits, involved in the existence of a social order. As a preliminary approach to the problem of isolating and describing the meaning of the term "revolution," we might therefore suggest the following: Revolution is a sharp, sudden change in the social location of political power, expressing itself in the radical transformation of the process of government, of the official foundations of sovereignty or legitimacy and of the conception of the social order. Such transformations, it has usually been believed, could not normally occur without violence, but if they did, they would still, though bloodless, be revolutions. The concept of a sharp, sudden change is no doubt a relative concept; what appears to the participants as the slow, gradual evolution of a new style of life may, to later generations, seem a sudden and revolutionary change. At the same time, acknowledged revolutions are rarely sharp and sudden enough to take place at a clearly defined point in time, or to reveal themselves unequivocally as revolutions at the very moment of the formal transfer of power. The violent outburst that heralds the beginning of the revolution for the chronicler may be understandable only as the product of important, if less spectacular, social changes that preceded it; the task of distinguishing a revolutionary outbreak from a *coup d'état* or a rebellion may be impossible until we see how the new masters use their new-won power. But unless we confine the term "revolution" to the field of *convulsive* changes we shall find revolution everywhere, all the time.

The history of the term "revolution" as a political concept has been traced for us in a scholarly work by the German sociologist Eugen Rosenstock-Huessy.[1] The men of the Italian Renaissance had

[1] Eugen Rosenstock-Huessy, *Revolution als politischer Begriff in der Neuzeit* (Breslau: 1931). There is a short summary of Rosenstock's argu-

used "revolution" (*rivoluzioni*) to describe the motion of the planets under the iron laws of the celestial spheres. In transposing the term into the field of politics, they meant to recognize in the rise and fall of princes a superhuman, astral force—the revolving wheel of fortune that raised up one prince or government and threw down another. This concept of a revolution as a total, fundamental and *objective* transformation, as a natural catastrophe, Rosenstock-Huessy calls the *naturalistic* concept. It persisted, according to him, right up to the French Revolution. When the Duc de Liancourt informed Louis XVI of the storming of the Bastille, the King exclaimed, "But good God! That is a revolt!" "No, Sire," replied the Duc, *"c'est la révolution"*—meaning that this was a force of nature completely beyond human control.[2]

With the French Revolution, Rosenstock argues, a new concept of revolution, the *romantic* concept, comes to the fore. Revolution is now seen as the heroic, romantic deed, as the assertion of human subjectivity, of man as the master of history. Before the Revolution Voltaire and Condorcet had laid down the elements of this view; Robespierre became its spokesman; the barricades of 1848 and the Blanquist faction in the Paris Commune were its visible expression. But in reality, the romantic period in Europe was short-lived. By 1850 it had lost most of its force. In the Italian *Risorgimento,* the realist Cavour replaced the romantic Mazzini; Germany moved into the age of Bismarck; the Republican opposition in the France of the Second Empire falls under the sway of the Comtean positivist Gambetta.[3] We enter a new period in the history of the idea of

---

ment in Sigmund Neumann, "The International Civil War," *World Politics,* 1 (1948–9), pp. 333–350. For a brief but independent confirmation of some of Rosenstock's findings, see Arthur Hatto, "Revolution: An Enquiry into the Usefulness of an Historical Term," *Mind,* 58 (1949), pp. 495–517.

[2] Cited by Neumann, *op. cit.,* p. 336. The naturalistic concept of revolution retained the cyclical conception of astronomy and of Classical political philosophy; the term "revolution" was associated with a concept of restoration, of the wheel of fortune returning to its original mark. It is for this reason, as Hatto points out (*op. cit.,* p. 505), that Clarendon called the events in England in 1660 a "revolution," that is, a *return* to the rightful order of things. For the opposing party, 1688 was the return or restoration, occurring, as they were delighted to note, precisely one hundred years after the expulsion of the Papists from England. The year 1688 was thus their "revolution": the Glorious Revolution that marked the restoration of their fortunes.

[3] Cf. David Thomson, "Scientific Thought and Revolutionary Movements," *Impact of Science on Society,* VI (1955), pp. 23–24.

revolution, the general trend of which is only confirmed by the defeat of the Paris Commune. It is the period of the *realist* concept of revolutions.

Rosenstock-Huessy is in the Hegelian tradition; he sees the realist phase as the dialectical negation and synthesis (*Aufhebung*) of the two previous phases. Revolution is no longer seen as an unpredictable result of superhuman forces; to that extent, naturalism is overcome. But revolutions are seen as dependent on objective conditions; they come when the time is ripe for them. To that extent, naturalism is preserved. Neither are revolutions the mere product of human will, they can occur only in a revolutionary situation. Thus, romanticism is overcome. But for the revolutionary situation to become effective, there must be a class ready to do its work, or a decided leadership able to recognize, articulate, and direct the revolutionary forces of the time. Thus, romanticism, the importance of subjectivity, is also preserved. It is because Karl Marx, the outstanding "realist," combined and yet transcended the naturalistic and the romantic views of revolution, that he and his disciples could claim to be neither the astrologers nor the poets of revolution, but its scientists.

The realist theory of revolutions has yet one more important component, which die-hard Hegelians, no doubt, might seek to interpret as the *Aufhebung* of cyclical repetition and lawless leaps into the future. This is the concept of progress. Revolutions were the milestones in humanity's inexorable march toward true freedom and true universality. Each revolution, Marx and Engels write in the *German Ideology,* is the work of a particular class, but during the revolution it appears as the representative of the whole society; as we pass from aristocracy to *bourgeoisie* and from *bourgeoisie* to proletariat, we pass to an ever-broadening base of social power; each revolution is thus truly nearer universality than the last.

The ascription of responsibility in history is governed by much the same psychological mechanisms as the ascription of responsibility in morals and law. A revolution, like a street accident, results from the interaction of a number of factors, each of them necessary but not sufficient to produce the result. We are constantly tempted to pick out as *the* cause the factor that we consider unusual or improper, the factor that lies outside the normal range of our expectations. The young Marx, accustomed to think of governments and social structures as rigid, and greatly impressed with the comparatively recent consciousness of the far-reaching economic changes taking place in society, saw revolution as caused by these changes. By the turn of the century, there was a new generation of Anglo-American thinkers, accustomed to think of far-reaching economic changes as the norm of social life: To them, *the* cause of revolutions seemed the rigidity of governments, the lack of social mobility and political flexibility, repression, and administrative incompetence.[4]

Though the emphases differ, the position is basically the same. Revolution, says Marx, is the bursting of the integument by the repressed forces of economic and social development; revolution, say later sociologists as different as Ward, Ellwood, Pareto, and Brooks Adams,[5] is the conflict between advancing classes or groups or interests in a society and the rigid structure or elite that holds them back.

Karl Marx, who saw revolutions as the violent conflicts between classes, defined these classes as purely economic groups, whose behavior and attitude were determined by their relationship to the means of production. Contemporary sociologists have been very strongly aware not only of the difficulties of Marx's class position in general, but of its particular weaknesses in dealing with revolutions. The leaders of the French revolution, for the most part, were not merchants, but lawyers, notaries, and bailiffs—professional men. The Russian Revolution in 1917 depended heavily for its success on the leadership of that very special noneconomic class, the intelligentsia, and on the fact that a significant number of peasants had

[4] Cf. the passage in L. F. Ward's *Pure Sociology* (p. 230): "Only the labile is truly stable, just as in the domain of living things only the plastic is enduring. For lability is not an exact synonym of instability, but embodies, besides, the idea of flexibility and susceptibility to change without destruction or loss. It is that quality in institutions which enables them to change and still persist, which converts their equilibrium into a moving equilibrium, and which makes possible their adaptation to both internal and external modification. . . . When a society makes for itself a procrustean bed, it is simply preparing the way for its own destruction by the on-moving agencies of social dynamics." Charles A. Ellwood puts the position even more strongly: the causes of revolution are the causes of social rigidity—the breakdown of those habits and institutions (free discussion, public criticism, etc.) that make a government responsive to the need or demand for social transitions. See Ellwood, "A Psychological Theory of Revolutions," *American Journal of Sociology*, II (1905–6), p. 53.

[5] V. Pareto, *The Mind and Society*, Vols. III and IV, esp. pp. 2050–2059, 2170–2203, and 2227; Brooks Adams, *The Theory of Social Revolution*, passim.

been converted, for a period, into soldiers. In these circumstances, most modern writers on revolution have turned, consciously or unconsciously, to Max Weber's conception of class as composed of those who share the same chance in life (*Lebenschance*)—a definition that enables us to cope with intellectuals and, in certain circumstances, with racial or national conflicts and the politics of minorities.

The conception of revolution as connected with members of a Weberian class seeking to improve their life chance, throws into relief once more the role of social rigidity in the production of revolutions and the mitigating influence that we might expect from the existence of a fairly high degree of social mobility, or from the strong belief in its possibility. Members of a class may ascend as individuals; they may ascend collectively as the result of objective conditions; or they may seek the revolutionary path of destroying the privileges of an upper class and reducing its life chances until it ceases to exist as a separate class—normally in the belief that a gain in average life chances will result. Collective ascent as the result of objective conditions is usually slow, but it can be extremely significant. Few people would doubt that the gradual collective ascent of the working classes of Western Europe and North America between 1815 and 1914 did a very great deal indeed to contain and even discredit revolutionary forces and movements. The extent and significance of individual ascent is much more the subject of controversy; but again, one might reasonably assert that the significant chance of individual ascent offered by the assisted migration schemes in England from the 1860's to the 1880's played a marked role in averting the revolutionary situation, or at least the sustained atmosphere of revolt, that might have resulted from the agricultural depression.

An important allied point about revolution was first hinted at by Karl Marx in *Wage Labour and Capital*[6] and put quite decisively by Alexis de Tocqueville a few years later:

---

[6] "A noticeable increase in wages presupposes a rapid growth of productive capital. The rapid growth of productive capital brings about an equally rapid growth of wealth, luxury, social wants, social enjoyments. Thus, although the enjoyments of the workers have risen, the social satisfaction that they give has fallen in comparison with the increased enjoyments of the capitalist, which are inaccessible to the worker, in comparison with the state of development of society in general." Marx and Engels, *Selected Works*, vol. I (Moscow: 1955), p. 94.

Revolutions are not always brought about by a gradual decline from bad to worse. Nations that have endured patiently and almost unconsciously the most overwhelming oppression often burst into rebellion against the yoke the moment that it grows lighter. The regime which is destroyed by a revolution is almost always an improvement on its immediate predecessor. . . . Evils which are patiently endured when they seem inevitable become intolerable when once the idea of escape from them is suggested.[7]

The final sentence is the crucial one. Part of the difference between a revolutionary uprising and a rebellion is the difference in the beliefs and expectations of those involved; rebels seek the redress of grievances, the return to a former state of comparative justice or prosperity; it is amazing, when we look back, just how limited the demands of that Great Peasant Rebellion in Germany in 1525 actually were, and how ready its leaders were to accept the authority of princes and kings. Revolutionaries, on the other hand, have great expectations; they think in terms of a new order, of progress, of changing times that need changing systems of government. For nearly two thousand years, China witnessed civil wars, rebellions, secessions, and *coups d'état*; but until the European revolutions came, there had been not one revolution in China. For revolutions, as Crane Brinton found,[8] require among other things an economically advancing society, the conception of progress, of the human ability to bring about fundamental social change, which seems, as far as we can tell, to be exclusively associated with the conception of a market economy. Rebellions and *coups d'état* occur everywhere; revolutions, it is fascinating to note, seem to have occurred only in *cities* and, until comparatively recently, in Western societies. The revolutions in other types of social structures, I shall argue, rest on the permeation of Western economy and ideology; they are revolutions by contact and imitation.

Revolutions are not produced by the forces of the market economy alone; they require the belief in human power and in the possibility of vast material improvement, but they require also anger and the prospects of success. They require, that is, the support of a significant section of people not normally given to revolt. This tends to occur when two requirements are fulfilled. First, there must have

[7] Alexis de Tocqueville, *The Old Regime and the Revolution*, transl. by John Bonner (New York: 1856), p. 214.

[8] Crane Brinton, *Anatomy of Revolution*, rev. ed. (London: 1953), pp. 277f. ("Some tentative uniformities").

been a strong rise in people's expectations, such as an economically advancing society normally produces, which is suddenly vitiated by a sharp decline in satisfactions. As James C. Davies puts it, "Revolutions are most likely to occur when a prolonged period of economic and social development is followed by a short period of sharp reversal. People then subjectively fear that ground gained with great effort will be quite lost; their mood then becomes revolutionary."[9] Davies attempts to show that this was in fact what happened just before Dorr's (unsuccessful) nineteenth-century rebellion in Rhode Island in 1840-42, in the period preceding the Russian Revolution, and in postwar Egypt before the fall of Farouk. Revolutions, he concludes, do not take place in a society where there is the continued, unimpeded opportunity to satisfy new needs, new hopes and new expectations; neither do they take place in a society in which there are no hopes, no expectations, but only hardship and hunger as long as men can remember.

The second requirement is related to the need for prospects of success, but is often intimately connected with the economic reversal that satisfies the first requirement. In every revolution that I can think of, the state against which the revolutionaries fought had been strikingly weakened by financial failure, administrative incompetence, lack of self-confidence and, in a very high number of cases, by defeat in war.

This latter point should not surprise. For if revolutions are the milestones on the way to the development of an advanced industrialized economy, they are also bloody battles, desperate struggles against the authority and power of the previously existing state. As Borkenau puts it:

> Every great revolution has destroyed the State apparatus which it found. After much vacillation and experimentation, every revolution has set another apparatus in its place, in most cases of quite a different character from the one destroyed; for the changes in the state order which a revolution produces are no less important than the changes in the social order. The revolutionary process itself is in the first instance a struggle for political power. And whatever may be the deeper driving-forces of a revolution, the struggle for the State always appears as its immediate content (!); indeed to such an extent that the transformation of the social order often appears not

---

[9] James C. Davies, "Toward a Theory of Revolution," *American Sociological Review*, 27 (1962), p. 5,

as the goal of the revolution, but simply as means used by revolutionaries to conquer or to exercise power.[10]

Contemporary political thinkers molded in the background of Western democracy are extremely conscious, in recent years, of the ruthless internal logic of revolutions, of the fraudulence of their claim to transfer power to "the people." Most of us today would accept what Borkenau calls "the law of the twofold development of revolutions. They begin as anarchistic movements against the bureaucratic state organization, which they inevitably destroy; they continue by setting in its place another, in most cases stronger, bureaucratic organization, which suppresses all free mass movements."[11] The Thermidorian reaction seems to us no longer a possible danger that revolutions must avoid, but a necessary consequence of the very nature of the revolutionary ideology and the revolutionary struggle. So clear, and so apparently inevitable, is the centralizing, dictatorial trend of revolutions that for the first time in human history we actually find revolution cynically used as a *means* for welding together a diffuse society, for creating centralized authority and power.

It is tempting, in these circumstances, to merge into one concept the successful rebellion, the revolution, and the *coup d'état*. Peter Amann, in a recent paper,[12] tries to do just this. Revolution, as he defines it, "prevails when the State's monopoly of power is effectively challenged and persists until a monopoly of power is re-established."[13] This approach, he argues, avoids such traditional problems as that of distinguishing a revolution from a *coup d'état*, the uncertain differentiation between wars of independence, civil wars and revolutions, and the difficulty of deciding how much social change is necessary before a movement may be called a revolution. At the same time, the definition recognizes the possibility of suspended revolutions, where we have the prolonged co-existence of two antagonistic governmental power centers, e.g., the Army and the Government in the Weimar Republic or in the post-Peron Frondizi regime in Argentina.

[10] F. Borkenau, "State and Revolution in the Paris Commune, the Russian Revolution, and the Spanish Civil War," in *Sociological Review*, 29 (1937), p. 41.

[11] *Ibid.*, p. 67.

[12] Peter Amann, "Revolution: A Redefinition," *Political Science Quarterly*, 77 (1962), pp. 36–53.

[13] *Ibid.*, p. 39.

Such simplifications are always attractive and, in a sense, they are not wrong. Words have no natural definitions; social events have no clearly manifest essential character. *Eadem sed aliter* is the motto of history and of nature. The distinctions we make, the connections and similarities we emphasize, are made for a purpose, an explanatory purpose. For some purposes, we may be interested only in the breakdown of the governmental monopoly of public power; for these purposes Amann's use of the word "revolution" may well be a useful shorthand. For other purposes—and they are the ones with which I and most students of revolution are concerned—it misses crucial distinctions. It is, I think, important to recognize the role of rising expectations and of ideology in revolutions, to be able to say that revolution is different from peasant uprisings and slave rebellions in respects crucial to understanding the process, and that there have been no revolutions in Asia and Africa until this century. To understand why this is so, we need a concept of revolution that is no doubt trickier to work with, but that has also far greater explanatory power, than the formalized concept that Amann proposes.

We have noted the naked emergence, in the twentieth century, of the centralizing motif in revolutions—the open preoccupation with power that lends plausibility to Amann's suggested redefinition. But even here there is a crucial distinction between, say, the Indonesian Revolution on the one hand and the old Chinese Triad movement to "overthrow the Ch'ing and restore the Ming" on the other.[14] Revolution has come to Asia because Europe has come to Asia; the change of power is no longer seen as a restoration, but as a leap forward, a leap forward into the universalized, industrialized society of the West. The Indonesian rebellion against the Dutch was utterly different from the Jewish rebellion against the Romans: it was not merely a movement of national liberation from foreign masters, but a struggle for *control* over political, social, and economic processes that were now recognized as the key to the future. In this sense, it seems to me, the movements of national liberation and the more or less peaceful transfers of power in Asian, African,

[14] The T'ai-p'ing T'ien-kuo rebellion of 1850–64 marks the transition; on the one hand, it drew on the traditions of southern separatism and hostility to the Ch'ing (the Manchus), on the other hand it drew from European missionary influence and the penetration of European trade a Messianic character that laid some of the groundwork for the revolutionary movement in China.

and Pacific countries have to be seen not only as revolutions, but as *revolutions within the history of Europe,* the transfer of social power from one governing class to a new class. It is only because Asia, Africa, and the Pacific have entered the history of Europe that such true revolutions have become possible to them. It is because Turkey had entered the history of Europe that Kemal Pasha Atatürk's *coup d'état* aspired to become a revolution.

In the advanced, industrial countries of the West, on the other hand, one is inclined to say that the age of revolutions is over. As R. S. Parker put it recently: "If . . . we consider preindustrial societies where the population pressed hard on the means of subsistence, we invariably expect to find direct power relations playing a larger part in the distribution of material welfare. . . . Comparatively speaking, high average living standards and the economic and social mobility that go with them in a country like Australia conduce, other things being equal, to a general acceptance of the economic processes of bargaining and exchange, and reduced need for the exercise of power in arranging the allocation of material values."[15] For the first time in human history technological advance has become so great that society can, as Toynbee notes in his *Reconsiderations,*[16] support a vast proliferation of bureaucracy without a sharp decrease in the sub-bureaucratic standard of living; the cyclical law of the rebellion against bureaucratic rule no longer applies. At the same time, the ideology of the market has found its political counterpart in the procedures of representative government. While popular political control is no doubt as imperfect as the consumer control extolled by capitalist apologetics, it is nevertheless there. Representative government *has* produced, in conjunction with the radically "capitalized" society, a comparatively flexible, responsive social structure able to make the transitions for which revolution and uprising were needed in the past.

This is not to say that the present political structure of advanced industrial societies has no tendencies that might lead to rigidity, or that a sharp discrepancy between people's economic expectations and their economic satisfactions might not once more arise, produc-

[15] R. S. Parker, "Power in Australia," a seminar paper delivered in the Institute of Advanced Studies, Australian National University, on October 8, 1962, and circulated to participants in the seminar on "The Sociology of Power," pp. 2–3.

[16] See Arnold Toynbee, *A Study of History,* vol. XII (London: 1961), esp. pp. 200–209.

ing a decidedly rebellious, revolutionary mood. But from the stand-point of the classical conception of revolutions, there will be fundamental differences in any such future situations. The concept of universality has been exhausted, for all practical purposes, in the attaining of representative government and reasonable economic affluence. The revolution of the future in advanced, democratic, industrialized society could only be a counterrevolution, a seizure of power by a group intent on re-establishing despotic rule and a status society. The intensification of military struggle or of popu-lation pressures on food resources could make such a possibility seem far more real than it does today; but they could hardly convert such a coup from its obvious place with Roman dictatorships to an af-finity with the French, the Russian, or even the Chinese and In-donesian Revolutions.

In the Communist world, future revolutions in my sense of the word do not seem to us impossible. The Hungarian revolt was in-deed part of a tradition that goes back to the French, Polish, and Russian Revolutions; it might even have ended, if successful, more happily than any of these. For the revolutionary in the Communist world the problem is the concentration of power in the hands of the modern state, the comparatively blurred nature of the class against which he is rebelling, and the fact that his revolution—unlike previous revolutions directed against idle aristocrats, absentee land-lords, and brokendown bureaucracies—would be against a class playing a significant role in the process of production.

The problems of social theory will not be solved by any careful, preliminary analysis of concepts. The definition of revolution is not the beginning but the end of an inquiry into social upheaval, social change, and the translocation of power. There is not a right defini-tion and a wrong definition, there are only fruitful distinctions and less fruitful distinctions, terms useful in one context and useless in another. In this paper I have tried to suggest that we should not abandon too readily the economic strand in the realist conception of revolutions. The Leninist emphasis on revolutionary theory as a manual for the seizure of power has led many contemporary so-ciologists to seek to treat revolution in static terms, as a situation in which the state monopoly of power is being effectively challenged. This emphasizes the undoubted connections between revolutions, re-bellions, civil wars, wars of liberation, and *coups d'état;* it is useful in deflating revolutionary pretensions about the elimination of power in human affairs and bringing out the centralizing tendencies inherent in bitter conflict. But this static, cross-sectional treatment of societies in the throes of conflict seems to me totally inadequate as a foundation for examining the causes and more general consequences of such conflicts, for understanding when and why they are likely to occur. For these purposes, we do need to distinguish between a *coup d'état* and a revolution, between the inauguration of a new dynasty and the inauguration of a new social order. The distinctions cannot be made sharply; social events run together, they vacillate between one category and another, they end where no one dreamed at the beginning they would end. Kemal Pasha's *coup d'état,* I have suggested, aspired, through its association with the Young Turks, to become a revolution; and for some purposes it may best be understood as such. The transfer of power in India, with its momentous revolutionary implications, has perhaps not succeeded in realizing them; one might easily query whether the India of 1963 is a new India in comparison with the India of 1938. Nevertheless, distinctions that can be blurred, or that can fail to be helpful in some situations, may still be vital to understanding the general picture. To do this, I have suggested, we need a *dynamic* concept of revolutions, a concept of political revolutions that sees them in their intimate relationship to the more general class of social revolutions of which they are part rather than to the allied classes of rebellions, uprisings, and wars.

REVOLUTION, IDEOLOGY, AND INTERNATIONAL ORDER

7

REVOLUTION AND IDEOLOGY IN THE LATE TWENTIETH CENTURY

C. B. MACPHERSON

The revolutions and the ideologies likely to be most important in the second half of the twentieth century are those of the underdeveloped countries. This proposition does not denigrate the obviously great continuing importance of the Communist revolutions of the first half of the century or of the Marxist ideology. They will go on working themselves out. But the new revolutions, having altered the terms on which the senior revolutionary ideologies can continue to be influential, may be regarded as the critical new factor in the problems of revolution and ideology of the next several decades. The revolutionary and ideological currents in the underdeveloped countries, currents which are not formed entirely from either Marxist or liberal-democratic ideologies, are already having

139

and will increasingly have an effect on the Communist and Western structures of power and of ideas.

PROBLEM AND TERMS DEFINED

I want first to show that the new revolutions depend to an unusual degree on ideology, that the new states built on these revolutions will continue that dependence, and that their ideologies are not likely to conform either to the Communist or the Western pattern. I will then offer some speculations on the possible effects of this fact on the Western ideology.

Throughout I use *ideology* in a neutral sense, neither implying, with Marx, an idealist philosophy and "false consciousness," nor, with Mannheim, contrasting ideology and "utopia." I take ideology to be any more or less systematic set of ideas about man's place in nature, in society, and in history (i.e., in relation to particular societies), which can elicit the commitment of significant numbers of people to (or against) political change. This does not exclude a set of ideas essentially concerned with merely a class or a nation, if it relates the place and needs of that section of humanity to the place of man in general. Thus liberalism, conservatism, democracy (in various senses), Marxism, Populism, Nkrumaism, pan-Africanism, and various nationalisms are all ideologies. Ideologies contain, in varying proportions, elements of explanation (of fact and of history), justification (of demands), and faith or belief (in the ultimate truth or rightness of their case). They are informed by, but are less precise and systematic than, political theories or political philosophies. They are necessary to any effective political movement, hence to any revolution, for they perform the triple function of simplifying, demanding, and justifying.

By *revolution* I mean a political overturn more far-reaching than a *coup d'état* or "palace revolution." I take revolution to mean a transfer of state power by means involving the use or threat of organized unauthorized force, and the subsequent consolidation of that transferred power, with a view to bringing about a fundamental change in social, economic, and political institutions. How long a period of consolidation is to be included in the revolution itself is a matter of theoretical convenience; here it will be convenient to consider the revolution to extend for as long as ideological zeal is needed (and is forthcoming) to secure a sufficient basis for the new institutions.

My interest in the revolutions and ideologies of the underdeveloped countries arises from my concern with the prospects of liberal-democratic political theory. The present widely-felt inadequacy of liberal-democratic justificatory theory is, I think, due to the posssessive quality of its basic individualism. I have argued elsewhere[1] (a) that the philosophy of liberalism has been, from its origins in the seventeenth century, permeated by possessive individualism, which assumes that the individual is human *qua* proprietor of his own person, that the human essence is freedom from any but self-interested contractual relations with others, and that society is essentially a series of market relations between these free individuals; (b) that this individualism was ethically adequate for societies dominated and vitalized by competitive market relations; (c) that it becomes ethically inadequate once the natural rightness or inevitability of market relations is challenged or denied by substantial sections of the people (as it began to be in England and Europe from the middle of the nineteenth century); but (d) that possessive individualism cannot simply be discarded from the justificatory theory of liberal democracy because liberal democracy is still in our day coterminous with market-dominated societies, so that the assumptions of possessive individualism (though now ethically inadequate) are still factually accurate. The question about which I now speculate is whether the impact of the underdeveloped countries' revolutions and ideology may provide some basis for the requisite change in Western political theory or ideology.

IMPORTANCE OF IDEOLOGY IN THE REVOLUTIONS OF THE UNDERDEVELOPED COUNTRIES

Compared to the classic revolutions of the seventeenth to nineteenth centuries, the revolutions of the underdeveloped countries in our time depend to a much higher degree on ideology. Two reasons are evident: (a) The new revolutions, in order to move toward their goal of bringing backward peoples rapidly into the modern world, must in most cases virtually create a nation. They must do in a few years what the classic European revolutions either did not have to do at all or were able to do with much less difficulty, that is, create a sense of primary loyalty to a political nation, rather than to local, tribal, or feudal communities. The leaders of

[1] In my *Political Theory of Possessive Individualism* (New York: 1962).

the new revolutions, themselves generally intellectuals,[2] politicized by training abroad, have had to bring a prepolitical people to a sense of nationality and national self-esteem, to create a political and national consciousness, and to infuse a hope and a faith that great things can be done by the new nation.[3] This is a task for ideology. And the leaders, being intellectuals, have been able to provide the ideology. They have generally proceeded by setting up the nation as the charismatic object, in place of the tribe, the kinship group, feudal or royal rulers, priests and magicians, in which the ordinary man hitherto had found the sacred quality.[4] But however the new ideology is brought into existence, its creation and spread are indispensable to the revolution.

(b) Just as the immediate aim of the revolution—the transfer of power from an outside imperial government to an indigenous national government—requires a high degree of ideology, so does the longer term but equally necessary aim of rapid economic development. The classic Western revolutions of the seventeenth to nineteenth centuries came, generally speaking, when there was already an enterprising *bourgeoisie* ready and able to press ahead with economic development. In the new revolutions there is, generally speaking, no indigenous *bourgeoisie* and no indigenous accumulation of private capital. The desired economic development has therefore to be undertaken by state initiative, state accumulation and investment of capital, state planning and controls. The accumulation of capital, and the provision of incentives which will convert the ordinary people into a modern labor force, obviously require, and will require for a long time, heavy reliance on ideology.

[2] "The gestation, birth, and continuing life of the new states of Asia and Africa, through all their vicissitudes, are in large measure the work of intellectuals. In no state-formations in all of human history have intellectuals played such a role as they have in these events of the present century." Edward Shils, "The Intellectuals in the Political Development of New States," *World Politics* (April 1960).

[3] "Differences of caste, tribe, clan or religion must be integrated into the political process, and it is precisely because they loom so large as an obstacle to the creation of the modern nation-state that the leaders place great emphasis on the primacy of 'the nation' and the elimination of traditional status differentiations. . . . The first requirement is the implementation of the common ideal of universal participation in the nation." Paul E. Sigmund, Jr. (ed.), *The Ideologies of the Developing Nations* (New York: 1963), p. 7.

[4] See Edward Shils, "The Concentration and Dispersal of Charisma: Their Bearing on Economic Policy in Underdeveloped Countries," *World Politics* (October 1958), pp. 3–4.

In short, both of the practical objectives of the new revolutions—the change from colony to viable independent nation, and the promotion of rapid economic development—require and will continue to require a high degree of ideology. In the nature of the case, the ideology has to be developed by the political elite, who are at once the intelligentsia and the political leaders. They do not, of course, create ideologies out of nothing. Where they can, they find historical roots in the precolonial cultures and polities of their own lands. And they draw, of course, on the ideological traditions they find in the advanced countries, both Western and Communist. What sort of ideologies have resulted?

REVOLUTIONARY IDEOLOGIES NEITHER COMMUNIST NOR LIBERAL-DEMOCRATIC

One may say in general of the new ideologies that they are neither Communist nor Western (using Western to mean pluralist, liberal-democratic, bourgeois-individualist). One may say also that it is not very useful to try to place them in a continuum stretching from Communist to Western. They see themselves as outside that continuum. For them, the polar division of the world is not between communism and liberal capitalism but between the rich nations and the poor nations. They know where they stand now in that division, and they know where they want to move. In order to move, they will take from both the Marxist and the liberal-democratic traditions whatever seems to them to go to the root of their problems.

As a brief analysis will show, they have, on the whole, taken something from Marxism, while refusing to identify themselves with Soviet Communism; they have rejected almost wholly the liberal individualist utilitarianism of the West, but have drawn heavily on its earlier democratic tradition, the tradition of Rousseau and Populism. Indeed, it is where Marxism and this original Western democratic ideology overlap that the leaders of the modern underdeveloped countries' revolutions find themselves ideologically most at home.

We may look first at what they have taken from, and what they have rejected in, the Western ideology. The clearest thing about the new ideologies is their rejection of the capitalist ethos. Whether or not they accept, or how much they accept of, the thesis of Lenin's *Imperialism,* they tend to have a strong moral aversion to the ethics of competitive individualism. This goes deeper than the natural reaction of an exploited colonial people to the ethos of their former exploiters and to any fear that they may still be exploited economically even after winning political independence. It goes back to their traditional culture, which saw no intrinsic value in wealth getting and gave no respect to the motive of individual gain.[5] These traditional roots might, of course, have been pulled up, just as the traditional reliance on the prepolitical local community is being uprooted. But there has been neither need nor inclination to try to do so, for it has seemed clear to the revolutionary leaders that the rapid national economic development they demanded could come only through social control of the economy; to have left it to private capitalist enterprise would have meant leaving it to foreigners, which would have negated the revolutionary goal of national independence.

Thus both the traditional ethos of the prepolitical society, and the political needs of the revolution, have operated against acceptance of the Western capitalist ethos. Added to this has been a strong moral egalitarianism, which may be explained partly in traditional terms and partly as revulsion against the dehumanizing contrast of poverty and wealth which they see in capitalism. All these forces may be expected to continue to operate against acceptance of the capitalist ethos.

At the same time that the economic ethos of capitalism has been rejected, so has the political ethos of liberal pluralism. And here too, traditional outlook has been reinforced by the requirements of a modernizing revolution. The local, community-centered society traditionally made its decisions by discussion between equals. The more primitive the society, the less do plural interests exist and demand recognition. In the underdeveloped societies generally there was little basis for pluralism, or for the Western system of competing political parties and pressure groups. Furthermore, the requirements of the struggle for independence generally favored the emergence of a dominant single party or movement, and this has been carried into the postindependence structure in most cases as a single-party or

[5] The "autonomous movement of the economic system is thought undesirable even if possible." It "is believed that no intrinsic value resides in the economic sphere—in the way in which the religious and political spheres possess the intrinsic value connected with sacred things. The only truly respected motives are those generated by authority, the exercise of that sovereignty, religious or political, which entails communion with the sacred." Shils, *World Politics* (October 1958), p. 2.

single-party-dominance system.[6] The political leaders, as ideologists, find no difficulty in justifying one-party rule, both as fitting the indigenous traditional idea of democracy and as necessary for the task of making and consolidating the national revolution.

While the practical basis of the antipluralist ideology is the revolutionary need for unified command and unified popular support, the moral basis is found in a Rousseauan concept of a general will. This concept is the moral basis also of the economic side of the ideology—the rejection of competitive capitalist individualism. Just as Rousseau found the source of social ills, of moral depravity, of dehumanization and loss of human freedom, in the institution of inequality, and believed that the secular redemption of mankind could be got through a purified general will (which, to be operative, would require the institution of substantial economic equality and the absence of effective interest groups), so do the new ideologies. To them, the period of colonialism was the period of inequality forcibly or fraudulently imposed in place of an original equality. Inequality had destroyed the human dignity and freedom of the people. Dignity, freedom, and humanity could be restored by re-establishing equality. This required not only the political revolution but also a moral revolution—an assertion of the will of an undifferentiated people as the only legitimate source of power.

It is less important to stress the Rousseauan parallels than to notice that the essential assertion—the ultimate moral worth of the freedom and dignity of the individual, which can however only be realized by the operation of an undifferentiated popular or mass will —goes back to a preliberal democratic tradition. In England, the classic home of liberalism, democracy was feared, down to the middle of the nineteenth century and even later, by the most enlightened liberals, as being inconsistent with liberal society and the liberal estate. If the ideology of democracy was then inchoate, it

---

[6] A recent study of new states in Africa shows that, of the independent states in which an indigenous majority participates in government (i.e., excluding the Republic of South Africa, Southern Rhodesia, etc.), all but four (Libya, Egypt, Sudanese Republic, and Ethiopia, in which no parties are permitted) have a single-party or single-party-dominance system. Single-party-dominance means that more than one party exists but one party has an overwhelming legislative majority and employs its legal, police, and political powers to restrict the competitive position of opposition parties and groups. M. L. Kilson, "Authoritarian and Single-Party Tendencies in African Politics," *World Politics* (January 1963), pp. 262–263.

was strong enough to be dreaded. It is this earlier tradition of democracy that the new leaders have tapped. They have seen that, historically, it has as good a claim to the title democracy as has the now more familiar pluralist liberal democracy. This has given the leaders confidence that their regimes are in a genuine sense democratic. If they have deserted Rousseau in the matter of the representation of the general will, they have not deserted Robespierre; the party and its leaders are the bearers of the will of the people.

This egalitarian general-will ideology is likely to become firmly established. It feeds and is fed by the necessary nationalism of the underdeveloped countries' revolutions. And it is a highly valuable, if not indispensable, support to the position of the revolutionary leaders; it upholds their one-party or dominant-party state, and validates their authority as leaders of it. Without such authority they cannot hope to carry through the program of economic development necessary to consolidate the revolution. They may therefore be expected to use all the resources of state and party to strengthen that ideology.

We may say, then, that the leaders of the underdeveloped countries' revolutions, rejecting the ideology of contemporary Western liberal democracy, have anchored themselves in the earlier Western ideology of preliberal democracy. Just as they have rejected alignment with either Western or Communist power blocs, and have seen themselves as outside the capitalism-communism continuum, so in rejecting contemporary Western ideology they have swung not to Communist ideology but to a position historically outside of both the dominant contemporary ideologies, a preliberal-democratic and pre-Marxist position.

It is in this light that the measure of their acceptance of Marxism may best be understood. Even the new nations whose ideology has come closest to Marxism, e.g., Sékou Touré's Guinea, can be seen to accept only those elements of Marxism that fit in with the pre-Marxian democratic position. Thus they gladly accept the basic moral position of Marx's humanism, which has its roots in the Rousseauan tradition. Although they may not be versed in the latest scholarly debates about the role of alienation in Marxism, they find immediately and deeply attractive the general thrust of Marx's analysis of the dehumanization of man by capitalism, and the Marxian belief that man can remake himself and can overcome his alienation, by concerted revolutionary action. But they do not accept as applicable to their countries or to the contemporary world the Marxian theory of class struggle as the motor of history, nor the theory of the state as essentially an instrument of class domination, both before the proletarian revolution and in the postrevolutionary dictatorship of the proletariat. Nor, consequently, are they interested in the withering away of the state. For they insist that their own countries are now classless societies, that the new national state (or the dominant party) consequently speaks for the whole of the people, and that its authority emanates directly from the whole of the people.

With this view of their own society as classless, they are able to accept what looks like the "vanguard" theory of Lenin's but which is not quite the same. Lenin argued, as early as 1902 in *What Is To Be Done?* that a working class by itself, under capitalism, could not reach more than trade-union consciousness, that only a vanguard of dedicated intellectual Marxists could see through to reality, and that it must therefore be their task, by building round themselves a tightly organized party, to lead and control the revolution. The vanguard, rather than the proletarian mass, was made the effective agent of the revolution. In thus clearly separating the function of the vanguard from that of the proletarian mass, and asserting that the vanguard could make a revolution before there was a thoroughly class-conscious proletariat, Lenin made it easier for the later underdeveloped revolutions to speak in Marxist terms. The fact that they had no industrial proletariat did not now matter; they had an intellectual vanguard.[7] Yet the theory and practice of the vanguard in most of the underdeveloped countries' revolutions is not exactly Leninist. The role of the vanguard is not to end class domination but foreign domination. It is to seize and wield power not in the name of a not yet fully conscious proletariat, but in the name of an undifferentiated people who are never to become a proletariat because industrialization is not to be allowed to take place under capitalist auspices.

Thus, in the matter of the vanguard, as in their beliefs about the sources of their people's dehumanization and the way to overcome it, the new ideologies have taken over less from Marxism or Lenin-

---

[7] This point was made by Eduard Heiman, "Marxism and the Underdeveloped Countries," *Social Research* (September 1952), who argued then that the addition of the vanguard theory had made Marxism readily transferable to the underdeveloped countries without distortion.

ism than from a pre-Marxist radical tradition, suitably reformulated
to meet the needs of underdeveloped peoples in a highly developed
world. The new ideologies may, in a sense, be said to have bypassed
Marxism. For the conditions in which their revolutions are rooted
are neither those envisaged by Marx nor those envisaged by Lenin.
They have no industrial proletariat, and do not intend to have one.
In the scales of Western economic history, they are peasants at most.
Yet a colonial people may be called proletarian in a deeper sense.
For, in the measure that the colony was fully subject to the purposes
of the metropolitan economy, the people were held to their economic
position not, as the prerevolutionary Russian peasant, by feudal or
precapitalist relations of production, but by capitalist relations of
production, albeit imposed by an economic force from beyond their
own borders. In this sense their revolutions might be called proletarian, for they have been made by peoples subjugated by capitalist
relations of production in order to throw off those relations. But the
classic Marxist and Leninist categories do not fit them exactly. An
underdeveloped people caught up in capitalist relations is, so to
speak, at once nonproletarian and more completely proletarian than
the trade-union-conscious labor force of an advanced capitalist society. It is nonproletarian in that it has not the industrial worker's
factory discipline and subordination to the machine (which Marx
counted on to produce proletarian consciousness, and which Lenin
counted on too, though with some impatience). It is more proletarian in that it, rather than the working classes of the advanced
countries, has experienced the immiseration (*verelendung*) that
Marx predicted for the latter, and in that virtually the whole people
rather than just one class has been immiserized.

The attractiveness of Marxism to underdeveloped revolutionaries
is no doubt due to this fact. Yet an underdeveloped people is not a
Marxist proletariat even when they develop a consciousness of their
common subjugation by capitalism, for their consciousness is not a
class consciousness but a national consciousness. They intend, as the
immediate aftermath of their taking power, not a dictatorship of
the proletariat (or of a vanguard in the name of the proletariat)
over a *bourgeoisie,* but the dictatorship of a general will,[8] or of a

[8] Cf. Sékou Touré's concept of "democratic dictatorship." He begins by
defining dictatorship as the exercise of sovereign power, so that all conceivable governments are dictatorships. Democratic dictatorship is then defined as government based on the sovereignty of the people. "A democratic
state comes from the will of the people. Its program is therefore necessarily

vanguard in the name of the general will, over a people undifferentiated by class (for once the imperial power has been driven out, there is no *bourgeoisie* remaining to be dominated).

Yet if the ideologies of the underdeveloped nations have bypassed Marxism and rooted themselves in an earlier radical democratic tradition, it should also be noticed that recent Soviet Marxism has been making an effort to catch up. The Soviet leaders have abandoned the nineteenth-century Marxist view that the world trend to communism must come through proletarian revolutions, and see it now as coming through colonial revolutions which, though they set up non-Communist systems, may be encouraged to move into the Soviet orbit. "It was no doubt with this prospect in view," Robert Tucker has written, "that Soviet doctrine was amended by Khrushchev in 1956 to provide for a 'peaceful' mode of 'transition to socialism.' In his report to the 20th Party Congress, he particularly singled out countries where capitalism is weak and relatively underdeveloped as the most likely places for the 'peaceful' mode of transition."[9]

One further factor must be taken into account in assessing the probability of Marxist penetration of the new ideologies. Most of the new nations have, from the beginning, taken a stand on nonalignment with either the Soviet or the Western powers. Whatever aid they receive from either bloc, they have remained uncommitted. They are likely to remain so, partly because their ideology has a strong moralizing element—a disapproval of power politics as such; partly because they hope, by remaining neutralist (even though not acting as a neutralist third bloc) to diminish the chances of conflict between the two great power blocs (an open conflict between which would finish their chances of economic development); and perhaps fundamentally because they are beginning to have some confidence that *they* see the long-range problem of a peaceful world order more realistically than those who are still caught up in the cold war. Whatever the reasons for it, their deliberate nonalignment

---

in conformance with the interests of the people. Likewise, its force, its authority, the powers it exercises, the discipline it imposes—in short, the dictatorship it exercises—arise exclusively from the interests, the requirements, and the principles of popular sovereignty." *La Lutte du Parti Démocratique de Guinée pour l'Emancipation Africaine* (1959), as translated in Sigmund, *op. cit.*, p. 163.

[9] Robert C. Tucker, "Russia, the West and the World Order," *World Politics* (October 1959), p. 18.

with either bloc entails some reserve about Soviet theoretical principles, and thus throws up a barrier to their acceptance of a full Marxist ideology. Indeed, to the extent that the third of the reasons suggested above is operative, they will be apt to regard Soviet ideology (as well as Western) as less realistic than their own.

I have argued that the ideologies of the underdeveloped countries' revolutions are, and are likely to remain, neither liberal-democratic nor Communist; that while they may be said to have adapted elements both of Marxism and of liberal democracy, they may better be understood as having their roots in a pre-Marxist and preliberal notion of democracy. The new ideologies are not so much eclectic compilations of bits from the two competing ideologies of the advanced countries as they are growths from an earlier stem, with such grafts from the two modern plants as the original stem will take. Grafts are needed because the new soil is not entirely congenial to the old stem.

I have suggested also that the emergence of the new nations and the new ideologies has already had some effect on one of the two advanced ideologies—the Soviet theory has been adjusted to the fact and the prospects of the underdeveloped revolutions. Can Western ideology also be adjusted to them?

POSSIBLE EFFECTS OF THE NEW REVOLUTIONS ON WESTERN IDEOLOGY

We may notice first that the requisite Western adjustment is not simply one that would make Western ideology more attractive to the underdeveloped countries. The notion of currying favor is as unnecessary as it is distasteful. What is needed is an ideology that would allow the West to maintain a position of world importance in a world one-third Communist, one-third uncommitted, and one-third Western (I assume that Western leaders will come to recognize that world dominance is no longer a feasible aim). I assume also that it is recognized by the leaders of both West and East (though not yet by the whole people or all the influential groups) that in the present and any future condition of nuclear armament no great power can maintain or improve its position in the world merely by a show of force. It follows that the West requires, beyond its military forces, a set of values or an ideology by which it can co-exist with, while contesting with, the other two-thirds of the world. A viable Western ideology must be built on the recognition that the world is no longer a Western preserve. This is difficult but not impossible.

In the second place we may notice that the requisite adjustment of Western ideology does not involve altering or abandoning the values on which the West most prides itself. It would, however, be misleading to suggest that the Western adjustment would be simply related to means, not ends, as the Soviet theoretical adjustment has been. The Soviets have not given up any of their values. They are still Communist, and still intend to further the "transition to socialism" outside the Soviet bloc. They have merely dropped their insistence that class war and dictatorship of the proletariat are the only possible ways to achieve their ends. The Western adjustment would involve not only an alteration in the theory of means but some alteration in the theory of ends as well. For the Western ideology treats as ends not only the ethical values of liberal democracy but also the ethos of capitalist enterprise, or what I have called the values of possessive individualism. As stated above, possessive individualism regards the individual as human in his capacity as proprietor of his own person; the human essence is freedom from any but self-interested contractual relations with others; society consists of a series of market relations between these free individuals. I have argued that these assumptions have been built into the value system of liberal democracy, and they are no longer an adequate ethical basis for it. The point here is that a Western ideology that is to be internationally viable from now on will have to abandon this possessive individualism. The reasons may be reduced to two. First, it is, of all the Western values, precisely this possessive individualism which has been rejected by the uncommitted nations. Secondly, possessive individualism entails continual capitalist aggrandizement; a nation devoted to possessive individualism must be, in Harrington's phrase, "a commonwealth for increase," and this is what the Western nations can no longer expect to be.

The real question, then, is whether possessive individualism is so built into the Western ideology that it cannot be dropped or decisively modified. This is too big a question to try to deal with here in all its aspects, but we can consider one specific aspect: Is the fact of the underdeveloped countries' revolutions (added to the preceding fact of the Communist revolutions) itself a new force making for Western abandonment of possessive individualism?

To consider this question we must notice that Western ideology is not simply (as I have so far by implication defined it) a compound of pluralist liberal democracy and possessive individualism, but that it has defined itself increasingly in the last two decades as a cold-war ideology. It has done so by embracing the assumption that there is between East and West not merely a long-term contest for world influence but an implacable and absolute hostility, such that Western nations must bend their whole effort to forcibly defeating, or not being forcibly defeated by, the East. This assumption has fused with the other two elements in Western ideology to produce a new compound. *The* Western value becomes "the free way of life," a concept in which the values of liberal democracy, of possessive individualism, and of anticommunism, are merged. They are merged in such a way that, of the two original elements, one particularly, possessive individualism, draws much of its vitality from the hostility to communism.

To the extent that possessive individualism has been so fused with cold-war anticommunism, anything that produces a Western move away from the latter will also carry Western ideology away from the former. The emergence of the underdeveloped nations may alter the Western cold-war ideology in two ways.

First, in the measure that the world effect of the underdeveloped countries' revolutions is realistically assessed in the West, it must modify the cold-war attitude of the West. I assume that as neither East nor West can now hope to advance their power or influence by war, and as the two now have comparable technical and economic strengths (at least when rates of growth are taken into account), the future relative world strength of East and West depends mainly on who wins (or does not lose) the good will of the uncommitted parts of the world. On this assumption, a Western policy of peaceful coexistence with the East becomes the rational policy, for coexistence is the only policy the uncommitted nations can regard as rational for others as well as for themselves.

Second, the revolutions of the underdeveloped countries have already, as we have seen, led to substantial modification of the Soviet doctrine of class conflict. Soviet abandonment of the doctrine of the necessary class war and proletarian dictatorship should increase the possibility of peaceful coexistence between East and West. In both these ways the underdeveloped revolutions have set in motion forces tending to moderate the cold-war ideology and thus, on our earlier assumption, to carry Western ideology away from possessive individualism.

The possessive individualism of the Western ideology may be affected by the underdeveloped revolutions in a third way, operative even if cold-war attitudes are not greatly reduced. Even on cold-war assumptions, there is no ground for implacable hostility between the West and the underdeveloped new nations. Their ideology does not commit them to proletarian revolution or world revolution. Their goals are more modest. They seek only to realize an egalitarian humanism, and that only for their own countries. The West can co-exist with these ideologies. The longer the West lives with them, and the more widely they are propagated, the more the ethical contrast between their egalitarian humanism and possessive individualism (which is already under wide attack by theologians, philosophers, and publicists in the West) will be borne in on the conscience of the West. In recognizing the merits of the new ideologies' humanism, the West would be going back to the roots of its own democratic tradition.

None of these prospects, it must be said, can be counted upon to reduce the possessive quality of our modern individualism to a point consistent with the requirements of twentieth-century liberal-democratic theory. But there is at least a possibility that Western recognition of the new world alignment of our time, in which the underdeveloped revolutions are playing the final decisive part, will be enough, coming as it does on top of the other new fact that individuals throughout the world are now equally insecure in face of the possibility of nuclear war,[10] to overcome the dominance of possessive individualism in Western ideology.

---

[10] The possible role of this new equality of insecurity in providing some part of a sufficient sense of equality to serve as an ethical base for a modern theory of liberal democracy is discussed in my *Political Theory of Possessive Individualism, op. cit.,* chap. VI, sect. 2.

8

WORLD REVOLUTION AND
INTERNATIONAL ORDER

RICHARD A. FALK

The relevance of revolution to the organization of international society is not a new subject. It was a dominant concern in the decades following the French Revolution when the Great Powers sought to reconcile the independent character of sovereign states with the defense of the principle of dynastic legitimacy. The development of collective procedures of intervention to protect the European monarchies against republican revolution was the most significant outgrowth of the Congress of Vienna. In fact, the response of the nineteenth century to the French Revolution resembles in many respects the response of the twentieth century to the Russian Revolution.

Thus it is certainly true that a successful national revolution in

154

a major state has long been perceived as relevant to the maintenance of order in international society. If a revolution includes an ideological challenge, then it threatens all governments that resemble the first victim of the revolutionary cause. An example has been set; the discontent is probably latent throughout international society, not just in the society that experienced the outbreak. Contradictory interventionary pressures arise both to hasten the spread of the revolution and to staunch the revolutionary flames. The prevalence of intervention based upon ideological cleavage is profoundly inconsistent with the basis of order in an international society composed of states supposedly sovereign and independent. So long as there are no predominant supranational institutions in existence, one serious consequence of an active revolutionary movement is to undermine the ideological basis of international society, that is, of a society of nation-states, and thereby to restrict the effectiveness of the normative element in international life.[1]

The background of relevant experience is, however, scant. There have been very few revolutionary movements in the history of international relations that have attained such a magnitude as to have relevance for the conduct and character of world politics. In fact, the only two clear cases are the French and Russian Revolutions. There is, however, a wider conception of revolution that embraces any political, social, and scientific facts that challenge and transform the prevailing bases of international order. This essay adopts this wider usage, thereby treating the history of international relations as a sequence of numerous revolutions.

By using this broader conception of revolution, attention can be given to nonpolitical facts that threaten international stability and are, at the same time, intimately connected with the phenomenon of political revolution on a national scale. The connection between these various kinds of facts must be studied to achieve an understanding of the over-all challenge to international order. In this respect, it is important to consider the impact of nuclear weaponry upon patterns of international conflict, the drive toward modernization in the new states, and the growth of supranationalism on a

---

[1] On the comparative role of international law in revolutionary and non-revolutionary systems, see Stanley Hoffmann's "International Systems and International Law," in Klaus Knorr and Sidney Verba, eds., *The International System* (1961), pp. 205-237.

regional and global level. These radical modifications of the international environment are crucial aspects of the revolutionary situation in world politics today.

This essay also assumes that it is useful to study international politics as if it were carried on within a single political system.[2] The international system tends toward revolutionary transformation whenever there is present a combination of forces (including a transnational revolutionary movement) that imperil the prevailing modes of organizing international life. The most obvious focus for these forces today is to contrast the adequacy of the nation-state as the basic unit in the system during the period between 1815–1914 with its declining adequacy since 1914. For this purpose "adequacy" is defined as the ability to advance human welfare and maintain the security of social groupings.

These preceding paragraphs sketch the orientation that controls the analysis that follows. The rest of the chapter is a preliminary attempt to depict the revolutionary situation that exists in contemporary world politics and to develop certain categories that seem crucial if we are to begin making an analysis of revolution as an attribute of international politics, as well as of national politics. Without the development of such an intellectual perspective it will become increasingly difficult to understand the unstable quality of international society.

I

The contemporary Western mind tends to visualize the actual and optimal constituents of international order in topical terms as a response to the overlapping dangers forced upon the world by the combination of nuclear weapons and Communist ambitions. From such a perspective, the desiderata of international order become a system that reliably prevents the coercive expansion of communism and that reduces the risks of nuclear war to tolerable levels. Profound disagreements surround the selection of the means available to accomplish this goal. There is, first of all, the need to assess this alleged expansiveness of communism. Do Communist leaders entertain the prospect of a Leninist-Marxist world as a matter of conviction or of rhetoric? It may be possible, in part, to as-

[2] For the contrary argument that it is not yet proper to consider international politics as taking place within a single system, see Kenneth S. Carlston, *Law and Organization in World Society* (1962), pp. 66–69.

cribe the ideological rift between the Soviet Union and China to this issue, that is, to China's contention that Soviet policies are tantamount to a repudiation of revolutionary strategy. Can the Soviet Union, or, for that matter, China be so transformed from without and within as to become a state that is content to refrain from force in the pursuit of its foreign-policy objectives?

Another set of disagreements about revolutionary prospects surrounds the extent to which current patterns of international conflict are war prone and, in particular, whether they are nuclear war prone. Can we rely permanently upon alliances and postures of deterrence to keep the nuclear peace? It is, of course, true that the deterrent systems developed in prenuclear periods have never been able to avert major war. Does, however, the unprecedented potential for nuclear destruction add enough intimidation to restrain nations over an extended period of sustained conflict and recurrent crisis? Those observers who are distrustful of such reliance make demands for a greatly altered system of international order. Often, those who are most sensitive to the risks of nuclear war are also those who are less alarmed by the threat of further Communist expansion, either regarding it, even if it takes place, as an insignificant evil compared to nuclear war or considering it something that is no longer likely to occur in any significant extent. This viewpoint produces an enthusiastic advocacy of major disarmament and support for greatly strengthened international institutions.

The revolutionary position includes demands to change international order by downgrading the role of the state in world politics. It favors the progressive displacement of states as the primary actors by the growth of multinational federations and international organizations, and especially by the United Nations.

There is, in contrast, a more prevalent conservative attitude toward international relations. The conservative emphasizes the intransigent quality of international conflict and human nature, de-emphasizes nuclear weapons as transformative agents, and voices skepticism about the possibility of interfering with the dominance of nations in the international political process. This conservative view may or may not be receptive to minor adjustments in response to the proclaimed dangers created by an intense bipolar struggle in a nuclear age, but it either is opposed to accepting the risks that attend fundamental alterations of the existing system of international order or is convinced that environmental restraints make fundamental changes politically infeasible and therefore highly improbable. Reform—or, for instance, "stabilizing the deterrent"—is consistent with the conservative or nonrevolutionary viewpoint.

The non-Communist revolutionary viewpoint is at once more skeptical and more hopeful about engineering a system change. It believes that fundamental changes in the existing international system are essential for the maintenance of nuclear peace. It is more dubious about the virtues claimed for the existing system and hence fearful that unless something is done soon a catastrophic war is quite likely to result. On the other hand, this viewpoint is more hopeful about the capacity of human reason and will to respond to the present dangers by devising an utterly new arrangement for social organization on a world level. Nuclear weapons have rendered the old system of nations and military self-sufficiency and self-help so obsolete, it is contended, that traditional reliances upon national security can and must be abandoned. The revolutionary viewpoint has not penetrated deeply into the behavioral patterns of nations, nor has it been acknowleged as valid by elite members of major states—although such events as Pope John XXIII's *Pacem in Terris* encyclical, President Kennedy's "Towards a Strategy for Peace" (June 1962) commencement address at American University, and the commitments of all states to the goal of general and complete disarmament have given some encouragement to the adherents of the revolutionary approach.

This contrast between conservative and revolutionary has been overstylized, here, to put in bold relief the conventional perception of the link between revolution and international order in the world today. There is a compatibility between the two viewpoints that may be stronger than their opposition to one another. We may seek to improve the existing system and, at the same time, work toward the creation of a new system. Such a dual concern does raise the question of the transition from one system to another. This is perhaps the crucial question for those persons working to improve the quality of international order. It is itself susceptible to useful analysis in terms of revolutionary and nonrevolutionary attitudes, depending, for example, on the extent to which one believes in the potentialities for evolutionary transition from one system to another as distinct from violent or traumatic transition. There are many people who think that only a considerable nuclear war can create the possibility of a reconstitution of international order on a scale sufficiently grand to be called a system change. Such a conclusion, I think, correctly emphasizes the strength of system inertia, even when once a particular system has been widely perceived as inadequate, that is, out of joint with objective circumstances. A "revolution" in the context of such a transition might be regarded, then, as a nuclear war, although we must distinguish between a revolutionary analysis and a revolutionary strategy.

A prediction about how the new international order can be brought about is not, even among those who regard it as an urgent necessity, the same as advocating such a course. The international Communist movement illustrates the coupling of a revolutionary analysis with a revolutionary strategy. In fact, the weakness of the revolutionary movement in the non-Communist world arises, in part, from the absence of any very powerful explanation of how to accomplish a system change other than by making a reluctant reference to the prospect of a nuclear war. The Communists, however, propose that a Communist imperium, brought about by a series of national Communist triumphs, will bring about the reconstitution of international order in a world that no longer possesses the bases for substantial conflict. Thus, the strategy to achieve the world revolution (or system change) is made contingent upon the successful outcome of a series of national revolutions (or unit changes). This may involve a violent transition, but the violence is broken up into subconventional war compartments (national revolutions) that appear to keep political violence within those limits traditionally regarded as tolerable. Such a vision of the transition is more plausible than the evolutionary image and less catastrophic than the traumatic image; it gives communism a way of reconciling its aims with the dangers of the nuclear age. Once again, the Sino-Soviet dispute is compellingly relevant. First, because the intensity of the conflict, especially when the defections of Yugoslavia and Albania are noted, casts considerable doubt that a fully communized world would be a solution, even in Moscow's or Peking's terms, to the transition problem. And, second, the battle between the Soviets and Mao is partly a matter of the extent to which the selection of a transition strategy should be influenced by the danger of nuclear war; more specifically, it concerns the risk of escalating a local war into a nuclear war by attempts to intervene on behalf of the radical insurgents. Maoists argue that unless the risks of escalation are assumed the Communist solution of the transition problem will be permanently frustrated. The Soviets claim, on the other hand, that the compulsion of spontaneous historical forces can bring about the Communist transition without any need for Communist states to export substantial violence across national frontiers.

II

The basic distinction between revolutionary and stable systems is predicated on the failure of international relations at a given period to adapt to important changes in their environment. This distinction also depends upon the objectives of the major actors and the extent to which those objectives are promoted by unauthorized violence. If disputes between states involve controversies about the application of existing norms, then the system is stable, even though fierce wars may be fought to establish a frontier or to secure possession of a province; the political identity and legitimacy of existing actors is accepted. Conversely, in a revolutionary system, the significant actors seek to eliminate certain other actors or to change their basic identities by force. The stakes of conflict are so large that they induce antagonists to adopt any expedient means to protect their interests. Such an atmosphere generates lawlessness. The obligation to adhere to norms cannot influence crucial decisions by those actors who either are trying to overturn the existing system or are compelled to fight in order to survive. If the revolutionary challenge is substantial, as it was after the French and Soviet Revolutions, it then generates counterrevolutionary pressures. In other words, *the revolutionary component, if significant, determines the characteristic behavior of all major actors in the system*. The Afro-Asian states today direct a revolutionary challenge toward Portugal's control of Angola and toward the Republic of South Africa; if there were no other revolutionary currents in the international system, then those actors interested in stability could probably moderate the challenge and constrain the tendencies to depart from basic norms. However, this challenge, posed in an environment that includes the revolutionary presence of the Communist states, produces revolutionary patterns of conduct—for instance, the overtness of the sanctuary and the support given by the Congo to Angolese rebels. Even more revealing is the extent to which the opposition of the United States to Castro's Cuba takes on a revolutionary form of normlessness. Oddly enough, the behavior of nonrevolutionary actors may serve as a better indicator of the revolutionary condition of the international system than does the behavior of revolutionary actors.

Is it possible to affirm the existence of an international order in a revolutionary system? Every system, no matter how revolutionary, discloses that actors accept certain limits upon the means available for the pursuit of their objectives. A description of international order in a revolutionary system requires the discernment and delineation of the limits that remain applicable. The popular assumption that revolutionary systems are characterized by the absence of limits is a dangerous exaggeration, tending to undermine respect for those norms that might otherwise remain operative, and thereby prevent intense conflict from degenerating into anarchy.[3] Even before revolutionary and antirevolutionary actors were intimidated by the development of nuclear weapons, there was a general willingness to accept certain restraints upon conflict as being in the common interest. For example, expectations continue high that, in the event of military conflict, most of the laws of war will be upheld, including such important restraints as prohibitions against the use of gas and bacteria. A revolutionary system weakens rather than destroys international order by its tendencies to induce certain dramatic departures from crucial norms (e.g., aggression) and to include explicit repudiations of some traditional norms (e.g., the legitimacy of colonial administration or the sanctity of foreign investment). But no revolutionary actor can participate for long in the international system without a fundamental willingness to adopt hallowed procedures and to abide by routine norms (e.g., diplomacy and diplomatic immunity). In this respect, it is worth noting the retreat of Soviet theory and practice from its original repudiation of the entire system of international law as an international manifestation of class dominance by the *bourgeoisie*. More recent Soviet jurisprudence accepts international law as a valid constituent of international order, while reserving for attack several specific norms contrary to Socialist values. The dependence of actors upon mutual contact and communication is the most visible expression of an interdependence that requires some minimum form of international order, despite the otherwise contradictory values and objectives of revolutionary and nonrevolutionary actors.

[3] This is the principal argument of my book *Law, Morality, and War in the Contemporary World* (1963).

III

It may advance our understanding of international relations if we are able to detach ourselves from immediate anxieties. This will permit a more abstract conceptualization of the relationship between revolution and international order, and thus direct our attention to more essential characteristics. It is fashionable nowadays to characterize as "revolution" change in any circumstance to which we wish to call attention; it is a way of letting people know that the change is important or, at least, that we think it is. The following items have each been called revolutionary: nuclear weapons, decolonialization, the loss of Christian faith, the cycle of rising expectations in poor countries, the increasing role of non-Western states in world affairs, and improved transportation and communication facilities. Thus conceived, a revolution is not just a national political movement that makes use of violent and illegal means to bring about a radical new social structure; it is a whole series of developments in political, moral, scientific, and economic life that are perceived as very important. This usage involves a debasement of language, seeking to appropriate the glamour of the word revolution for other kinds of happenings whose importance is more difficult to convey unless it is connected with a theory of international society. This loose usage does, nevertheless, introduce a suggestive richness of connotation for the word revolution. From the viewpoint of international relations, there is a high functional equivalence among those unsettling events in economic, social, political, technological, and moral spheres of human activity that is highlighted by the use of a single dramatic word like revolution.

International order is an even vaguer term than revolution, especially since the concept frequently confuses descriptive and normative categories. Are we identifying the kind of order that exists, such as it is, or are we trying to specify the requisites of minimum and optimum order in various international environments? Is "order" something that is invariably present in every social system, or are there social systems that lack the qualities implied by our use of the word order? It seems useful to delineate order in broad terms but to insist that it be understood as a descriptive concept; it will thus be possible for order to be evaluated as good or bad, as adequate or inadequate, or as increasing or decreasing. We propose to define order in international relations primarily by reference to peace and, therefore, to consider a given international order as consisting of the rules, procedures, and institutions available to control unauthorized political violence in international affairs. This definition is sufficiently broad to encompass the ordering claims of international law, international diplomacy, and international organization; in fact, the traditional separation of these approaches to international affairs inhibits the growth of an integrated awareness and understanding of the political factors that operate in international relations. The diplomat, the lawyer, and the official of an international organization are working on different aspects of a single process, and could benefit from the coordination of their travail.

There is one further difficulty: The word "international" has been used in a way that violates its literal meaning and its Latin origin. The world is now composed of a network of actors that are national, infranational (individuals, corporations), transnational (political parties, trading associations), and supernational (regional and global international organizations). "International order" can no longer be usefully understood as referring only to the quality of order that exists in the relations among states. Even if one, in a polemic fashion, wishes to emphasize that states retain pre-eminent power and discretion in the international system, it remains essential to acknowledge the descriptive point that many new classes of actors have status and functions in the adjustment of relations affecting world affairs. Thus, it would be semantically progressive to substitute the label "world order" for "international order"; however, I prefer to retain the title "international order" to emphasize the extent to which a concern exists with the improvement of techniques for the prevention of interstate violence and to assert the importance of historical approach to the study of war prevention, suggesting how much we have to learn from the successes and failures of earlier forms of international order—that is, from forms in which states were the only significant actors.

Some substantive problems arise from a focus on the characteristics and requisites of international order. It makes less obvious the link between domestic violence and the maintenance of international order in the existing system. An expanding aspect of the existing system is the extent to which supranational control is claimed over domestic events that produce, or threaten to produce, violence that might in turn become an arena for an international confrontation. The Congo illustrates a supranational effort to maintain international order even though the violence took place within the borders of a single state; the internal wars of Southeast Asia have disrupted international relations because they are both civil encounters between rival domestic factions and, at the same time, tests of the ideological, economic, and military strength of the major cold-war antagonists.

The attitude assumed by international institutions and by dominant national actors toward such civil strife is a crucial ingredient of any attempt to describe and assess international order. The dispute between passive and active sponsorship of "national liberation movements" is a primary way in which the Soviet Union and China express their current disagreements; one preferring the stability that seems to result from a passive role, the other the revolutionary dynamism that is claimed for an active role. The same kind of attitude leads us to insist that the obligations of the United Nations Charter to promote human rights be treated as an aspect of international order. Humanitarian interventions, which were previously prompted by the persecution of a national or religious minority, indicate that the processes of international order have long been accepted as relevant to the conditions *within* a nation, as well as the contacts *among* nations. This link between peace and human rights is accented, at present, by the formation of a world-wide consensus favoring equal status for all people—a consensus that can be increasingly acted upon because of the ever improving communication and transportation systems and by an ever more impatient United Nations.

It may appear that these "domestic" events—civil wars and struggles to promote human rights—have little relevance to a study of the connections between revolution and international order. But the connection is vital, if not always visible. Civil wars are often revolutionary in character for either of two reasons: because the insurgent is a revolutionary faction, or because the civil war is treated by the Communists as part of the world revolutionary process that they are eager to promote, or so perceived by the West. If a civil war is defined as a national war of liberation, it is then almost certain to attract Communist-bloc support, at least to the extent of opposing or offsetting aid to the incumbent; this, in turn, generates a Western response designed to neutralize internal and external Communist influence. The denial of human rights is often the prelude to revolutionary action; as such, supranational intervention to establish certain minimum conditions of human dignity can be evaluated as a way to forestall national revolution, as well as to provide a safeguard against the outbreak of international violence.

IV

A systematic study of the relationship between revolution and international order requires a variety of perspectives. Seven categories seem worthy of study. First, a consideration of environmental changes that tend to revolutionize the character of international relations; a discourse on historical causation. Second, an analysis of the behavior of revolutionary and nonrevolutionary actors in a revolutionary system of international order; a survey account. Third, a study of the reception given by the international system to the appearance of a revolutionary nation; norms and practices correlated with the condition of the system. Fourth, the response of the international system—patterns and norms—to civil wars in which one of the factions possesses a revolutionary outlook; an array of responses and justifications. Fifth, the outlook of a revolutionary nation—its claims and demands; impacts on the status of particular norms and upon the security of the system. Sixth, the regulation by the international system of the transmission of revolutionary energy from one nation to another; historical case studies in system responses to ecumenical revolutionary movements. And seventh, the extent to which international order itself depends upon revolutionary undertakings.

Environmental Causation. Various kinds of political, social, economic, and technological events may undermine the stability of international relations. The central moral authority of the Pope was a target of the Reformation; the *levée en masse* was an outgrowth of the French Revolution; the rules of naval warfare could not be adapted to deal with the advent of the submarine and airplane; the doctrine of neutrality could not be adjusted to the requirements of "total war"; norms of nonintervention and self-determination are incompatible with the struggle for power in a revolutionary system; the scope of sovereign discretion with respect to force is progressively curtailed in response to the increasing destructiveness of warfare; assumptions of immunity for sovereign activities are rejected in face of the growth of state-trading and of the decline of laissez-faire economics; norms of independence are qualified by facts of interdependence and by the gradual appearance of an international welfare system in the form of foreign aid and international capital financing;

sovereignty as an indication of national autonomy is reinterpreted in the light of the assertion of effective claims against the nation on behalf of a world community increasingly more organized on a regional and global level; the necessity of national consent is being eroded by the authority of community consensus. This list of examples tries to illustrate the dependence of international order upon all dimensions of human activity.

Today we are engaged in the process of trying to adapt the international system to the new realities created by the existence and diffusion of nuclear weaponry. No structural changes, such as a new distribution of power, seem presently feasible. It is possible to attribute a more cautious style of risk taking in world politics to the presence of nuclear weapons. There are also some specific steps taken by nations to reinforce precautions against accidental and unauthorized military provocations. Perhaps the most important impact of nuclear weapons has been that of decreasing the incentive of the major states to commit overt aggression or to get involved in wars. An apparent willingness to continue the traditional structure of power and authority premised upon the primacy of nations and national defense systems remains, despite the vulnerability of every state to substantial destruction in the event of a major nuclear exchange, and despite the failure of deterrent systems in prenuclear periods to maintain peace indefinitely.

A second crucial change that is even less assimilated, is the emergence of articulate non-European states as independent actors in world affairs. In addition to the disturbance of the Western dominance, other problems are beginning to arise as a consequence of the glaring economic disparities between rich and poor states.[4] A restored stability for international affairs will depend, it is submitted, upon the gradual development of a supranational welfare mechanism that accomplishes a major redistribution of the world's wealth. This development, ideally coupled with disarmament and the supranational control of population expansion, is essential if the accommodation of the new nations is to be more than temporary and expediential.[5]

[4] On this, see Gustavo Lagos, *International Stratification and Underdeveloped Countries* (1963), pp. 3–34; and S. J. Patel, "The Economic Distance between Nations: Its Origin, Measurement, and Outlook," *The Economic Journal* (1964), 119–131.

[5] For a study of the connection between disarmament and the realloca-

Certainly, this is not a period of international anarchy. The United Nations, the development of regional and international specialized agencies, and the quasi-formalism of nuclear deterrence indicate the degree of the existing concern with ordering world politics. Nevertheless, nuclear weapons and the new nations create a revolutionary situation that threatens to destroy the present system of order. The responses of the system have so far been gestures of accommodation, falling far short of what seems necessary to avert an eventual catastrophe. A lag separates the procedures used to maintain minimum order from the changes that have occurred in objective circumstances. This lag makes these procedures insufficient and causes what might be described as a climate of pessimism with regard to the future of mankind.

Behavior in a Revolutionary System. We need an account of the methods and objectives of the actors in the system. It is, today, a revolutionary system not only because the methods of conflict are potentially destructive but also because the existence and identity of important actors have been formidably challenged on ideological and humanitarian grounds. There is no universal consensus about the character of legitimate government. This is symbolized by the high incidence of nonrecognition and of premature recognition; normative approaches to the recognition of governments and states are strong evidence of the existence of a strategic controversy in world affairs about the nature of political legitimacy. This doctrinal controversy, in its intense phases—both today and following the French Revolution—leads to action in the form of subversion and intervention. The Organization of American States finds Cuba to be "incompatible" with the hemispheric system because it is a Marxist-Leninist government. African states are ready to accord status to hastily formed exile groups that are busy preparing to overthrow the remnants of African colonialism. China, Yugoslavia, and the Soviet Union argue about the quality and quantity of support to be given national wars of liberation. The United States arms and trains armies for reactionary governments throughout Asia.

A revolutionary system, especially when the costs of strategic conflict are as high as at present, exhibits widespread interventionary and counterinterventionary behavior and experiences a consequent

tion of the world's wealth and income, see Neil W. Chamberlain, *The West in a World without War* (1963).

weakening of respect for those norms that assure the autonomy, independence, and equality of states. The Spanish Civil War illustrates a refusal of the dominant nonrevolutionary actors to perceive the transformation of the system into a revolutionary one; they scrupulously adhered to a nonintervention system while revolutionary actors were intervening to the full extent of their capability. Only after the conflict with the Soviet Union was perceived as a revolutionary struggle for world dominance did the United States adopt the style of behavior appropriate for a revolutionary system.

It should be noted that the search for means to restore stability to international relations as a result of the dangers of nuclear war and the presence of the new states is quite inconsistent with optimal participation in a revolutionary system. All nations strive to find the right mix for their varying interests in system stability and system change; the superstates strive, in addition, to achieve system dominance. This generalization is sufficiently broad to include the outlooks of revolutionary, modernizing, and status quo nations.

Reception. A revolution that occurs in a significant state usually arouses a hostile response from other states that identify their social system with the prerevolutionary government. This is especially true if the revolutionary elite has an ecumenical outlook, considering itself to be the herald of a new form of government and social organization. In this respect, wars of liberation, often called revolutions (for instance, the American Revolution or the recently concluded Algerian Civil War) are to be sharply distinguished from revolutions that seek to bring a new social and political system into being everywhere. A revolutionary nation in a previously stable system of international relations is often disturbing because it threatens the security of domestic governments that resemble the victim of the revolution.

A stable international system usually includes a consensus about the character of legitimate government. The fact of revolution—the seizure of national power by illegal and violent means—is compatible with all systems of international order that have existed at various historical periods. The incompatibility arises from the radical reordering of the domestic system; the tendency of this radical program to encourage discontented groups to imitate the revolution and the inclination of ideological revolutions to spread their system to foreign nations. These conditions induce a variety of responses, a few of which will be mentioned.

The Formation of Antirevolutionary Coalitions. Status quo powers join together to oppose the spread of the revolution. This happened after the French and Soviet Revolutions; it is happening today. The minimum objective of a conservative coalition is to resist the expansion of the revolutionary system through external wars.

Intervention. Coalitions often give rise to interventionary patterns and practices. The minimum goal is to prevent the balance of internal forces from reaching a revolutionary outcome. It supplements collective defense arrangements by trying to prevent the expansion of the revolutionary system through internal wars. The Protocol at Troppau, adopted by the leading monarchies of Europe in 1820, was a most explicit commitment: "States which have undergone a change of government, due to revolution, the results of which threaten other states, *ipso facto* cease to be members of the European Alliance, and remain excluded from it until their situation gives guarantees for legal order and stability. If, owing to such alterations, immediate danger threatens other states, the powers bind themselves, by peaceful means, or if need be by arms, to bring back the guilty state into the bosom of the Great Alliance." Note should also be taken of the Declaration of Pillnitz (1791) in which the Emperor of Austria and the King of Prussia pledged themselves to secure the restoration of the French monarchy by joint force, if necessary. The action taken against Cuba at Punta del Este in 1962 is a modern equivalent of the eighteenth-century concern of European monarchs.

Nonrecognition. The system of international order allows nations the discretion to refuse formal relationships with a revolutionary nation. Prolonged nonrecognition is used to express disapproval and to isolate and harass a revolutionary government. It is also used as a bargaining counter. Recognition is withheld in the hope that certain guarantees can be extracted in exchange for a willingness to grant status and maintain diplomatic contact. The United States failed to recognize the Soviet government until 1933; it fails now to recognize the People's Republic of China even though more than fifteen years have passed since that government acquired secure control of mainland China. With the advent of the United Nations, an antirevolutionary consensus can also seek to deny China representation in and admission to the United Nations. Conservative states demand evidence that the militant revolutionary state will abide by the constraints of the system that it is pledged to oppose.

International order, then, includes practices and rules that permit antirevolutionary states to organize against the threat posed by the emergence of a powerful revolutionary state. Presumably, a recourse to force to implement an antirevolutionary alliance is illegal under the Charter of the United Nations and is impractical in view of the defensive strength of the existing revolutionary coalition. But, short of force, states are authorized to form defensive alliances and build regional security systems to resist the expansion of the revolution.

Civil War.[6] In stable systems, a civil war is regarded as a domestic event; in a revolutionary system, a civil war is frequently a confrontation between representatives of the antagonists in the struggle for world dominance. This is especially true in the present revolutionary system since the danger of nuclear war inhibits the assumption of high military risks; participation in a civil war is the most intense form of unauthorized violence that is characteristic of the behavior of major nations.

Traditional norms of international order strongly emphasize the irrelevance of civil strife to the rights and duties of other states. Notions of domestic jurisdiction and self-determination express this insulation that was perhaps developed to prohibit the justification of intervention by outside powers. Domination by the Great Powers was often a by-product of an intervention allegedly carried out to maintain or restore order; the United States exercised, until 1933, such rights in relation to Latin America, often claiming the need to protect resident Americans and their property.

Classical international law both allowed outside states to help the incumbent early in a civil war and obliged them to refrain from aiding the insurgent. If, in a state of war, the challenge to domestic control was sustained over time and space, then a state of belligerency could be established that obliged all third states that recognized it to maintain strict neutrality. Thus, the antirevolutionary interest in the security of government is displaced on a formal level by the interest in keeping the scale of violence small since it created duties of nonparticipation.

Such an approach is not suitable for a revolutionary system or even for the treatment of civil wars in which the insurgent is a revolutionary in the full sense of possessing a radical social program

---

[6] I have made a more detailed study of the problems in this section, "Janus Tormented: The International Law of Internal War," in James N. Rosenau, ed., *International Aspects of Civil Strife* (1964).

and a universal ideology. Then, the stakes in the outcome, especially since the French Revolution and the Spanish Civil War, are too great to make norms of nonparticipation effective. Modern communications and transportation systems put exiled leaders easily in touch with domestic groups. The same technology, available to the modern state, allows the suppression of discontented groups that lack foreign support. For all these reasons, international order has no reliable ways to deal with civil wars in which the incumbent is being challenged by a revolutionary or counterrevolutionary faction. The absence of such means is a major source of instability and danger in the present system.

The existence of the United Nations suggests two possible modifications in the traditional treatment of civil war: first, the adoption of military measures to keep outside states from intervening on either side and, second, the organization of United Nations' interventions to prevent national interventions and to shorten civil strife. The Congo illustrates this use of the United Nations, but it also discloses a Soviet hostility to such enterprises if they appear to diminish the prospects for a revolutionary outcome. For this reason, the United Nations should be encouraged to anticipate the outbreak of a civil war by intervening to secure basic human rights. Once the revolutionary challenge has been posed in a system that contains major revolutionary actors, it is already too late.

The Revolutionary Actor. The "true" revolutionary actor must be distinguished from other actors that assume control after a successful revolt. We are concerned only with actors that seek to transform the world, especially by spreading the ideals of their revolution to other national societies. The state is not the only revolutionary actor in world politics; there are political parties of transnational revolutionary significance as well as those groupings of revolutionary states known as blocs and regions.

An ecumenical revolution seeks to bring a new world order into being, although perhaps not immediately. There is, as after the French Revolution, a violent and multifaceted interaction between the hostile reception given by conservative forces and the aggressive policies adopted by a revolutionary actor. Each side comes to see that its security depends upon the elimination of the other side from the system; this leads to intervention and aggression abroad and to the repression of the opposition at home.

The revolutionary actor justifies its recourse to violence in terms of a necessity to overcome gross injustices in the former system and to forestall counterrevolutionary activity. There is also a tendency to feel strong sympathy for those insurgent groups abroad who seek to eliminate similar injustices. The American Revolution fostered, at the time, a national tradition of support for anticolonial revolts. As soon as a single major anticolonial revolt was successful, no colonial empire was secure. A model for decolonialization had been brought into existence. This catalyzed the formation and activity of anti-colonial groups everywhere.

It is difficult to generalize about those demands that the revolutionary actor makes upon the system. The demands depend, first of all, upon the reception that the system gives to the revolution and, second, upon the degree to which the leaders of the revolutionary and of the nonrevolutionary actors are aware of history. In 1848 the moderation of both the revolutionary demands and the conservative response was, in part, a consequence of the awful memories on both sides of the experiences in 1789 when unrestraint held sway.

The Soviet Revolution had, from its ideological conception, a universal outlook. This revolution was thought to be an expression of a necessary historical process that would eventually be duplicated everywhere. The restraining claims of the international system— that is, the pattern of international order—were regarded as nothing more than an externalization of the interests of the reigning social class; international law had no more legitimacy than did any other part of the state apparatus designed to carry out bourgeois domination. Law was a reflection of class dominance, and thereby reflected neither common interests nor social justice. The original Soviet denial of the international system by Marxian analysis gave way to patterns of selective repudiation and pragmatic participation. Thus, the Soviet Union denies both that the duty to compensate accompanies the right to expropriate and that colonial title to territory constitutes a valid exercise of sovereignty. Similarly, the Soviet Union participates actively, albeit ambivalently, in the United Nations, partly to retard its effective growth, partly to further its own national interests, and partly, we suppose, to help realize its own interest in the prevention of a major war.

A revolutionary actor, almost by necessity, favors unauthorized violence as a means to achieve revolutionary objectives. However, this violence may take the form of wars of aggression with imperial goals—such as Napoleon's or Hitler's—in which case it structures the international system for a major war. It may, on the other hand, involve the adoption of subversive and infiltrative strategies designed to spread the revolution—in which case, the international system is structured for intense conflict, but not necessarily for war. The presence of a revolutionary actor disrupts whatever consensus had previously existed about permissible political objectives. In so doing, it raises the stakes of conflict to a point where antagonists take added risks to achieve success. This drives the system toward total war. Other factors also have this effect: the growth of nationalism, the rise of bureaucratic centralism in the great states, the rapid improvements in military technology, and the creation of industrial systems capable of supporting long and costly wars.

There is always the possibility that a revolutionary actor will lose or at least weaken its revolutionary outlook. This happens when its mixture of perceived interests is so influenced as to emphasize other values, such as a higher domestic standard of living, the maintenance of peace, a preservative attitude toward what has been already achieved, an awareness that ideological similarity may not be a necessary condition for international solidarity, and a gradual realization that the revolutionary theory no longer provides a reliable guide to action. Revolutionary actors tend to become less revolutionary as time passes. If the international system can withstand the external impact of a revolutionary actor, it then seems likely that the mere passage of time will domesticate the revolution. It is, perhaps, interesting to compare the proscription of heresy in Catholicism with its assimilation in Hinduism and to consider these two lines of response as alternatives for the international system. In the history of international relations, the periods from 1789 to 1822 and from 1917 to the present illustrate chiefly the Catholic approach, whereas the reactions after 1776 and 1848 suggest the Hindu approach.

Containment. Following the failure of natural law after the Reformation to develop common standards and community judgments on the subject of recourse to force by states, the matter of war was left by law to the discretion of sovereigns who were restricted only by appeals to conscience and moderated by prudence and equilibrating coalitions (deterrence). There were contradictory affirmations of this right to wage war and of the rights of national independence, nonintervention, equality, and territorial jurisdiction. The French Revolution, at least in Europe, generated coalitions that were founded upon the legitimacy of coercive interventions designed to throw the revolutionary elite out of power.

In the present revolutionary system, revolutionary actors are strong and sufficiently well established to prevent the adoption of an interventionary coalition. However, there are alliances committed to resisting revolutionary penetrations. In Latin America, both before and after Castro, the OAS has identified Communist activity with extrahemispheric aggression so that it might create a legal basis for preventive intervention. In 1954 the United States intervened to help dislodge a government in Guatemala that was tending toward Communism; in Cuba, the identification of Castro as revolutionary came after his power was secure. Cuba's transfer of allegiance to the Soviet bloc seems firm; current efforts are designed to prevent the spread of Castroism to other parts of Latin America.

Containment is the basic norm of antirevolutionary strategy. There is some disposition to engage in pre-emptive interventions, especially within spheres of regional dominance, but the main effort is to prevent the *violent* expansion (by direct and indirect means) of revolutionary hegemony. The spread of the revolution by hostile propaganda, the training of exiled subversives, and the guidance and financial support of indigenous revolutionary groups all elude control.

The existing system of international order has made generally effective responses to overt aggression across boundaries; it is, however, less equipped to handle either indirect aggression or counterrevolutionary intervention. In fact, those internal wars that are fought to expand or to contain the expansion of the revolutionary bloc are *tolerated* as a proper arena of conflict; norms to keep these conflicts both subnuclear and physically within the boundaries of a single state are increasingly recognized and are accepted as binding by the opposing actors.

Revolutionary Intervention by the Organized Community.[7] There is an increasing prospect that the United Nations will sponsor changes in those domestic political systems that are of a revolutionary character. This does not imply the fostering of revolutionary nations, but it does suggest that domestic system changes are likely

[7] This analysis is more fully developed by Saul H. Mendlovitz and myself in "Toward A Warless World: One Legal Formula to Achieve Transition," *The Yale Law Journal*, 73 (1964), 399–424.

to be brought about by the exercise of supranational authority and force. The role of the United Nations in the Congo is illustrative, although its subsequent financial and political difficulties seem to suggest that too much action was attempted on the basis of the partial and temporary consensus that existed among the main members at the outset.

But social injustice, especially in the forms of classical colonialism and constitutional racism, has aroused increasingly coercive responses from the United Nations over the behavior of South Africa and Portugal. The Goa solution (military self-help), the Algerian precedent (prolonged civil war), and the Indo-China debacle in Vietnam, Laos, and Cambodia (rival cold-war interventions and prolonged internal war) lend support to those who advocate supranational coercion as the least destructive alternative.

Such interventions would try to keep the domestic struggle from becoming a part of the cold-war competition. In these missions, the United Nations may not be able to muster a great power consensus unless a general interest in war prevention takes precedence over the revolutionary struggle for system dominance. In fact, the use of supranational institutions to achieve revolutionary changes would be most successful if they acted before domestic violence occurred. Thus, a competence to secure minimum human rights might enable a genuine consensus of states to favor a revolutionary intervention —that is, an intervention that transferred sovereignty to a new elite pledged to uphold human rights.

Such a pattern of coercion is a revolutionary change in the allocation of authority between nations and the organized world community. At the same time, it serves as a potential source of stability in the international system and deserves consideration as a new aspect of the role of the United Nations in the maintenance of international order. Communist ideology connects support for national revolutions and for the completion of the world revolutionary process with a secure peace. It may be desirable for the West to exploit revolutionary opportunities by acting first and selflessly. The use of supranational institutions to bring about revolutionary changes, dangerous though this pattern could become, is one way to help bring into being the kind of international order that satisfies both our values and our interests.

One thing is certain. A revolutionary civil war for supremacy in a strategic nation is not a domestic event. It will attract foreign participation. The maintenance of international peace hinges upon the capacity to keep internal wars under control.

V

National revolutions are formally compatible with an interstate system of order. Yet if, in the contemporary world, a revolutionary movement possesses a Communist orientation, its attempts to seize power are likely to heighten cold-war tensions and to provide an occasion for a violent test of strength between the main rivals for world dominance.

There is little prospect of a breakthrough in military technology that would be of a magnitude sufficient to make recourse to warfare a rational means of achieving political expansion in conflict among the Great Powers. In this sense, the nuclear stalemate generates an image of a rigid, but safe, future. Yet, the existence of powerful military weapons in a revolutionary system leads actors to threaten one another in order to achieve transitional goals of foreign policy. Threats have utility in crises and can influence behavior. The credibility of threats depends on a willingness to carry them out. But to carry out a nuclear threat is to initiate a nuclear war, an act that is widely regarded as self-destructnve. Thus, there is a temptation to discount the threat as a bluff. This kind of crisis behavior makes the balance of terror unstable, especially because the stakes of conflict are high and because the revolutionary actors try to dominate and transform international affairs in order to fulfill their ideological mission. If the revolutionary quality of international rivalry at the strategic level were replaced by an *entente cordiale* or by a Soviet-American condominium, then the possession of nuclear weapons could possibly provide a rather stable peace. Through the retention of nuclear weapons, their nonuse could be reliably developed and secured to ensure that minimum cordiality persisted. At just this point, the prospects for serious disarmament might improve as a result of the new spirit of confidence—just then, and when it is much less needed, because a nonrevolutionary international system is far less dangerous.

This illustrates a familiar paradox in global politics: so long as international relations are conducted in a revolutionary system, there is a need for a system change with respect to war and the distribution of power and discretion, but the revolutionary nature of the conflict generates tensions and hostilities that are incompatible with system change. Without the revolutionary attribute, a system change may become feasible but it is much less essential, perhaps even undesirable; with the revolutionary attribute, system change is necessary but almost impossible to bring about. In that sense, revolution, as attribute and as challenge, is a decisive obstacle to the achievement of a qualitative improvement in international order.

The prevention of war, however, is not the only consideration. It may turn out that the adaptation of the international system to the needs of modernization in the poorer states is the most essential requirement for international stability, and is more fundamental than either of our obsessive concerns: the avoidance of nuclear war and the frustration of Communist objectives.

9

THE REVOLUTION OF MODERNIZATION IN NATIONAL AND INTERNATIONAL SOCIETY

MANFRED HALPERN

It is no longer revolutionary to suggest that we live in a revolutionary world. However, the task of understanding revolution remains.

These notes sketch, in a tentative fashion, some concepts and propositions that might lead, at a later stage, to a theory for analyzing the fundamental nature of our historical era, which I have called "the revolution of modernization." Readers who would try the new spectacles being offered here even before all the frames and lenses have been completed will certainly be pained to see old words used strangely, and new controversies raised in the attempt to move beyond customary conclusions. An incomplete view of a path which seems to be more promising than present roads is all I can now offer. I wish to bar no criticism; only false expectations.[1]

THE UNIQUE AND REVOLUTIONARY
CHARACTER OF MODERNIZATION

The central argument may be stated in one paragraph. The revolution of modernization involves the transformation of all systems by which man organizes his society—the political, social, economic, intellectual, religious, and psychological systems. That is what I mean by revolution, any revolution. The revolution of modernization, however, is the first revolution in the history of mankind to set a new price upon stability in any system of society; namely, an intrinsic capacity to generate and absorb continuing transformation. This constitutes both the unique opportunity and the unique requirement of the revolution of modernization. Still, elites in some societies may not wish to exercise this new option; others do not yet have the capacity to control or guide the transformation which, against their hopes, is changing their lives. There are different roads for achieving modernization or defending a society against it, but always at a cost determined by the new price of stability. By now, both the achievements and the failures of the revolution of modernization in national societies have created forces and tensions which are beginning to transform international society as well.

Our focus is on a unique type of transformation. The revolution of modernization demands of modern society the capacity to maintain continuously that ability which the species *Lepidoptera Rhopalocera* loses after having been successively transformed from caterpillar to chrysalis to butterfly. Modernization demands of all systems (by "system" I mean simply a patterned interaction of elements) the ability that the scientific community already possesses: to persist continuously in developing, maintaining, modifying, and disintegrating systems of theory, even though such systems thus also undergo revolution after revolution. That such scientific revolutions, even under the best of circumstances, tend to be discontinuous, conflict-ridden, and marked by considerable intervals of concentration on refining and enlarging existing systems, helps to make scientific

---

[1] These notes raise in a preliminary way some basic themes of a longer work on this subject now being pursued under the auspices of the Center of International Studies, Princeton University.

transformations particularly characteristic examples of the revolution of modernization.[2]

The revolution of modernization is not, however, the first rapid or fundamental transformation of human societies. Dozens of times before, kinship groups have—by conquest or conversion—become part of bureaucratic empires, and so transformed their political, social, religious, economic, and intellectual relations.[3] Often such empires have quickly yielded to, or become more slowly transmuted into, another such empire, or else kinship groups have evolved or empires devolved into feudal societies. I suggest, however, that all these earlier historical transformations shared a single quality. They all created closed systems. Dogma set boundaries to the search for truth; social norms severely restricted the number of roles that could be played and the manner in which they could be performed; technology, skills, and organization set sharp limits upon production, income, and economic growth; the continuing autonomy of kinship groups hobbled social and political integration and control. Such empires, feudalities, or tribes sometimes survived for millennia, depending on their capacity for maintaining or modifying their particular closed system or, at most, transforming it into a different closed system. A traditional system thus differs from any modern system by its incapacity to deal with continuous systemic transformation: traditional societies were not faced continuously by system-transforming demands and when, usually only after centuries, they were confronted by a particular challenge of this kind, they were capable of responding only by disintegrating or by creating a new closed system.[4]

"Transformation," odd as it may seem, is a term rarely found in the literature of social change, whether dealing with the past or the modern age. Whether we can conceive of transformation at all depends, in part, on the level of abstraction on which we move. Many are the histories written about traditional bureaucratic empires in which one exciting event after another is related in detail, and

[2] See Thomas S. Kuhn, *The Structure of Scientific Revolutions* (Chicago: 1962).

[3] Such transformations have been systematically examined by S. N. Eisenstadt in *Political Systems of Empires* (New York: 1963). In a forthcoming volume, I examine the dynamics of change in traditional Islam.

[4] An open society, by contrast, would, of course, be a society whose stability rests on its intrinsic capacity to generate and absorb further transformation.

neither author nor reader notices that on another level (that of events affecting the integration of the system) nothing happened at all; everything remained the same. It is also possible to remain blind to transformation in the modern age by avoiding systemic analysis and exploring change only through the addition or substitution of specific traits, or through the alteration in particular combinations, frequencies, or intensities of factors present in all societies. As a result, it becomes easy to miss the unique character of system transformation in modern times. Certainly this revolution of modernization, which began at least six hundred years ago in Italy, two hundred years ago in the Ottoman Empire, and in Yemen suffered another fitful start in 1963, is not a process without ancestry, nor does it ever finally abolish the past. The modern peoples of the world, whether American, Russian, French, Mexican, or Japanese, remain different from each other because each has kept different facets of a different past alive. But if we remain content to see the world in this fashion, paying heed only to particular institutions or habits which often enough remain for long unchanged, we shall fail to perceive the very essence of this revolutionary age.

If, instead of studying particular individual factors or even clusters of variables as symptoms or indices of modernization, we expand our vision to analyze the system in which these factors, however ancient their origins, now constitute a part, and contrast it with the system of which they were once a part, we shall see that a revolution has taken place. It is usually an incomplete revolution, but a revolution nevertheless. The reason for calling the process of modernization a revolution is that this transformation involves a change in systems and that the new system is qualitatively different from any system which preceded it.

Transformation, at any time in history, may be defined as that kind of alteration of a system which results in the exclusion of some existing elements and linkages and the entrance of some new elements and linkages sufficient to be recognized, at a given level of abstraction, as a new system.[5] Any research strategy devoted to the

[5] The problem to be analyzed itself dictates the level of abstraction best suited for identifying, sorting, and interpreting the most relevant information. If, for example, you are concerned with the relationship of butterflies to other insects, it may be most useful to abstract them into the discussion as *Lepidoptera Rhopalocera*. If your concern is with the transformation of this insect, you will be more interested in the fact that in the form of a *caterpillar*, this animal can bite and chew, has six eyes, legs, but no wings;

modern transformation of societies would therefore be designed to bring into view: (1) the traditional system as a system; (2) the elements of the traditional system no longer present; (3) the traditional linkages that have been broken; (4) the new elements that have entered; (5) the new links being fashioned; (6) the new system seen as a system. Such a research strategy can thus help us to develop indices that will tell us when a particular society is entering the revolution of modernization.

To view this process in its entire scope, I would suggest that in all societies of the world modernization is uniquely marked, over time, by the following developments:

1. All premodern systems of a society disintegrate as systems, and so does the premodern pattern by which these systems interacted with each other, and so maintained their particular life processes. (This radical change is usually obscured by the fact that some—never all—of the elements and linkages of premodern systems continue to function, though with altered relevance and effectiveness.)

2. The revolution of modernization closes, as fully adequate responses for the successful survival of societies, all three roads which constituted the premodern alternatives for confronting stability and change: (a) changes *in* certain structures and functions within some systems of a society without altering the core pattern of the systems (e.g., accepting new tools without altering a kinship-based political system); (b) changes *of* some of the systems of a society and the patterns relating them to each other, but not involving a change of all systems or all patterns of relationship (e.g., the establishment of traditional bureaucratic empires based on certain free-floating resources available to a centralized authority, but combined with the continuing autonomy at least of kinship group; the

---

that in the form of a *chrysalis,* it can hardly move; and that in the form of a *butterfly,* it may have as many as 20,000 eyes, can only suck and not bite or chew, and can fly.

Such an approach provides no answer to the question: At what *point* does change within a system deserve to be called transformation? That is, despite appearances, not an interesting or useful question, for the same reason that asking *at what point* a snowball becomes an avalanche is not an interesting or useful question. Nobody needs an answer to this question for any practical reason except possibly to provide an alibi for political leaders who are short-sighted or hard of hearing. All we require are concepts that clearly distinguish the one from the other, and hypotheses about how, how soon, and why one structure may be transformed into another.

growth of "great cultures" combined with the persistence of "little cultures," etc.) ; or (c) resistance to change through isolation. By contrast, the revolution of modernization for the first time raises the opportunity and need (which represent at the same time the minimum and maximum modern chance for wedding stability and change) to create systems which derive their stability from their intrinsic capacity to generate and absorb continuing transformation. This conception of the revolution of modernization does not, therefore, apply merely to underdeveloped areas, but to the entire world.

3. On actual observation, one finds that the majority of contemporary societies have not yet been able to seize this modern opportunity. Instead, they are unstable in a peculiarly modern fashion: their systems are each imbalanced within and in relation to each other. This imbalance results, in part, from the persistence of structures from the premodern era which retain the capacity to fulfill their traditional function, and so frustrate the emergence of modern structures able to carry out required modern tasks that would also threaten the persistence of the traditional structure (e.g., the struggle between Church and state in the West, or between traditional chiefs and modern bureaucracy in Africa). This imbalance also results from a relationship that is entirely modern— namely the uneven development of modern structures, functions, and systems (e.g., the disparity between educated men and jobs available for them, between population and resources, between armies and political parties, between modern problems and theories relevant for understanding them).

In short, what we need to know in order to understand any modern system as a system is the interaction among three elements: the imbalances existing within and among the systems of a society, and the will and the capacity of society to transform these imbalances so that it may generate and absorb continuing transformation. By will I mean such factors as drive, imagination, interest, and courage. By capacity I refer to such factors as material resources, knowledge, skills, institutions, and procedures. The imbalances may be ascertained by inquiring into types, rates, and dynamics of change from any preceding system—by asking, for example: What new social classes are emerging? What traditional classes are surviving? What interests do they no longer share? What conflicts are turning into cleavages of opinion? What role are kinship structures coming to play in other systems of society? What aspects of society have become secularized, or have remained sacred or have newly become ritualized? How dependent has this society become on other societies for ideas, capital, skill, and security?

The types of interaction possible among will, capacity, and imbalances may be illustrated by suggesting that an imbalance between population and resources may inhibit capacity long before it lames the will to modernize society; an imbalance between aspiration and achievement may come to be used creatively to generate and absorb further transformation. This is obvious enough. What is different is the criterion for analyzing the relevance of actions—namely, whether they facilitate the process of transformation in the system as a whole, and in the relationship of that system to other systems in society. The point is not that transformation must or is likely to take place every day or even every year. Transformation will almost certainly take place discontinuously, with periods of inaction, friction, and renewal. What a political system must be able to maintain continuously is the capacity to engage in transformation.

This formulation has another advantage: It raises into autonomous issues the conditions under which violence may or may not accompany the revolution of modernization, and progress or degeneration marks its outcome at various times. All this framework of analysis is intended to supply is an elucidation of relevant facts and an assessment of alternatives open at any given point, and their cost. No change is, by itself, seen as being either useful or good, nor is anyone being called upon to admire, more than any other style of life, the process which involves adaptation to the revolution of modernization; that is, the generation and assimilation of transformation. I myself prefer it, though certainly an argument can be made that it may sometimes be temporarily more prudent for a society to live with the burdens and conflicts it knows than to accept the heavier, yet uncertain sacrifices in habits, savings, work, and freedom that may be required to transform that society more quickly. (Asoka Mehta, the Indian Socialist, has argued that if India could delay industrialization for several decades it would find that advances in technology would then exact a much smaller toll in political, social, moral, and economic sacrifice for modernization.) A society is also free to choose different paths to modernization. But in one respect our view of the revolution of modernization preempts, through theoretical analysis, a realm hitherto assumed to be a matter of preference only. We argue that in the longer run, the price of stability remains transformation; lacking it, the price will have to be paid, instead, in instability or repression. This is a lesson which some colonial overlords learned more quickly than others and some independent governments have not yet taken to heart.

If, from here on, I give priority to the consideration of political systems, it is not for reasons of loyalty to a discipline, but because I remain concerned about the transformation of societies. When a closed society disintegrates, no system within it may, for a time, be able to initiate the genesis of a new society. But of all systems drawn into the revolution of modernization, none has more potential capacity than the political for rapidly and decisively mustering coercive and material resources, mobilizing masses, and developing an ideology to substitute for the faith that was and the political culture that has not yet grown into being. The political system need not play at all times as weighty a role as it does during crises of transformation. Because the revolution of modernization constantly raises new system-transforming issues and demands, effective policy making, whether centralized or based on pluralistic interest-bargaining, becomes policy planning. The political system tends to retain its primacy because it possesses greater and more immediate power than any other system for maintaining, or altering, society's capacity to generate and absorb transformation.

Let us now look more closely at the political alternatives open to men throughout history. The three largest and most fundamental categories which may be suggested for political systems are "traditional," "transitional," and "modernizing." If these are familiar terms, they are being used here with a difference. I use the term "traditional" provisionally to describe the single, ideal-type traditional political system, already defined on page 180.[6]

The term "transitional" applies to any political system in which

---

[6] It may turn out in subsequent explorations that we are able to distinguish types of traditional political systems in terms of their capacity to deal with rebellion (or system renovation) and the dynamics of their system disintegration. These factors may be especially critical in helping to shape the subsequent genesis of modern political systems. For certainly no traditional system has the systemic capacity directly to transform itself. Critical elements and linkages of a traditional system must first disintegrate before a transformation can take place.

Portions of the next several pages were first presented in somewhat different form, in a paper, "On Comparing Political Systems in Process of Transformation," to the Annual Meeting of the African Studies Association, San Francisco, October 25, 1963.

the structural changes and demands set loose by the uncontrolled forces of transformation exceed the will or capacity of political authority to cope with them. Transition, therefore, is a term used without any predetermined judgment of the direction being taken by such a society.

A transitional political system may be engaged in selective modernization without coming any closer to achieving a capacity for that systemic transformation which is characteristic of the modernizing political systems defined below. It may transform some of its institutions in a manner that is likely to inhibit further transformation. For example, it may develop what Fred W. Riggs calls "clects," a blending of premodern clique and posttraditional sect, instead of maintaining religious brotherhoods or developing political parties.[7] A transitional political system may seek to fixate and ritualize the status quo it has achieved at a given moment, even though the unintended or uncontrolled forces of modernization continue to undermine the system in the long run. It may try to return to certain selected traditions. Any society is transitional which is no longer closed but not yet open, and whose destination remains uncertain.

The term "modernizing" applies to any political system which, by contrast to the transitional, has achieved the will and capacity to deal with social change. I would use the broader term "modern," therefore, to refer not to time but generically to transitional and modernizing systems. For the revolution of modernization is marked by the emergence of these two types of systems for the first time in history, whether they appeared five hundred years ago or have yet to emerge.[8]

To be a modernizing state is no firm, final achievement, but rather a persistent capacity for coping with a permanent revolution. There are only five certainties arising from the conceptions here proposed. (1) Countries intent upon modernization need not go through that phase of modern existence described here as transitional, though modernizing systems have their own problems of system genesis, system modification, and system maintenance. (2)

7 Fred W. Riggs, "The Prevalence of Clects," *American Behavioral Scientist* (June 1962), 15–18.

8 For the sake of clarity, I would prefer the term "contemporary" to refer to time, specifically our lifetime, and, by metaphor, to any systems in existence now. Hence, "contemporary" embraces primitive, traditional, transitional, and modernizing systems.

No amount of patience or persistence will lead a country in the transitional phase to its modernization. In a transitional society changes also take place, but they are predominantly unintended. They are not the consequences of a revolutionary act which is perpetuated in the deliberate self-conscious deeds of men engaged in the process of creating, maintaining, modifying, or transforming modern systems, but are instead the results of the historical process of revolutionary transformation. This concept comprehends all those forces which fundamentally alter the systems constituting society regardless of the intentions of the elites of that society. Such forces may originate beyond the control span of a particular elite, or persist because of inadequate will, knowledge, or resources for dealing with them.

(3) To analyze the fundamental nature of our historical era—which is to say, the revolution of modernization—we need not study all turnovers of governments, all forms of political violence, or all types of change or innovation. We need not examine revolt—action, however violent, which is intended to consolidate the existing political order by bringing into power leadership which will exercise customary authority with greater justice or greater partisan strength. A revolution, by contrast, is any action, however bloodless, which transforms the political order to transform society. Transformation to a modernizing society can be achieved only by a revolutionary act. This specific event may in fact be a political revolution (e.g., the French Revolution). It may be merely a *coup d'état* or even the radical change of course by an existing, but converted, elite. The distinguishing marks of a revolutionary act are not violence or illegality, but the initiation of the transformation of the political system in order to transform society. (4) Even a modernizing system may, under the pressure of the historical process of revolutionary transformation, lose the will or capacity to avoid slipping back into a transitional phase. (5) No modern political system, whether transitional or modernizing, can ever return to that traditional system through whose disintegration it was born.

Our theory thus is neither deterministically evolutionary nor does it postulate entirely open multilinear development. The challenge of the revolution of modernization faces all contemporary societies and cannot be avoided. There is no reason to assume, however, that all contemporary societies will succeed in modernizing, and good reason to fear that many may not.

It may, therefore, be helpful to discriminate further between transitional and modernizing political systems. Our criteria for selecting five transitional and three modernizing political systems are derived from what are obviously the most important distinctions as men organize to deal with the revolution of modernization; we try to conceive of systems exhibiting different will and capacity to deal with different kinds of imbalances arising in the course of modernization. We have, however, arbitrarily pared down the number of interesting systems for the present notes to those which most closely resemble currently existing or emerging societies.

TRANSITIONAL AND MODERNIZING POLITICAL SYSTEMS

Five transitional political systems seem especially worth discussing: the system of structured instability, the extremist system, the ritualized system, the oligarchic interest-bartering system, and the pluralistic interest-bartering system. None, it may be worth repeating, is a road to modernization; all are cases of arrested revolution.

The system of structured instability involves instability not merely of the specific government, as occurred even in traditional societies, especially in Islam or Byzantium, where rulers changed often and abruptly but the same political system endured for centuries. Here governmental instability reflects instead the instability of the political system itself; it lacks the capacity for orderly change responsive to the revolution of modernization. This typically transitional situation leads to instability in this particular type of political system for the following reasons: (1) the posttraditional consensus in such a society is deeply split by both differences and cleavages of opinion;[9] (2) even the differences of opinion involve not only different conceptions of interest but also different views on how to deal with existing cleavages, and hence with societal transformation itself; (3) all competing views are organized and no single political group can secure predominance; and (4) instability is structured (and thus perpetuated) by limiting access to positions of power to groups whose action is defined principally by their agreement to disagree, thus to check each other. Hence the groups

[9] This contrast between differences and cleavages of opinion is drawn from Maurice Duverger, *Political Parties* (London: 1954), pp. 230–239.

who share power in this manner avoid any action that would alter the existing system by removing the fundamental causes of cleavage that divide the groups. Neither do they usually deny participation in the political game to any group ready to adjust itself to the arrested revolution.

We have, of course, long been familiar with systems that show a persistent tendency to play a political game of musical chairs that is no longer confined to the traditional elite, but is not yet accessible to all claimants. The advantage of integrating this type of political system in a larger category of transitional systems is that it may provide systematic ways of comparing the dynamics of structured instability, for example, in contemporary Syria and Iraq and during much of the Third and Fourth French Republics, and so develop hypotheses regarding the dynamics by which such systems may experience genesis, maintenance, modification, transformation, or disintegration.[10]

In contrast to the system of structured instability, a system of pluralistic interest-bartering derives its greater stability from the fact that only differences and not cleavages of opinion are effectively organized in competition for power and benefits. The dominant decision-making groups, as in India, Nigeria, and the Philippines, share a broad area of agreement regarding system maintenance and modification, and a general opposition to system transformation.

Systems of this kind have probably given rise to stronger illusions than have any other transitional types in the considerations of Western observers, now that the oligarchic interest-bargaining systems have faded in popularity among them. The pluralistic transitional system seems to resemble the democratic modernizing system more than any other; it is usually willing to give scope to private economic enterprise; it tends to be less stridently nationalistic; it often shows as much amenability toward compromise on the international scene as it does internally. In short, it seems to represent the furthest advanced and already the most adjusted system on the road to modernization. It may be so, but usually it is not.

[10] It would not be too difficult to show, for instance, under what circumstances earlier attempts at Gaullist transformation of systems of structured instability failed in Iraq and Syria, and with the help of their experience, indicate what alternatives there may be to transformation under the mantle of charismatic transcendentalism.

The consensus built on the aggregation of existing dominant interests under conditions of great scarcity and rising frustrations is likely to grant inadequate place to newly emerging social classes, to the poor, and to the uprooted. Interest bargaining among those already possessed of power and influence tends to concentrate on the distribution of scarce resources and the reinforcement of existing relationships, rather than on the sacrifice of vested interests and of accustomed beliefs, values, and behavior which is the unavoidable price of productive transformation at this stage of development. There are few countries in Asia, Africa, or Latin America that possess the resources or the consensus to keep such a system from becoming a premature and usually also an invidious and squandering method of distributing benefits instead of mustering resources for modernization.

These weaknesses, which are likely to make the ultimate turn toward modernization more costly, are reinforced in the oligarchic system of interest bartering. The transitional authoritarian ruler, in contrast to the authoritarian modernizer, bases his power on a calculus of personal relations—upon the intimidation of one prominent man, the purchase of another, the expectation of future favors by a third, and the fear of losing privileges not earned on grounds of talent or skills. Or if diverse groups are already organized in response to the issues of modernization, the authoritarian ruler will deal with them also as if they were persons rather than embodiments of issues, playing them off against each other or jailing or silencing their leaders rather than resolving their grievances.

By the very nature of the ties that created their power, such transitional authoritarian rulers are barred from engaging in any reforms that would destroy the system in which politics remains synonymous with the calculus of personal relations. No specific project, however spectacular, and no additional policemen, however well-trained, are likely to hold such an authoritarian system together for long in modern times. The revolution of modernization has already brought into existence almost everywhere men who by virtue of their education and interests, their lack of personal connections, or sheer number cannot hope to find a place in such a transitional matrix. Their weight sooner or later cannot help but alter a system that refuses to contain them.

Political systems on the road to modernization may lose their will or capacity to adjust to continuing transformation. They may instead come to ritualize their transitional state.[11] The leader may ritualize rather than attempt to routinize the power of his charisma. Ideology comes to be valued as a catechism. The new salaried middle class converts itself into a new caste of functionaries.

Not only leaders but the masses may be tempted by the pseudo-traditional reassurance of the ritualized transitional system. Uprooted tribesmen moving into cities may, as in the Congo, form new solidarity networks that act as if they were tribes on the defensive. Men from the provinces, thanks to the advance of modernization, become literate for the first time and hence more transitional men begin to read traditional religious literature than did their forebears. The new is absorbed into the old, but immobilized by being ritualized.

The last of the transitional systems to be mentioned here—the extremist system—is best clarified by contrasting it with a modernizing system with which it is often confused—namely, the radical authoritarian system. I would call extremist any totalitarian system that institutionalizes terror and violence in order to impose dogmatic certainty in the midst of rapid social change. The radical authoritarian modernizer, by contrast, uses only as much power as may be required to muster sufficient strength to uproot survivals of the past that prevent new growth and to establish roots for modern ideas and institutions.[12]

The use of great power is thus, by itself, not a sufficient measurement of the difference between extremist and radical systems. The critical distinction here, as among other systems, derives from the particular relationship between capacity and will, and the imbalances to be faced. The radical authoritarian modernizers (for example, Nasser, Ben Bella, or Touré) tread a most difficult path; they face not only the corrupting temptations of power but also the fear, perhaps even the fact that they may not, after all, possess resources, skill, and power enough to avoid being overwhelmed by the uncontrolled revolutionary consequences of social change. Nonetheless, the distinction between dispossessing and killing landlords, or

[11] This formulation of the ritualized transitional system owes its inspiration to David Apter's essay, "Political Religion in the New Nations," in *Old Societies and New States*, Clifford Geertz, ed. (New York: 1963).

[12] I have enlarged on this contrast in *The Politics of Social Change in the Middle East and North Africa* (Princeton: 1963).

between restricting and liquidating dissenters still makes a major difference in terms of human lives and the corruption of human dignity.

In addition to radical authoritarianism, two other modernizing political systems deserve to be mentioned. The syncretic modernizing system is marked by the willingness of the traditional elite to accept, at any time, as much modernization as seems required to maintain its place in the evolving elite. The United Kingdom is the best example of such a system. The United States seems to fall somewhere between this and the radical democratic system. The latter is radical (in the same theoretical rather than ideological sense as the radical authoritarian system) in that it is committed as a system to deal with the roots of change. Unlike the authoritarian modernizing system, however, its capacity for generating and absorbing change is sufficient so that the political system need no longer monopolize the control and direction of change, but can plan to maintain and expand its society's enjoyment of freedom and diversity. By now it should be apparent that we do not measure a modern political system by its current set of accomplishments as much as by an evaluation of its current and (if its present trends persist) future will and capacity to deal with the imbalances of its society while developing systemic capabilities for generating and absorbing further transformation. (For this reason, we consider Egypt today a modernizing state, and Nazi Germany a transitional state.)

From these formulations, it must also be apparent that totalitarianism is a mark of transitional rather than of modernizing systems. It is an expression of inadequate will (as in Fascism) or capacity (as in Stalinism) to deal with the modernization of society. In either case, the threatened loss of political control is compensated for, at the cost of the perversion of both will and capacity, by the adoption of dogma and the institutionalization of terror. Extremist systems may appear anywhere along the transitional range of the continuum, (compare, for example, the Kenya Mau Mau, the Egyptian Muslim Brotherhood, and the German Nazis) just as radical systems may appear anywhere along the modernizing continuum. Each expression differs, depending on the kind and number of system-transforming demands with which political authority is being confronted, the demands it is willing to resolve through system-transforming action or else contain by repression, and the resources and institutions it can command for this purpose. As the certainty that even a totalitarian regime can successfully impose on a changing society is only partial, the analytical problem is always to determine whether the actual movement along the continuum is toward tradition, modernization, or fixation in place, and, in each case, at what cost. Thus Russia, which began to evolve as a modern state several centuries ago and experienced a number of different transitional systems until 1917, has, since the death of Stalin, been moving from a transitional extremist system to a radical modernization system.

Utilizing a similar approach, a pluralistic or consociational system is not, from our perspective, a moderate and moderating system automatically equidistant from all extremes. Instead, it may appear on the traditional, transitional, or modernizing range of the continuum, its particular expression depending on the balance of tasks, responses, and resources involved in the system in question. A regime that encourages only limited innovation, like that of Libya or King Faisal's Saudi Arabia may not be conservative; by its very caution, it may fail to conserve anything. Moderate regimes like the Moroccan and Pakistani may pave the way for extremism by failing to confront their immoderate problems.

More broadly speaking, it also follows that no transitional system can lead to modernization except as the unintended consequences of the actions of a transitional elite, or the uncontrolled consequences of the historical process of transformation produce a revolutionary act which, in turn, alters the political system. Even this incomplete typology and explication of political systems conceived in relationship to the revolution of modernization may be sufficient to show that this comparative approach is more fruitful than one which presupposes that our understanding or practice must be restricted to the great particular models (U.S.S.R., China, United States, or Japan), or can prudently be confined only to particular institutions, or depends entirely on our ideological preferences or else had best remain descriptive. Theory can help us analyze alternatives and costs in the revolution of modernization.

THE REVOLUTION IN INTERNATIONAL SOCIETY

This mode of analysis and the conclusions which flow from it also alert us to the fact that the revolution of modernization is transforming not only national but also international society. What fundamentally divide the world today are not the remaining differences in cultural tradition but the different responses (shaped only in part by contrasts in cultural inheritance) of societies to the same world-wide revolution of modernization.

Yet most analysts have found it even more difficult to perceive the revolution of international society than the transformation of national societies. There is only one contemporary international society, and its contrasts with earlier international systems still appear to be less than many anticipated, feared, and hoped for since the advent of nuclear weapons, missiles, or the tripling of UN membership. Though, indeed, some of our worse fears of say, 1948, regarding the U.S.S.R., European recovery, colonial independence, and war have justifiably lessened by now.

Nonetheless, I argue that despite such appearance, international society is in process of being fundamentally transformed. The transitional political system that now marks that society—a system which, without straining the analogy with national society, may be termed one of structured instability—is being fundamentally altered. The kind of new system that may be born is not yet clear, at least not to me, but that the new system is being formed is no longer in doubt. What is the evidence for this systemic transformation?

If we look for transformation (and not merely change or innovation), then it is interesting, but not decisively significant, that the number of sovereign actors in the international political system has tripled. That is the kind of change that can normally be handled within an existing system. What really matters is that new types of actors have entered the system in the nations that are fundamentally unable to exercise the role called for by the existing system; namely, to act in sovereign independence. This is the fate not only of the Congo, or of many countries overwhelmingly dependent financially, politically, or militarily on one great power, but threatens to be the case of countries such as Indonesia, Pakistan, Nigeria, and many others. Most countries of the world have not yet succeeded in the revolution of modernization sufficiently to enter present international society in roles which, if not equal to others, would at least allow or encourage them to maintain the rules of the games of the present system.

Instead, the existing international political system is faced by the system-transforming demands of these new nations and hence the system-transforming responses of the older nations. Among these revolutionary changes, the following may already be observed:

The economic interdependence among nations today is already such that if trade or aid were significantly reduced, the consequence for most nations would be systemic transformations within their societies.[13] This interdependence is another result of the progress of the revolution of modernization in national societies.[14]

The revolution in international society is also caused by the unevenness of development among national societies in response to the revolution of modernization. The absolute and relative gap between industrial and underdeveloped societies continues to grow at a time when the great majority of the politically active around the world share similar economic aspirations and face similar problems of political and social reconstruction, at a time when this gap is more visible than before, and poverty more curable, at least, in terms of the resources and technology available to international society as a whole.

It is our great good fortune that we and the culture from which we derive our traditions have had about five hundred years in which to adjust ourselves to this revolution, whereas the majority of mankind has had only decades. We are also fortunate to belong to that one-third of mankind which produces 80 per cent of the world's goods, or to put it even more dramatically, to live in the United States, where about 5 per cent of the world's population produces about 40 per cent of the world's goods. It is one thing to experience this revolution gradually and in great comfort; it is quite a different thing to experience revolution in telescoped time, and with far fewer resources and skills.

This is a division of the world far less easy to heal than the division between ourselves and the U.S.S.R., wherein the latter, in the view of the poor nations of the world, is coming to represent the "communism of the rich." Egypt, for example, the largest Arab

[13] This change in the realm of trade is perhaps especially dramatically evident in the Middle East, where ten years ago a stoppage of oil sales would have risked little for Iran, Iraq, or Saudi Arabia, but today it would fundamentally undermine politically necessary development programs.

[14] In this sense, the nationalization of production—through preclusive sovereign control over national boundaries—is likely to be far more important to the future of the revolution of modernization in international society than the form of nationalization to which we primarily pay attention; namely, the establishment of sovereign national control over particular properties.

country and the second most populous state in Africa, must build the world's biggest dam, the High Aswan Dam, to increase its cultivated land by one-third during the next decade—an extraordinary achievement. Egypt's population will grow by one-fourth during the same period; this will not leave much of a margin. As for the increase in electric power as a result of the dam, it must also be added that even a doubling of present industrial employment would hardly absorb the annual increase in the total labor force. Moreover, the trend in Egyptian industry as elsewhere is toward the introduction of labor-saving machinery to allow it to compete in international markets. Present industrial production in Egypt's large factories can probably be doubled with hardly any increase in employment.[15]

For another measure of the problem in most of the world, Eugene Black, the recently retired President of the World Bank, has put forth the following example of India. Let us disregard, he says, rural housing in India "on the somewhat optimistic assumption that it can be carried out entirely with local materials and labor." Let us consider only urban houses for India's growing population. "A sober estimate of the cost suggests that in the thirty years between 1956 and 1986 a total investment of roughly $25 billion will be needed." This figure, however, represents over four times the money lent by the World Bank to all countries of the world.[16]

The majority of the peoples of the world live in the Alice in Wonderland domain of the Red Queen where one has to run very fast in order merely to stand still. In the face of this growing gap between rich nations and poor nations even the most remarkable achievement of the poor leaves a bitter taste and may not prevent political violence.

For example, Egypt may come close to doubling its per capita annual income from $100 to $200 during the next ten years, thanks to very hard work; given its resources it is unlikely to push the ceiling of poverty much higher thereafter. During this same period of time, America will no doubt increase its per capita annual income from $2,300 to $3,300. Hard work has ceased to be a match for technological inventiveness combined with nonhuman energy.

It is this invidious poverty, unnecessary today in terms of the

---

[15] Frederick H. Harbison and Ibrahim Abdelkader Ibrahim, *Human Resources for Egyptian Enterprise* (New York: 1958), pp. 22, 136–138.
[16] *The New York Times,* October 11, 1963.

resources and skills of international society, and the resultant continuing *dependence* of the majority of newly *independent* states on the industrialized countries for capital, military security, skills, and ideas that makes anticolonialism a live issue even though there are scarcely any colonies left and they are doomed to an end of European rule. It is this continued fact of dependence that feels and smells like colonialism that rankles a new-found pride, that remains a powerful undercurrent embittering relations between ourselves and the underdeveloped world. More important still, it is doubtful that to the majority of the poor an international system will justify itself when it maintains an order permitting the rich nations to get richer and the poor nations, poorer.[17]

At this stage, these new norms of international behavior are being expressed through historically unprecedented bilateral and multilateral aid programs. However, the elites of most of the nations of the world have not yet become sensitive to the full dimensions of the revolution; and in the less developed nations many governments still lack the will or the capacity to call upon international society (or their own) for help and participation in the required transformation. The rate of change continues to accelerate, however, especially among the poor and ill-prepared nations of the world. Birth control cannot be made retroactive, and the intellectual, institutional, and economic foundations which are not established now will be much costlier and more difficult to build three decades hence, when the world's population may have doubled. Even if we assume that international society will possess the capacity for deterring military aggression on the part of these nations, the leading industrial powers will also, by that time, have become even more vulnerable to foreign-organized plots of sabotage and assassination.

In this context, the conflicting ambitions of half a dozen national societies to transform all or part of the structure of international society according to their particular world view also confronts international society with radically new challenges in norms and the possibilities of violence. Unlike the ambitions of world conquerors preceding this century, such hopes need not be pipe dreams. At a price, it is possible now to conquer the entire world, and certainly

[17] This point is developed by Richard A. Falk, "The New States and International Law," a report prepared for the International Bar Association, Tokyo, 1964; by B. V. A. Röling, *International Law in an Expanding World* (New York: 1960), pp. 83–86; and G. Clark and L. B. Sohn, *World Peace Through World Law* (Cambridge, Mass.: 1960), pp. 206–213, 345–358.

the price of preventing such conquests has already become one of the heaviest burdens upon the world.

In part these ambitions stem from older concerns for national power and prestige. In part they arise from ideologies intended to come to terms with the revolution of modernization. Victory through ideological conversion rather than military conquest, therefore, also has a significance no religious conversions had in the past. Today conversion results in the transformation of societies and thus helps to determine the further course of a revolution of world-wide scope.[18]

For the first time, international society is being transformed by a new kind of capacity among its members for intervention in each other's internal affairs. The encouragement of treason from abroad is an ancient art. If it intends to be relevant to the revolution of modernization, intervention today does not encourage rebellion or bother with political games of musical chairs. To intervene responsibly today—whether by granting or withholding economic aid or by supporting or denying support to governments in domestic political crises when such foreign support might prove decisive—is to intervene in the process of history.[19]

Such revolutionary, that is, system-transforming, interventions are made feasible and likely in large part by the uneven progress of modernization in international society. While causing new forms of interpenetration of political authority within international society, these interventions are facilitated by other forms of interpenetration born of the revolution of modernization. For the first time in history, a single intellectual system spans the entire world. Though men continue to disagree, they have little difficulty in communicating in scientific thought and in the realm of ideology involving nationalism and social welfare. For the first time in history, also, similar internationally crucial types of individuals may be found nearly everywhere in the world. Decades ago Thorstein Veblen, in an essay on the Jews, perceived the peculiar advantage of their condition in being at once insiders and outsiders in their society. Being Jewish

[18] The issue of both violent and nonviolent conversions is examined in Cyril E. Black and Thomas P. Thornton, *Communism and Revolution* (Princeton: 1964), and the broader context will also be treated in Black's forthcoming *Modernization: Essays in Comparative History*.

[19] I have expanded on this view in *The Morality and Politics of Intervention* (New York: 1963), and in "The UN in the Congo," *Worldview* (October 1963), 4–8.

in this sense has by now become a universal condition experienced by intellectually, socially, and politically important segments in every society. Styles of leadership in transitional and modernizing societies are emerging as related types, and their representatives at the United Nations can communicate and collaborate to a degree that remains unattainable among contemporary tribal leaders or the upholders of traditional high cultures.

As a result of the scientific and technological changes that are part of the revolution of modernization, a number of national societies now also possess the power not merely to coerce other national societies but to annihilate the entire international society. Never before was this the possible cost of failure in the management of political conflicts in international society. Indeed, the political, social, and intellectual cost of maintaining the current structure of conflict management is itself a major cause of system transformation in national and international society.

All these transformations are creating a new international society whose current transitional mode of structured instability is systemically incapable of managing it politically. In terms of transitional or modernizing systems, international society has political options open to it similar to those of national societies, each with different costs of achievement and risks of violence. What this discussion suggests, above all, is that the resolution of conflicts in international society may lie far more in action upon the revolution of modernization than is usually suspected. Even if conflicts are not always limited to, or most easily resolved within, the confines of the field in which they originated, nonetheless, it is not sensible to neglect theory or action on underlying causes.

It may, therefore, be helpful to ask whether the cold war is the most important challenge facing the international political system, and indeed, whether most of its facets cannot better be understood and dealt with as one manifestation of the revolution of modernization.

Clearly the capabilities of the great powers to contend with each other in the cold war depend, above all, on their own success in generating and absorbing change within their own societies (including but not limited to their technological capacity). The chief protagonists are themselves self-conscious and proselytizing special models of modernization, and the very arena in which they act as powers is being shaped less by the rules of loose, asymmetrical tripolarity than by the revolution of modernization. The vast majority of the world's population so far remains victim rather than beneficiary of this revolution, living in transitional societies in which few values can any longer gain immediate assent, few institutions, implicit allegiance, and satisfactions are increasingly out of tune with aspirations.

In fact, as long as the existing balance between the United States and the Communist nations makes large-scale war unlikely, the conflicts of the cold war will be fought out primarily in terms of the revolution of modernization—through involvement in the internal warfare of nations or through peaceful competition in ideas, techniques, and goods. Already, the internal transformation of nations has given rise to more frequent acts of political violence than the cold war. The revolution of modernization is engendering around the world more enduring conflicts, and conflicts much harder to resolve, than most of the issues of power standing between us and the U.S.S.R. By the very nature of the problems involved, there can be no marching up the hill and down again all in one week as in the Cuban situation—either in the foredoomed failure of 1961 or the brilliant success of 1962.

On guard against the threat of instability in other countries, we have tended to concentrate on the risks of external political coercion and propaganda. These are worth our attention. But by concentrating on the threats of instability, rather than the problems of revolution, we have also been inclined to neglect the more subtle, yet more decisive ways in which power can today be exercised over greater distances than before. Pressures for transformation of national societies can be generated by shifts in terms of trade, the rise of new models of organization or thought, or by any revolutionary changes that accompany the transformation of international society.

We miss these revolutionary consequences if we merely relax in the comfort we may derive from the fact that, contrary to conventional expectations, these pressures do not lead to the acceptance of any of the great powers as architects or prototypes of revolution. Nationalism is one of the first and most powerful manifestations of the revolution of modernization, representing, among other things, the search for new individual and social identity. Nationalism, although utilized for both combat and protection, has proven a remarkably effective ideology for organizing new units for collective bargaining. Mobilization alone is not enough. The growing turn toward social transformation in the world is not due, however, to the expanding influence of the U.S.S.R., China, or Cuba, but to the fact that, in most of the world, governments can be readily captured by coup and (not excluding a number of democracies) ruled on many vital issues by the decisions of small minorities. It is these minorities who speed the spread of revolution—either by bringing it increasingly under their guidance or control or by letting the uncontrolled historical forces of change continue to mount.

In turn, the balance of power, the orientation, health, and stability of the international system are vitally affected by the success or failure of local elites in dealing with the social, political, economic, intellectual, and psychological modernization of their countries. No rulers can pursue these tasks in sovereign isolation. Increasingly, their choice is whether to achieve such complex and difficult domestic goals through free international collaboration or to suffer them to be directed through the subversive intervention of the stronger nations in the instability and violence that mark the internal politics of the unsuccessful. In the latter case, domestic failure thus also helps to enlarge the area of hostile confrontations among the great powers.

MISSING THE REVOLUTION

If what has been presented here in rudimentary form has been sufficient to allow readers to begin to understand an exploration that has just begun, there may nonetheless be reservations. Why so many assertions in the face of so few answers? Why such seeming certitude in view of the likelihood that politics, being an art, not only a science, will always foil systematic analysis and projected estimates to a significant degree? Why such novel concepts when we have barely begun to develop perspectives that already have more solid anchoring?

There are indeed few answers being offered here. What are the prerequisite and requisite processes of interaction for the genesis or disintegration of a modern political system? What are the necessary conditions for maintaining a system's capacity for transformation? What are the dynamics of change from one transitional system to another? These are the kind of questions that have not been answered yet. I submit that it is the virtue of the suggested framework that it raises and underscores the relevance of such questions, and seems to me to give more promise of helping us to develop answers in the future than earlier perspectives on modernization.

I accept the fact, however, that we shall probably never be able to do better in political analysis than to speak, without final certainty, of tendencies and trends. Still, I think that we may be able to recognize more of these, and speak of them more systematically than we have supposed. As for developing further the concepts and approaches we already possess, we shall now have to examine what may be deficient in accepted perspectives.

For example, I recognize that the radical view that has been offered here regarding the opportunity and requirement of the capacity for system transformation contrasts with the more widely held assumption that men of culture, prudence, and good will naturally strive to combine the best of the old with the best of the new.

Nonetheless, I submit that two things that cannot be combined at all are the best in traditional society and the best in modern society. Indeed, before anything significantly traditional can be combined with anything significantly modern, a revolution must first have torn apart the closed system of tradition so that it may not merely add or substitute the new, but become capable of assimilating it.

To illustrate this argument, let us consider the problems of transformation for traditional Islam, which was, and to a considerable degree still is, the way of life of about 400 million people from West Africa and Yugoslavia to Indonesia and the Philippines. If I had to select among the many significant accomplishments of Islam the three aspects of it that Muslims themselves would be most eager to preserve in the modern age, I would choose: (1) the Muslims' belief that they received God's final revelation to mankind, a revelation which, being final, cannot ever be altered or amended; (2) the Muslims' belief that all things in existence are related to each other and that no distinction is possible between the sacred and the secular (as opposed to the Christian separation of the things of God from those of Caesar); and (3) the Muslims' extraordinary achievement of a way of life that endured 1,300 years because of a system of balanced tensions in which political violence and what may be called antagonistic collaboration became integrative and homeostatic rather than destructive forces in society.

It is quite clear that one cannot combine the best aspects of the modern age, say the spirit of scientific inquiry, rational bureaucratic administration, and an increasingly interdependent world order, with these major tenets of the Islamic world.

Japan is sometimes cited as an illustration of a traditional society that successfully entered the modern age without a revolution that tore apart the fabric of the traditional society. Modernization proceeded in the name of a time-hallowed symbol, the Emperor, and took advantage of military, feudal, and traditional bureaucratic values to inspire great disciplined effort.

I think the Japanese success has commonly been misinterpreted in several ways. From Japenese experience, one may well argue that pouring new wine in old bottles remains a shrewd form of manipulation and persuasion in politics. One would have to add, however, that the purpose of this approach in Japan was to achieve economic and military power by modifying the traditional system but avoiding its social and political transformation. I believe that the rise of military fascism in Japan during the thirties and its imperialist expansionism were intimately related to this decision to keep modernization confined within too rigidly limited structures of power, habits, and benefits. The corresponding maladjustments of a transitional rather than a truly modernizing society helped to produce aggressive reactions both at home and abroad. This lesson, which I think is also to be drawn in an even more developed form from the growth of German fascism, remains an important warning for our time: modernization is a process; it cannot be arbitrarily contained except at great peril.

And there is a third fallacy among some who have thought about the Japanese experience. It is not a relevant model for the modernization of other still underdeveloped areas, not merely because of the specific distortions I just mentioned, but also because of the tremendous importance of the time at which a society joins in this world-wide revolution. In Japan during the late nineteenth and early twentieth century, as in Turkey during the Atatürk modernization in the 1920's, it was still possible to confine the power and benefits of modernization to a segment of the educated urban class, and to neglect the rural countryside except as a source of revenues. The widespread awareness of the unevenness of development in all systems of society today and the consequent aspirations and demands are such that no leader can ignore workers and peasants even at the outset of his march into the modern age. For that reason, a modernizing leader in the underdeveloped areas today must be able to mobilize more people for modern tasks and achieve more faster than did either Atatürk or the Japanese.

It is also true that analysis of the revolution of modernization has been suffering from a scarcity of facts about most of the world— Africa, Asia, and Latin America. For the great majority of the countries of the Middle East and North Africa, for example, we possess not a single work of any merit discussing the political system factually or theoretically as a system in process of transformation.[20]

It is not enough to deplore that. What facts are we looking for, and how can we best put the facts that are available into order and hence give them significance? This is a problem even for those interested only in answering questions about particular structures or particular functions *within* a political system. However, for that purpose at least, structural-functional analysts have already helped us greatly to refine our concepts. But suppose that you are interested instead in asking questions about the dynamics of the political system as a whole, and particularly about the transformation of a political system. Then you discover that your first obstacles to analysis are not so much scarcities of fact but present theories and present philosophies.

A recent "Reconsideration of Theories of Social Change" concluded that the mere "mention of 'theories of social change' will make most social scientists appear defensive, furtive, guilt-ridden, or frightened."[21] And one of the principal architects of structural-functional analysis, Talcott Parsons, tells us there is no use trying to explain the transformation of a system. He writes: ". . . a general theory of the processes of change of social systems is not possible in the present state of knowledge. The reason is very simply that such a theory would imply complete knowledge of the laws of process of the system and this knowledge we do not possess. The theory of change in the structure of the social system must, therefore, be a theory of particular sub-processes of change within such systems, not of the over-all processes of change of the systems as systems." And a little later, Parsons adds, "When such a theory [concerning the change of systems] is available, the millennium

[20] I have enlarged on this point in "Middle Eastern Studies: A Review of the State of the Field with a Few Examples," *World Politics* (October 1962), 108–122.

[21] Wilbert E. Moore, "A Reconsideration of Theories of Social Change," *American Sociological Review* (December 1960), 810.

for social science will have arrived. This will not come in our time, and probably never."[22]

Now true enough, Parsons can, within his own framework, account for several types of changes that can be integrated by the existing structure of the system: inventions and discoveries that can be exploited to support or enhance the existing system; cyclical movements, growth or differentiation in size or complexity in certain already present variables of the system; and repeated fluctuations around the equilibrium position.[23] What he cannot explain are revolutionary transformations of the system, which is to say, the most decisive historical trend in world history today.

But we need not share Parsons' pessimism about the millennium. The reason is that it is not going to arrive from the direction in which he is looking. To understand the transformation *of* a political system, we do not need to possess "complete knowledge of the laws of process" *within* the system. A theory that can help explain how things function within Morocco or Egypt today is useful, very useful, but complete knowledge about every structure and every function within Morocco or Egypt is not a necessary precondition for understanding the forces transforming the political system, in the same manner that most of what we can and should learn about a caterpillar will not prepare us to understand a butterfly. A static theory may even mislead us about the nature, depth, and direction of a revolution by identifying observed troubles and discontents only as being dysfunctional *within* the existing system when, very often, they actually turn out to be the agents and elements of a new system.

These are not merely questions of convenient definition. Much more is at stake. Aside from any differences in political values and political interests, it is, implicitly or explicitly, on this ground that rested the difference in perspectives of those who argued since 1945 that Algerian discontent was not merely evidence of inadequate reforms and inadequate police—that is, of dysfunctional aspects of the existing system—but rather of a new system of ideas and actions being born. It is our failure to achieve a theoretical understanding

[22] Talcott Parsons, *The Social System* (New York: 1951), pp. 486, 534.

[23] Most of these formulations regarding changes that do not threaten the fundamental integration of a system I owe to a doctoral dissertation by Mohammed Guessous on Theories of Social Change, Department of Sociology, Princeton University.

of systemic transformations which, whatever our stand on issues of
political values and interests, prevented most social scientists from
providing, plainly, convincingly, and in time, a theoretical understanding of two of the primary systemic transformations of the past
two decades in Africa, Asia, and Latin America—from the colonial
system to independence, and from the nationalist revolution to the
social revolution. We have been served well by a number of studies
of fundamental changes in charismatic and bureaucratic leadership,
communication, political parties, armies, and ideologies—but by far
fewer dealing with the transformation of the political system perceived as a system.

That is perhaps not surprising, considering that no one has yet
developed a conceptualization of the political system that fulfills the
theoretical requirement of comprehending it in process of transformation. Harry Eckstein has recently presented a critique of all
attempts so far made and found them wanting on even more modest
grounds, even though some progress has been made.[24] We no longer
find any reputable political scientist who supposes that the political
system of a society is merely its legal government or formal institutions. But most of the conceptualizations that have since taken
its place, as Eckstein points out, suffer either from including too
much, by urging the study of power and decision making in all
social interrelationships, without systematically identifying those
which are politically crucial either to the goal attainment or the
transformation of the system, or else they suffer from including too
little, by selecting inputs, outputs, or functions which constitute elements, but surely only some of the elements of a political system.
But the point that really concerns me is that none of the formulations presently available succeeds in conceptualizing (or perhaps
I should say more accurately, attempts to conceptualize) the political system that is at stake in the politics of social change.

Eckstein's own formulation does, I think, greatly advance us over
earlier conceptions. "A political system," he writes, "consists of the
most inclusive structures in a society that have recognized responsibility for performing, at a minimum, the function of goal-attainment
by means of legitimate decisions." This conception usefully es-

---

[24] Harry Eckstein, "The Concept 'Political System': A Review and Revision," a paper prepared for delivery at the Annual Meeting of the
American Political Science Association, New York, September 4, 1963.

tablishes the field of action (and inquiry) for many existing political systems and also sets out the minimum which others must yet achieve. From another perspective, however, we remain still without help, nor is Eckstein's conception entirely intended to help us from that viewpoint. For, in perhaps a majority of states, a political system, thus conceived, has either not yet been attained or the structures, the responsibility, the performance, the minimum, the goals, the means, and the legitimacy of decisions remain the fundamental issues of political strife, the outcome of which is uncertain. Yet we need a conception for a political system of this kind. It does not constitute merely a melee of fragments; genesis no less than transformation has its persistent patterns and rules of movement.[25]

The discussion of the revolution of modernization also has been hampered rather than illuminated by the fashion in which ideology has been associated with it. We have tended to expose prevailing ideologies as either intellectually shallow or mischievous, or as rationalizations of particular interests, or we have accepted, rejected, or revised them for our own use. We have seldom analyzed the essential usefulness (or the failure to be useful) of an ideology in confronting problems of modernization which we have first examined from a theoretical perspective.

The characteristics of the present discussion of the role of ideology may be illustrated by recalling the distinction Hannah Arendt draws between the American Revolution on the one hand, and the French Revolution, the Russian Revolution, and most Afro-Asian revolutions of this century, on the other. The American Revolution, Arendt declares, was a revolution that involved only questions of authority. The other revolutions include an attempt to resolve fundamental social issues by political means. It is this extra burden that exacts the grave toll of these revolutions. She writes: "The whole record of past revolutions demonstrates beyond doubt that every attempt to solve the social question with political means leads into terror and that it is terror which sends revolutions to their doom.

[25] The genesis of a modernizing system requires, among other things, the tearing asunder of the traditional system as a system, a transformation of the role of the traditional elite, the re-creation of a legitimate authority, the creation of an ideology relevant to the tasks of transformation, and the organization of a political movement capable of mobilizing mass support—tasks at which Algeria by 1964 had made considerable progress and the Congo almost none.

. . . Nothing . . . could be more obsolete than to attempt to liberate mankind from poverty by political means; nothing could be more futile and more dangerous."[26]

Hannah Arendt has been answered primarily by men who offer a different ideology, or who oppose to Arendt's philosophical considerations the practice of most political systems, which have increasingly accepted social tasks, or who persist in policies which come most naturally to Americans. We tend to rest our hope in revolutions that seem as pragmatic as Americans are, without asking whether such societies already possess the structure of experience, skills, and values which give *ad hoc* solutions some promise of becoming constructive.

This is a fruitless kind of debate. Nations cannot be created nor societies transformed merely by outlining this project or that. Neither can those who are intent upon becoming the organizers, rather than the victims, of social change build any longer in most of the world on inherited and generally accepted philosophy, custom, or institutions; nor do they possess, as yet, any consensus on the means and objectives of governments intent on moving out beyond tradition. Under such circumstances, ideology (conceived not as dogma, though all ideologies, including pragmatism, can be so converted, but seen only as an explicit framework of means and ends for society) plays a crucial role in developing a new political culture when the traditional political culture is disintegrating. Ideologies take the place of inherited, inner-directed certainty and serve as the frame of analysis, the inspiration of action, and the touchstone of accomplishments.

Although ideologies have become more important than ever before, we cannot and need not start our analysis by making ideological distinctions between the public and the private realm or between democratic and nondemocratic systems. Such distinctions come later, after the theoretical foundations have been laid, and then appear in a more complex form, thanks to a more systematic beginning.

Consider, for example, the role of the individual in the revolution of modernization, and let us suspend ideology in favor of empirically based theory for a moment. We observe that when the traditional structure of accepted patterns for expressing personal demands has been broken, private demands are likely to become

[26] Hannah Arendt, *On Revolution* (New York: 1962), p. 108.

public issues. That is, adult conditions turn out to be radically at variance, and discontinuous with, childhood conditioning, and political socialization also becomes an uncertain and conflict-laden process. It is no longer clear what one's duties are as a tribesman and not yet clear what they are as a citizen. But not only are private demands, in so far as these are the product of conditioning by the social and political system, no longer being assuredly shaped by traditional systems. As accustomed social controls wane, private neurotic conflicts and demands can also be more readily politicalized. And, an area of research perhaps most neglected by all political analysts, ontological demands (i.e., the issues arising from the existence of man as man, from the nature of his being, the questions about man's fate, and man's death, and the meaning of life, and the responsibility one bears for one's self and others) become politicalized.

This transformation of private demands into public issues invariably takes place in a politically crucial minority and in a part of the uprooted but politically still inexperienced masses some time before the first ideology or political system is formed to meet these new challenges. This sequence raises two interesting points for the development of suitable theory. First, it helps to raise the inquiry into the requisites and interactions by which a political system transforms itself to accommodate new kinds of human beings demanding modern kinds of satisfactions to the level of a fundamental historical question. Second, if this is the sequence of events and analysis, theoretical rather than ideological distinctions are first in order at this point. At this stage in the analysis it is too soon to inveigh against trying to solve social problems by political means. We must first come to grips theoretically with the fact that the burden on political systems in process of modernization is far greater than we may know. The unavoidable political task may, at a particular stage in the revolution of modernization, include not only the social and economic realm but the politicalization of personal demands and personal conflicts as well. A criticism of ideologies intended to deal with the revolution of modernization must therefore be based first on a theory that can assess the relevance of ideologies to actual problems posed by this revolution and their costs before there can be grounds for philosophical and moral judgments.

To understand political systems that are characterized by not yet being what they may become or not remaining what they are, we cannot rely on philosophical strictures or test these systems by their deviations from our ideology. We cannot be content with studying selected indices or terms of reference, or utilizing a set of theoretical categories derived from empirical evidence drawn solely from political systems already in existence, and neglecting all potentialities. We find inadequate those theories that start from a conception of order to comprehend change, and so glance off a crucial part of their target. Actual history in Africa, Asia, and Latin America, and originally in Europe, started from an order unaccustomed to systemic change through a transformation which, when present, establishes an order based on change.

I have suggested, therefore, that we conceptualize a changing political system in terms of fundamental historical questions of will, capacity, and imbalances which, at different times during the revolution of modernization, shape its systemic character and especially its capacity to persist, whenever necessary, in the process of systemic transformation. This led, in turn, to the proposal to give new significance to the terms "transitional" and "modernizing." It may be too much to suggest such alterations in the use of established terms. Yet there are advantages in rejecting the present ambiguous concepts of political modernization. "Transitional," as commonly employed, is a term without roots in any particular historical era. As soon as Adam had tasted of the tree of knowledge and Eve was shaken by their ejection from Paradise, Adam could already reassure her by saying that they would have to get used to the fact that they were living in an age of transition. Several thousand years ago a Persian ruler, asking his wise men for the one truth which would always endure, received the reply, "And this too, shall pass away." The term "transitional" masks the revolutionary nature of our era, and the crucial distinction between those who have come to grips with the revolution of modernization and those who have not.

Nor is it useful for any but limited policy purposes to retain the distinction between "underdeveloped" or "developing" societies on the one hand, and "developed" or "industrial" societies on the other. The revolution of modernization is world-wide in scope, and the alternatives available for dealing with its challenges, world-wide in relevance. Thus Germany possessed a modernizing political system in 1928 and 1964, but a transitional system from 1933 to 1948; Fascism and its aftermath are not simply German problems; they raise issues of world-wide comparisons. The United States itself is not exempt from participating in this revolution merely because of the events of 1776. American ideas, American values, American institutions are not yet sufficiently developed to meet the challenges that face us—for maintaining peace, eliminating poverty, ending ignorance and bigotry, for dealing with the sheer growth in the number of people, institutions, and facts, for mastering our technology, and for preserving and spreading beauty. In this respect, the fortunes of the underdeveloped areas are a more dramatic and more intense reflection of our own lives, and their leaders are sometimes more sensitive to the problems of change than ours (and in this sense, more advanced), if not always more skilled in meeting the challenge.

There is a gain also in abandoning the most popular of all ways of defining modernization; namely, in terms of the means (especially economic) relevant to the process of modernization, or of indices most amenable to quantification, or of small clusters of variables selected, usually, from the earlier Western experience of modernization. Any analysis of such particular factors is likely to underestimate, if not miss altogether, the underlying and contextual relevance of systemic transformation. It is also likely to be mistaken, since almost all factors commonly used in such indices may be found separately in traditional societies, and in clusters in some societies we have here called transitional, which must nonetheless be acknowledged as modern societies.

This customary type of factor analysis is likely, also, to mislead the policy maker into supposing that economic development or universal literacy or nation building is modernization. In the context of the revolution of modernization, economic development is destabilizing, by creating, for example, the *nouveaux pauvres*, men who for the first time turn their poverty into an issue because they have learned that it can be remedied.[27] Economic development needs to be destabilizing—for unless old habits, values, and institutions are exchanged for new, investments cannot be creative, or even secure. Economic development must also be restabilizing; but its achievements are tested historically not merely by lusty growth rates or even by capacity to outstrip population growth, vital as that is. The crucial historical pay-off of economic development lies in its

---

[27] See Mancur Olson, Jr., "Rapid Growth as a Destabilizing Force," *Journal of Economic History,* 23 (December 1963), 529–552.

capacity to provide means for overcoming the imbalances created by the revolution of modernization. It must be able to satisfy aspirations, which usually grow more rapidly than population. Such aspirations do not normally qualify under the economist's concept of effective demand, but that is no reason to ignore the fact that they can readily be turned into effective political demand or inhibited, in the absence of systemic transformation, only at the cost of instability or repression.

This same type of analysis applies to education, the emergence of new social classes, new ideologies, and even to the emergence of the most essential of modern men—the competent innovator. In the context of the revolution of modernization, the appearance of none of these constitutes an index, by themselves or in clusters, of the achievement of modernization. They indicate only that there is in process a revolution that must be and will be destabilizing and may or may not be restabilizing, depending on the society's success in systemic transformation.

Stability, commonly defined as persistence and effective control by the elite in power, cannot, therefore, be the criterion for assessing the success of modernization. In the midst of the revolution of modernization, both stability and instability have their cost. Stability, for example, may inhibit modernization and, in the longer run, may well serve to raise the cost of system transformation. Stability, too, is a term that must be defined dynamically. Depending on the cost of the means employed to secure stability and also on the imbalance of pressures in society that need to be resolved through systemic transformation, stability may accompany a revolution, as in Egypt from 1952 to the present. Or stability may raise the cost of a revolution, as in Stalin's U.S.S.R., just as instability may also raise the cost of revolution, as in contemporary Brazil. If we concentrate our analysis and action on stability, and correspondingly on order, we may blind ourselves to the revolution with which, in the modern age, stability and order are now irrevocably entwined.

The main task of theory building and policy planning relevant to the revolution of modernization is not that of finding explanations and remedies for the maladjustment of specific factors in a society thrown off balance. When a system is being transformed, only a system-oriented view will allow us to say what the improved functioning of one structure (e.g., foreign military aid for a Middle

Eastern army) will cost in terms of the rate and direction of change of the entire society. The most crucial questions are: What transformations are required of men whose traditional systems for organizing life are irrevocably disintegrating? What are the alternatives and costs for creating systems that derive their stability from their intrinsic capacity to generate and absorb continuing transformation? What are alternative paths and costs for avoiding the construction of a society that would thus differ so radically from all previous societies? All other questions—concerning governmental structures, economic development, law, violence, or foreign intervention—achieve their fundamental meaning and significance primarily in relation to these historical issues.

We can, of course, continue to respond, as most scholars and most political leaders have responded, by neglecting questions about the system that is evolving and concentrating instead on particular tasks: tribal integration, economic development, party organization, civil rights, and so on. Scholar or politician, one can accomplish much this way. The price of such an approach, however, is that one cannot, in this way, come to know whether one has taken account of all significant relationships, given emphasis to the most crucial interactions, validly assessed relative costs and values, or, above all, understood the direction in which the system as a whole is moving. A piecemeal approach in scholarship or politics is practical enough, provided it is intended as a contribution to the understanding or functioning of a changing system. Otherwise, the approach remains merely particularistic.

Concern with the capacity and direction of system transformation in societies comes, however, at a high price. It is hard, in a language and culture focused on essences and forms, to think of process, transformation, and interaction. It costs more in all realms of life to build and pay for the capacity to deal with the revolution of modernization for ourselves or others than it does merely to build roads or train technicians. It is more painful to transform societies, ideas, or one's self than it is to maintain, enlarge, or modify what we already possess.

Yet as long as we, as a nation, neglect the underlying revolution, we are likely to respond only to its crises which allow only for yea-or-nay decisions, and reinforce, even in American society, the tendency toward hierarchy, secrecy, and pure power. By contrast, a political system oriented toward interventions in the process of history, whether in national or international society, thrives on intellectual collaboration and discussion to guide both analysis and purpose. One of the greatest contributions the United States could make to the conscious transformation of the present unstable world order would be to develop an insightful theory about the character and potentialities of the revolution of modernization.

MARXIST REVOLUTION:
ITS MORAL DIMENSION

10

THE MARXIAN REVOLUTIONARY IDEA

ROBERT C. TUCKER

In his parting word about Marx at Highgate Cemetery, Engels characterized his friend as "before all else a revolutionist." This was a true summation of Marx both as a man of action and as a thinker. For as a theorist Marx was before all else a theorist of revolution. The revolutionary idea was the keystone of his theoretical structure. Marxism, as he fashioned it with the assistance of Engels, was in its essence a theory and program of revolution.

Like many another powerful teaching that becomes the ideology of movements carried on in its name and dedicated to its realization, Marxism has not always reflected its original inspiration. It has tended at various times to lose its "revolutionary soul" (to borrow Lenin's phrase). This happened with the revisionist Marxism of Eduard Bernstein, who forsook even the revolutionary theory of

Marx in favor of a doctrine of evolutionary socialism. It was reflected too, if less obviously, in the orthodox Social Democratic Marxism of Karl Kautsky, whose fidelity to Marxist revolutionism in theory went along with an abandonment of it in practice. A similar if less pronounced discrepancy is becoming apparent in some present-day Soviet Marxism. Its exponents rather resemble the German orthodox Marxists of a generation ago in their tendency to talk Marxist revolutionism while pursuing a relatively unrevolutionary policy. But all these instances of the decline of the revolutionary impulse in the Marxist movement belong to the story of what happened to Marxism after its founder's death. Our subject here is Marx's Marxism, and this was the *Weltanschauung* of a revolutionist.

It was so, moreover, from the beginning of his intellectual career. Marx's first independent act of theorizing, contained in notes to his doctoral dissertation of 1841, was an essay on the necessity of a complete revolutionary transformation of the world in the name of the "realization of philosophy," meaning the Hegelian philosophy of humanity's apotheosis in history. Marx was thus in some sense committed to the idea of world revolution prior to his conversion to the notions of socialism or communism, and he only accepted the latter a year or so later when he found a way of assimilating them into the philosophy of world revolution that he had evolved as a Young Hegelian philosopher. Marxism was born of this fusion in an intellectual process recorded in Marx's *Economic and Philosophic Manuscripts of 1844,* whose publication in the present century presaged a new era in Marxian scholarship in the West.

As a form of socialist doctrine, then, Marxism was inseparable from the idea of revolution. It conceived of socialism or communism (these two terms were always used by Marx and Engels more or less interchangeably) as a radically new state of the world, and of man in the world, which was to be achieved by revolutionary means. This, according to the *Communist Manifesto,* was what distinguished Marxism from the main currents of earlier socialist thought and most earlier socialist movements, which were essentially reformist rather than revolutionary.

The idea of revolution is present in nearly everything that Marx wrote. It is the theoretical axis of his early philosophical writings. It is the *leitmotif* of his great political pamphlets on the 1848 events, the *coup d'état* of Louis Bonaparte, and the Paris Commune. It informs almost all that he has to say on the strategy and tactics of the Communist movement. It is a favorite subject in the voluminous correspondence that he carried on with Engels and others. And his major work, *Capital,* together with his other economic writings, is essentially a political economy of revolution, an inquiry into the conditions of capitalism's revolutionary self-destruction. In a basic sense, therefore, revolution was the master theme of Marx's thought, and an exposition of the Marxian revolutionary idea in complete form would be nothing other than an exposition of Marxism itself as a theoretical system.

It follows that the Marxian revolutionary idea has as many dimensions of meaning as Marxism itself. Revolution for Marx is a social, an economic, a technological, a political, a legal, and an ideological phenomenon. It is even, in its way, a natural phenomenon, for it involves the appropriation of the man-produced world of material objects that Marx describes in his early writings as "anthropological nature" or the "nature produced by history." Furthermore, revolution means transformation of man himself. In Marx's words, "the whole of history is nothing but a continual transformation of human nature."[1] He especially looks to the future Communist revolution as the source of a radical transformation of man or "change of self," and here we touch upon the moral and religious dimensions of the Marxian revolutionary idea. Finally, revolution for Marx is a historical category. The whole of his theory of revolution is set in the frame of the materialist conception of history. His theory of society is a theory of society-in-history, and his theory of revolution is a theory of the transformations of society in history, a theory of history itself as a process of man's revolutionary evolution.

Marx always maintained that his theory of history arose as a metamorphosis of Hegel's. The materialist conception of history was the Hegelian idealist conception turned "upside down" or "back upon its feet." The meaning of this enigmatic contention has only become clear in the light of the 1844 manuscripts, which show that Marxism was indeed born as a metamorphosis of Hegelianism.*

Hegelianism treats world history as the self-realization of God or Spirit (*Geist*). Historicizing the creation of the world as con-

---

[1] *The Poverty of Philosophy* (Chicago: n.d.), p. 160.
* An extended exegesis of Marxism in these terms is presented in the author's *Philosophy and Myth in Karl Marx* (1961).

ceived in the Judaeo-Christian theology, this philosophy pictures creation taking place in historical time as the process by which God becomes fully God *in* the world. Having at first externalized itself in the form of nature, Spirit, acting through humanity, creatively externalizes itself in a succession of historical civilizations or culture worlds, which it appropriates in thought stage by stage through the minds of the great philosophers down to Hegel. History is thus seen as a process of production. God becomes fully God in the course of it by becoming aware of himself as such, for in Hegel's definition self-knowledge or self-consciousness belongs to the nature (or "concept") of God. For God to become aware of himself as such is, moreover, to become aware of himself as infinite being, or of all reality as Spirit, as subjective. Each historical episode of self-knowledge begins with Spirit confronted by a seemingly objective world of "otherness" outside and beyond it. This experience of being bounded by an object is portrayed by Hegel as an experience of finitude, which in turn is an experience of "alienation" (*Entfremdung*). The knowing mind, in other words, experiences the given objective world as alien and hostile in its otherness before recognizing it as Spirit in externalized form. Hence knowing for Hegel is de-alienation whereby the given form of external reality produced by Spirit is stripped of its illusory strangeness and made "property of the ego."[2] The terminal point in the historical process of self-knowledge (which Hegel also describes as a progress of the consciousness of freedom through the overcoming of the fetters of finitude) is the stage of "absolute knowledge" when Spirit finally beholds the absolute totality of creation as Spirit and thus achieves complete self-realization in the knowledge of itself as Absolute Being. This self-knowledge, on Hegel's premises, is reached in Hegelianism—the scientific demonstration of the entire process of world history just summarized.

Marx originally formulated his materialist conception of history as a conscious act of *translation* of this Hegelian phenomenology of history into what he considered realistic or truly scientific terms. Following a lead given by Ludwig Feuerbach, he assumed that one had to draw a distinction between the manifest content of Hegelianism, which was mystical, and the latent or "esoteric" content, which was scientifically sound. What Hegel was esoterically talking about in his philosophy of history as the self-realization of God was the self-

<hr>

[2] *The Phenomenology of Mind* (1931), p. 97.

realization of humanity, the human historical process. Hegelianism was a philosopher's fantasy picture of real human history. The task was to demystify it, which one could do by turning it upside down. That is, one had to switch the subject and predicate in the key propositions of Hegelian theory.

Thus man was not *Geist* in the flesh; rather, *Geist* was the thought process in the head of real material man. History was not the process by which God becomes fully God in man; rather, Hegel's image of history as such a process was a mental representation of actual history as a process by which man becomes fully human. The world-creating activity going on in history was not thought production, not something going on in God's mind; rather, the production of the world by Spirit was Hegel's mystified rendition of the real fact that the world is produced in a historical process of *material* production carried on by man in his economic life. Hence the true and scientific conception of history esoterically present in Hegelianism was a "materialist" one that views man as the universal creator and material production—the production of material objects —as the basic kind of human productive activity. By the same token, Spirit's experience of self-alienation in the presence of an alien and hostile world of its own creation was simply Hegel's mystified way of expressing the real fact that working man experiences alienation in the presence of a world of material objects that he himself has created in "alienated labor" in the service of another man—the capitalist—who appropriates the product as his private property. Appropriation (*Aneignung*) was not, therefore, something going on in the philosopher's mind; rather, the Hegelian notion of the cognitive appropriation of the world by Spirit was an inverted representation of the material appropriation of objects in history, the accumulation of capital. Further, the overcoming of alienation was not a process that could take place simply in thought. As the alienated world was a world of real material things and productive powers, the appropriation of it by the exploited and alienated producers, the proletarians, would have to take place in a real revolution—a Communist revolution consisting in the world-wide seizure and socialization of private property. And finally, Hegel's picture of the ultimate stage of "absolute knowledge," when Spirit contemplates the whole world as Spirit in the beatific moment of complete self-awareness in freedom, was the philosopher's fantasy of ultimate communism, when man would achieve self-fulfillment in creative activity and aesthetic experience of the no longer alienated world surrounding him.

Such was Marxism, or the materialist conception of history, in its original presentation in Marx's 1844 manuscripts as an inverted Hegelianism. Much was refined and added in the subsequent development of the system by Marx and Engels. Yet this "original Marxism" was the matrix of the mature Marxist *Weltanschauung*. Even where a seeming break occurred, as in the abandonment of the category of "alienation" in the mature restatements of the theory beginning with Marx's in Part I of *The German Ideology,* we find an underlying continuity of thought; for the content of the idea of alienation lives on in the special meaning assigned in mature Marxism to the concept of "division of labor."

The fundamental ideas of original Marxism remained, explicitly or implicitly, the presuppositions of Marx's thought. Having defined history in the 1844 manuscripts as man's "act of becoming," he continued to see it as the process of self-development of the human species or society. For Marx, history is the growth process of humanity from the primitive beginnings to complete maturity and self-realization in future communism. Since man is conceived in this system as a creative being or producer in his essential nature, his developmental process is, as Marx had called it in his early manuscripts, a *Produktionsgeschichte* or history of production, with material production as the primary kind of productive activity. It proceeds through a series of epochs marked by the division of mankind into warring classes toward the postulated Communist future. The transitions from epoch to epoch are revolutionary, for "Revolutions are the locomotives of history."[3]

Understandably, much of the literature of and about Marxism as a revolutionary theory has a political orientation. Marxists beginning with Marx and Engels have been deeply concerned with the politics of revolution, and very many students of Marxist thought have interested themselves in this too. It is perhaps a measure, and in any event a symptom of this bias, that Lenin's principal treatise on Marxist revolutionary theory, *State and Revolution,* is almost wholly devoted to revolution as a political phenomenon. Now there

[3] Marx, *The Class Struggles in France 1848–1850* (New York: n.d.), p. 120.

is no doubt about the great importance of this aspect of the Marxian revolutionary idea. For Marx, every revolutionary transition from one social epoch to the next involves a political revolution—the overthrow of the existing state and conquest of political power by the revolutionary class. But to Marx's way of thinking this is not the core of the revolutionary process. Here, indeed, we encounter a certain difference of emphasis between the Marxism of Marx and that of Lenin, for whom the political process of revolution was of supreme importance both theoretically and practically. Without ever slighting the significance of the political dimension, Marx, on the other hand, always saw *social* revolution as the fundamental revolutionary fact. In the analogy between revolution and the birth process that recurs from time to time in his writings, the social revolution is the whole organic process by which a new society comes into being; the political revolution is merely a momentous incident occurring at the climax of the process. The principal question to be considered here, therefore, is what Marx meant by a social revolution.

In *The Social Revolution,* an influential little volume written in 1902, Kautsky answered this question in behalf of German orthodox Marxism by defining social revolution as "the conquest of political power by a previously subservient class and the transformation of the juridical and political superstructure of society, particularly in the property relations. . . ." As Kautsky himself pointed out, this was a "narrower" view than Marx's own as expressed in the well-known preface to the *Critique of Political Economy.*[4] It also suffered from superficiality. Although the supplanting of one ruling class by another is integral to social revolution as Marx conceives it, this formula fails to convey the substance of what he means by social revolution. To arrive at a more adequate formulation, we must first consider Marx's conception of society.

Marx the sociologist is inseparable from Marx the theorist of history. The view of society presented in his own mature writings and those of Engels is governed at every point by the basic premises of the materialist conception of history. One of the expressions of this is the fact that Marx as a social theorist recognizes the existence of societies on a national scale but does not see in them the fundamental unit of society. For him the real social unit is the species, the human collectivity at a given stage of its historical

[4] *The Social Revolution* (1913), pp. 6, 8–9, 27.

growth process. Each such stage constitutes a social epoch dominated by a particular "social formation." Any national society, such as the German, English, or French, is but a concrete expression of human society as a whole in the given epoch, although it may be a case that exhibits the general pattern of the existing or emerging social formation most clearly and in most mature development. Marx, for example, saw contemporary English society as the model and most advanced form of a universally emerging "bourgeois society" of the modern epoch. This bourgeois or capitalist social formation, now becoming dominant on a world scale, had been preceded in history by feudal, antique, and Asiatic social formations, each of which represented the dominant form of human society in its time. An important implication for Marx's theory of revolution is that he always sees a social revolution as universal in scope, as an event of world history. It may express itself here and there on a national scale, as in the French Revolution of 1789, but such a happening is only a partial and local manifestation of a world revolutionary process. For Marx all social revolutions are world revolutions.

The materialist conception of history underlies all other aspects of Marx's sociology. Man being essentially a producer and his history a "history of production," society, to Marx's way of thinking, is in essence a productive system and process. The constitutive fact of society is that human productive activity, especially the material production on which all else depends, is social in nature. In other words, production, for Marx, is a process going on not simply between man and nature but also between man and man. This "social process of production" is the core of the social process per se. Human society is fundamentally a society of production, a set of "social relations" that men enter in the activity of producing. In the familiar formulation from *The Critique of Political Economy,* the social relations of production constitute the "basis" (*Basis, Grundlage*) of society, over which rises an institutional superstructure, and to which there corresponds a social mind expressed in various "ideological forms" (religion, philosophy, art, etc.).[5]

Since primitive times, according to Marx, the society of production has been a divided one. The social relations of production have been property relations between the immediate producers and those who, by virtue of their ownership and control of the means of production, have been able to appropriate the producers' surplus

[5] Marx and Engels, *Selected Works,* Vol. I (Moscow: 1958), p. 363.

product as private property: slaves and slave owners in ancient society, serfs and landowning nobles in feudal society, proletarians and capitalists in modern bourgeois society. Each one of these sets of social relations of production has been, in Marx's terminology, a specific form of the division of labor (*Teilung der Arbeit*) in production. This concept has a twofold meaning in Marxist thought. First, it refers to occupational specialization in all its forms, beginning with the division between mental and physical labor and between town and country. But it also refers to what may be called the "social division of labor," meaning the division of society as a whole into a nonworking minority class of owners of the means of production and a nonowning majority class of workers. As already indicated, Marx holds that such a social division of labor has been the essential feature of human society so far in history. The prime expression of the division of labor is the class division of society. In Engels' words, "It is . . . the law of the division of labor which lies at the root of the division into classes."[6] Marx makes the same point more concretely when he writes: "In so far as millions of families live under economic conditions of existence that divide their mode of life, their interests and their culture from those of other classes, and put them in hostile contrast to the latter, they form a class."[7]

The determination of the class structure of society by the nature of the social division of labor may be expressed in Marxist terms by saying that every society is characterized by its particular "mode of production" (*Produktionsweise*). Contrary to what one might suppose, this key concept of Marx's is primarily social rather than technological in content, although it has a technological element. The mode of production is not equated with the productive techniques or material "productive powers," which are included, rather, under the heading of "means of production" (*Produktionsmittels*). What Marx means by the mode of production is the prevailing mode of labor or productive activity as conditioned by the existing state of technology or means of production. Now productive activity, as already noted, is for Marx exclusively and essentially social activity. Accordingly, the mode of production is equivalent to the social relations of production viewed, as it were, dynamically or in motion, together with the conditioning state of technology. And inasmuch

[6] *Anti-Dühring* (Moscow: 1947), p. 418.
[7] *The 18th Brumaire of Louis Bonaparte* (New York: n.d.), p. 109.

as the social relations of production have, so far in history, been successive forms of the division of labor in production, the various historical modes of production may be described as forms of productive activity within the division of labor. Production within the division of labor has thus been the *general* mode of production in history. In Engels' formulation, "The basic form of all former production is the division of labor, on the one hand within society as a whole, and on the other, within each separate productive establishment."[8]

The central thesis of Marxist sociology is that every society in history has been characterized and, indeed, shaped in all its manifold aspects, by the nature of its particular mode of production as just defined. In ancient society the mode of production was slave labor, or productive activity performed within the social division of labor between master and slave. In feudal society it was serf labor, or productive activity performed within the social division of labor between nobleman and serf. And in modern bourgeois society it is wage labor, or productive activity carried on within the social division of labor between capitalist and proletarian. In every instance —runs the argument of Marx and Engels—the mode of productive activity has been the definitive fact of the social epoch, the determinant of the character of society in all of its superstructural expressions: political, legal, intellectual, religious, etc. To this way of thinking, every society fundamentally *is* its mode of production. Speaking of wage labor, for example, Marx writes: "Without it there is no capital, no bourgeoisie, no bourgeois society."[9]

It follows that a social revolution in the Marxist definition is a change in the mode of production with consequent change of all subordinate elements of the social complex. The feudal revolution would be defined in these terms as the change from slave labor to serf labor resulting in the general transition to feudal society; the bourgeois revolution as the change from serf labor to wage labor resulting in the general transition to bourgeois society. Historically, argue Marx and Engels, these revolutions in the mode of production and therewith, in society as a whole, have been changes of the *specific form* of productive activity within the social division of labor. They have been revolutions within the general mode of production based upon the division of labor in society and the produc-

[8] *Anti-Dühring,* p. 432.
[9] *The Class Struggles in France 1848–1850,* p. 42.

tion process, i.e., upon the class division of society and occupational specialization.

Turning to the technological aspect of the theory, Marx holds, as pointed out above, that every historical mode of production has been conditioned by the nature of the available means of production or state of technology. As he puts it in a vivid passage, "The windmill gives you society with the feudal lord; the steam-mill, society with the industrial capitalist."[10] On this view, the rise of a new technology, a new set of material productive powers, will necessarily prove incompatible with the perpetuation of a mode of production associated with an older one. The rise of modern manufacturing technique led to the bourgeois revolution against serf labor and feudal society and to the enthronement of wage labor as the mode of production. Marx further supposes that the transition from early capitalist manufacture to "machinofacture" in the Industrial Revolution has brought into existence a new set of productive powers—modern machine industry—that must and will prove incompatible with the perpetuation of wage labor as the prevailing mode of production, since the new powers of production cannot be fully developed under the system of wage labor. The destruction of wage labor, and with it, of bourgeois society, in a proletarian and communist revolution is the predicted outcome. Reasoning in this way, Marx and Engels frequently define a social revolution as the resolution of a conflict or "contradiction" between the productive powers and the social relations of production, or as a "rebellion" of the former against the latter.

This "rebellion" is not understood in mechanistic terms. A social revolution originates in technological change but actually takes place, according to Marx, in a revolutionary social-political movement of producers as a class. It is not the material powers of production themselves, such as the machines, that rebel against the mode of production; it is the men involved. This presents no problem of inconsistency for Marx, however, because he views working man as the supreme productive power. "Of all the instruments of production," he writes, "the greatest productive power is the revolutionary class itself."[11] It is this productive power whose uprising constitutes the actual revolutionary process. The revolt of the productive powers against the existing social relations of production finds its manifesta-

---

[10] *The Poverty of Philosophy,* p. 119.
[11] *Ibid.,* p. 190.

tion in class warfare in the economic arena, culminating in the political act of revolutionary overthrow of the state. If revolutions are the locomotives of history, class struggles are the locomotives of revolution.

What motivates a class of producers to rise against and revolutionize a mode of production and its social superstructure? Suffering caused by material want and poverty is one of the immediate driving forces of revolutionary action, especially with the modern proletariat. But in Marx's view, material satisfaction as such is never the actual aim of the revolutionary class in its struggle to overthrow and transform an established social formation. What is fundamentally at issue in the class struggle and in social revolution, as in history as a whole, is not the consumption interest but the production interest—this, however, defined in a special Marxist way.

It is man as frustrated producer rather than man as dissatisfied consumer who makes a revolution, and the need of man as producer is freely to develop and express his manifold powers of productive activity, his creative potentialities in material life. Under this heading Marx includes both the productive powers within men and also industry, or the material productive forces employed by the human species in its productive interaction with nature. Thus in *Capital* he describes the material forces of production as "the productive organs of men in society" and compares them with "the organs of plants and animals as productive instruments utilized for the life purposes of these creatures."[12] His thesis is that the source of revolutionary energy in a class is the frustration of man in his capacity of producer, his inability to develop new powers of production to the full within the confines of an existing mode of production or socioeconomic order. The bourgeois revolution, for example, results from the inability of the rising capitalist class to develop the new productive powers inherent in manufacture within the cramping confines of feudal relationships. And he believes—wrongly as it turns out—that a proletarian revolution will be necessitated by the impossibility of fully developing the productive potentials of modern machine industry within the confines of wage labor as the mode of production. In each instance the effect of the revolution is to eliminate a set of social relations of production that has become, in Marx's Hegelian terminology, a "fetter" upon the evolving pro-

[12] *Capital,* Eden and Cedar Paul, trans. (1933), p. 392n.

ductive powers of the species, and thus to "emancipate" these powers. The goal of all social revolutions, according to Marx, is freedom. But freedom in a specifically Marxist sense: the liberation of human creativity.

The obstacle to freedom, the source of human bondage, and thus the evil in history, is the division of labor. This fundamental proposition of Marxist theory has several meanings, all closely interconnected. Not only does each successive historical form of the social division of labor between an owning and a producing class become an impediment to the free development of emergent productive powers; the social division of labor is also a force for enslavement in that it subjects the producer class to the acquisitive urge of the owning class, the insensate greed for possession and power that Marx sees as the dominant motive force of historical development up to now. (We read in Engels: ". . . it is precisely the wicked passions of man—greed and the lust for power—which, since the emergence of class antagonisms, serve as levers of historical development. . . ."[13]) Man's life in production is thereby transformed into a life of drudgery, of forced labor or "alienated labor" as Marx called it in his manuscripts of 1844, and always continued to view it. Above all is this true in modern society where the worker, although legally free to seek employment wherever he will, is bound down to wage labor, which Marx calls "wage slavery" and describes, in *Capital* and other writings, as productive activity performed in servitude to the capitalist profit mania, the "werewolf hunger" for surplus value.[14]

Finally, every social division of labor is an enemy of human freedom, for Marx, in so far as it enforces occupational specialization as a way of life. "For as soon as labor is distributed, each man has a particular, exclusive sphere of activity, which is forced upon him and from which he cannot escape. He is a hunter, a fisherman, a shepherd, or a critical critic, and must remain so if he does not want to lose his means of livelihood. . . ."[15] It is Marx's view, in other words, that a division of labor under which men are compelled by economic necessity to devote themselves throughout life to one particular form of work activity, be it a specialized economic function, or a noneconomic calling such as a profession or governmental work, or even intellectual activity, is slavery. And this is by no means

[13] Engels, *Ludwig Feuerbach,* in Marx and Engels, *Selected Works,* Vol. II (Moscow: 1951), pp. 345–346.
[14] *Capital,* p. 269.
[15] *The German Ideology* (1947), p. 22.

a view that Marx, as it were, "outgrew" in the later development of his system. Thus he speaks, in the famous passage of "The Critique of the Gotha Program," on the higher phase of communist society, of the disappearance there of "the *enslaving* subordination of man to the division of labor."[16] Engels is just as explicit and even more concrete when he writes:

> not only the laborers, but also the classses directly or indirectly exploiting the laborers, are made subject, through the division of labor, to the tool of their function; the empty-minded bourgeois to his own capital and his own thirst for profits; the lawyer to his fossilized legal conceptions, which dominate him as a power independent of him; the "educated classes" in general to their manifold local limitations and one-sidedness, to their own physical and mental shortsightedness, to their stunted specialized education and the fact that they are chained for life to this specialized activity itself, even when this specialized activity is merely to do nothing.[17]

This is a theme that has not always been much emphasized or even noted in the literature on Marxism. An influential school of Soviet Marxists has even undertaken to expunge it from Marxism, denying that Marx was opposed to occupational specialization as a way of life.[18] But this is to deny the undeniable. The proposition that occupational specialization is slavery and that it can and should be done away with is met constantly in the writings of Marx and Engels, including such major works of mature Marxism as *Capital* and *Anti-Dühring,* and it is of fundamental importance in Marxism as they understood it.

Underlying their condemnation of the division of labor is the

[16] Marx and Engels, *Selected Works,* Vol. II (Moscow: 1951), p. 23. Italics added.

[17] *Anti-Dühring,* pp. 435–436.

[18] It should be added that among Soviet Marxists there are also some defenders of the authentic views of Marx on this question. One is Academician S. G. Strumilin, who has recently accused the dominant school of Soviet Marxists of resorting to outright falsification of Marx's language in its effort to misrepresent the true Marxist position on the desirability and possibility of doing away with the division of labor in the sense of occupational specialization as a way of life. This, he points out, was done by consciously mistranslating *Verteilung der Arbeit* as "division of labor" (the correct translation would be "distribution of labor") in a 1947 Russian translation of Marx's letter of July 11, 1868, to Ludwig Kugelmann. To prove that the mistranslation was deliberate, Strumilin mentions that the phrase was correctly translated "distribution of labor" in Volume XXV of the Russian edition of the collected works of Marx and Engels, published in 1934 ("Razdelenie truda i vsestoronee razvitie lichnosti," *Voprosy Filosofii,* No. 3, 1963, p. 39).

philosophical anthropology inherited by Marxism from earlier German philosophy, Hegelianism in particular. Marx's *Mensch* resembles Hegel's *Geist* in that both are imbued with a need for totality of life experience, for creative self-expression in all possible fields of activity. Thus Hegel speaks of Spirit as "manifesting, developing and perfecting its powers in every direction which its manifold nature can follow," adding: "What powers it inherently possesses, we learn from the variety of products and formations which it originates."[19] It is the same with the human species in Marx's image of it. And in view of the fact, noted earlier, that Marx constructed the materialist conception of history on the premise that Hegel's *Geist* was a mystified representation of man in his history of production, it is not at all surprising that the Marxist view of human nature shows this strain of Hegelian philosophical romanticism. Like Hegel's *Geist,* Marx's humanity develops and perfects its productive powers in every possible direction, and man as an individual shows this same tendency. A man's inherent bent— that is, his nature—is to become, as Marx puts it in *Capital,* "an individual with an all-round development (*total entwickelte Individuum*), one for whom various social functions are alternative modes of activity."[20] Consequently, the division of labor is unnatural and inhuman, an impediment to a human being's self-realization. A person who applies himself to one single life activity is alienated from his real nature, hence a self-estranged man. "In the division of labor," writes Engels, "man is divided. All other physical and mental faculties are sacrificed to the development of one single activity."[21] Even the division between town and country, between urban and rural labor, is on this view "a subjection which makes one man into a restricted town-animal, the other into a restricted country-animal."[22] And to be restricted to a particular kind of life or occupation is to be unfree.

The enslavement and dehumanization of man under the division of labor is a dominant theme of *Capital* and the other writings of Marx and Engels on capitalism and the proletarian revolution. They morally condemn capitalism not for being unjust as a mode of distribution (indeed, they hold that it is the only just one in terms of the sole applicable criterion of judgment), but for being inhuman

[19] *The Philosophy of History* (1956), p. 73.
[20] *Capital,* p. 527.
[21] *Anti-Dühring,* p. 435.
[22] *The German Ideology,* p. 44.

as a mode of production, an unnatural way for man to carry on his productive activity. What makes it so, they maintain, is above all the hideous extreme to which it develops the division of labor. The capitalist mode of production—wage labor in the service of the drive for surplus value—is a system of division of labor within the division of labor. That is, within the social division of labor between capitalist and proletarian, which Marx calls the "despotism" or "dictatorship" of capital, the worker is subjected to an increasingly oppressive form of occupational specialization. He is reduced to a mere detail worker bound down to a single mindless operation endlessly repeated. As capitalism evolves from the stage of "simple cooperation" into that of manufacture, it brings "the lifelong annexation of the worker to a partial function," which "cuts at the very roots of the individual's life" and "transforms the worker into a cripple, a monster, by forcing him to develop some highly specialized dexterity at the cost of a world of productive impulses and faculties —much as in Argentina they slaughter a whole beast simply in order to get its hide or its tallow."[23]

Moreover, the inner dynamism or dialectic of capitalist production is such—according to Marx's argument—that the functions become increasingly subdivided, the specialization more and more minute, and hence the fragmentation of man more and more monstrous, as the employers, under relentless pressure of the competitive struggle, strive for greater and greater technical efficiency through mechanization of work processes. The total dehumanization of the worker comes about finally under modern "machinofacture," the descriptions of which in *Capital* resemble a *Modern Times* without the Chaplinesque anodyne of humor. Of this stage—which he treats as the stage in which capitalist production becomes wholly unendurable—Marx writes, for example, that here all the means for developing production "mutilate the worker into a fragment of a human being, degrade him to become a mere appurtenance of the machine, make his work such a torment that its essential meaning is destroyed; estrange from him the intellectual potentialities of the labor process in very proportion to the extent to which science is incorporated into it as an independent power. . . ."[24] Progress in technological terms thus spells regress in human terms, and man sinks to the nadir of wretchedness and self-estrangement in the production

[23] *Capital,* pp. 381, 384, 390.
[24] *Ibid.,* p. 713.

process at the very time in history when his productivity, technically speaking, reaches its peak and, providentially, brings with it the possibility of a thoroughly human way of life in production. This "slavery" and "labor torment" under the division of labor represents a major share of the ever increasing misery of the proletarian masses that drives them at length, according to Marx's argument, to revolt against their mode of production.[25]

The human history of production is thus also a history of revolution. The growth process of society is propelled by a series of revolutions that center in major changes in the mode of production as a social process. These changes have been the very substance of the social history of man. It is true that Marx speaks of an "epoch of social revolution" as something occurring when a form of society nears its end.[26] Yet in a way he believes that history has always, up to now, been a revolutionary process, that man has always been at least incipiently in revolt against his mode of production. This, after all, is the sense of the opening statement of the *Communist Manifesto* that the whole of recorded history is a history of class struggles. Why it should be so on Marx's premises has been made clear. Every mode of production in history has been a form of productive activity within the division of labor, and the division of labor is bondage. In Marx's mind, history is a succession of man's revolutionary breaks out of the prison-house of the division of labor for freedom in the life of production.

No sooner has a new mode of production within the division of labor been established by revolutionary means than it too starts to become a "fetter" upon the ever developing productive powers of the species. Such is the revolutionary dialectic of the historical process as Marx expounds it. Just as men begin to die biologically as soon as they are born, so societies embark upon their own revolutionary dissolution virtually from the time of their revolutionary "birth pangs." So we shall look in vain in Marx for a sociology in the sense of a theory of how societies work. His is a sociology of revolution, a theory of the internal dysfunctioning of the several historical societies, leading to their disintegration and downfall. Thus *Capital*, which is Marx's principal treatise on society and revolution as well as his chief work of economic theory, treats of the revolutionary

[25] *Ibid.*
[26] "Preface to *The Critique of Political Economy*," Marx and Engels, *Selected Works*, Vol. I, p. 363.

rise, development, and fall of bourgeois society. And the whole thrust of the book is toward the "knell" of the proletarian revolution that it tolls in conclusion.

The proletarian revolution is described in various places in Marx and Engels as the overthrow of the bourgeois state and establishment of a proletarian dictatorship, accompanied by the forcible seizure and socialization of private property in the means of production. But this is only the external manifestation, the "phenomenal form" of the communist revolution. Like all previous social revolutions, the revolution of communism is, for Marx and Engels, essentially a change in the mode of production. And like all past revolutions again, it is both destructive, in that it does away with an old mode of production, and constructive, in that it establishes a new one in its place.

This presentation of the socialist or communist revolution, and hence of socialism or communism itself, as turning principally upon production, stands in substantial contrast with the view of most socialists, both of that time and now, that socialism is mainly concerned with the distribution problem. Marx and Engels were well aware of this difference. They often called attention to it in emphatic and even polemical terms. They argued that changes in the mode of distribution, leading to the practice of distribution according to needs in the higher phase of communist society, would only be incidental by-products of a change in the mode of production that would be the real substance of the revolution of communism. Marx, for example, attacks what he calls "vulgar socialism" for the "consideration and treatment of distribution as independent of the mode of production, and hence the presentation of socialism as turning principally on distribution." He states in the same passage that "it was in general a mistake to make a fuss about so-called *distribution* and put the principal stress on it."[27] In the same vein Engels pours scorn on Eugen Dühring for basing his "socialitarian" program on the unacceptable proposition that "the capitalist mode of *production* is quite good, and can remain in existence, but the capitalist mode of *distribution* is evil." He comments in this connection on "how puerile Herr Dühring's notions are—that society can take possession of the means of production without revolutionizing

[27] "Critique of the Gotha Program," Marx and Engels, *Selected Works,* Vol. II, pp. 23–24.

from top to bottom the old method of production and in particular putting an end to the old division of labor."[28]

If the communist revolution resembles all past revolutions in that it primarily revolutionizes the old mode of production, it also, according to Marx and Engels, differs from all other revolutions in history; and this thesis on the uniqueness of the projected world communist revolution is of the greatest importance in Marxist thought. The argument is that what undergoes revolutionizing in the communist revolution is not simply a particular form of productive activity within the division of labor (in this case wage labor), but the division of labor as such. Instead of replacing one form of productive activity within the division of labor by another, as the bourgeois revolution replaced serf labor by wage labor, the communist revolution will pave the way for a radically new mode of production that altogether abolishes and transcends the division of labor and therewith "labor" itself, in the sense in which mankind has always known it (i.e., in the sense of "alienated labor" in the terminology of the 1844 manuscripts). As the younger Marx formulated it, "In all revolutions up to now the mode of activity always remained unscathed and it was only a question of a different distribution of this activity, a new distribution of labor to other persons, whilst the communist revolution is directed against the preceding *mode* of activity, does away with *labor*, and abolishes the rule of classes with the classes themselves. . . ."[29] Over twenty years later the older Marx was saying the same thing when he wrote in *Capital* that the "revolutionary ferments" in modern capitalist society have as their aim "the abolition of the old division of labor."[30]

By the abolition of the old division of labor he and Engels mean, first, the abolition of the class division of society into owners of the means of production and nonowning workers. This will spell the abolition of wage labor after an interim during which old habits of working for a remuneration, and also the lack of full material abundance, will enforce a continuation of wage labor in a noncapitalist form, performed for social needs rather than in the service of the drive for profit. The disappearance of the latter as the motive force of production will make possible the withering away of the division of labor in all its subordinate forms—the division between

[28] *Anti-Dühring*, pp. 443, 445.
[29] *The German Ideology*, p. 69.
[30] *Capital*, p. 527.

mental and physical labor, between urban and rural labor, between different trades and professions, and between different functions in each. For as soon as man is no longer compelled by the imperatives of greed and need to engage in some one form of productive activity all his life, he will give rein to the natural human tendency (as Marx sees it) to become a universal man—"to do one thing today and another tomorrow, to hunt in the morning, fish in the afternoon, rear cattle in the evening, criticize after dinner, just as I have a mind, without ever becoming hunter, fisherman, shepherd or critic."[31] Within the factory the detail worker, annexed for life to a particular specialized function, will give way to the "individual of all-round development" for whom various functions in production are possible. Marx based this expectation, which may have been prophetic, upon the view that in modern machine industry, where machines themselves do highly specialized work, the technical foundation is established for liberating men from narrow specialization. "Since the integral movement of the factory does not proceed from the worker but from the machine," he reasoned in *Capital,* "there can be a continuous change of personnel without any interruption of the labor process."[32] Machine industry without the division of labor would thus be based upon rotation of jobs among highly trained and versatile machine operators, whose work would become a form of free productive activity owing to the constant variation and to the "almost artistic nature of their occupation."[33]

Since Marx and Engels believe that every form of society fundamentally *is* its mode of production, most of what they have to say about the future communist society (in its "higher phase") is naturally concerned with the anticipated new mode of productive activity. But the latter, as we see, is not analyzed in economic terms. This omission of an economics of communism from the theory of Marx and Engels is entirely logical considering that part of what they mean by communism is *the end of economics.* They assume that with the emancipation of the immensely potent productive forces inherent in modern machine industry from the "fetters" of capitalist wage labor, there will very soon be created a material abundance so great as to satisfy all proper human needs. At this point, which is the entry point into the "higher phase," the historic

[31] *The German Ideology,* p. 22.
[32] *Capital,* p. 449.
[33] *Ibid.,* p. 405.

scarcity of goods and resources ceases, and therewith the need for economics as a theory and practice of allocation of scarce goods and resources. "And at this point," writes Engels, "man in a certain sense separates finally from the animal world, leaves the conditions of animal existence behind him, and enters conditions which are really human. . . . It is humanity's leap from the realm of necessity into the realm of freedom."[34] For Marx and Engels this "leap" is a take-off not into affluence as such, but into the authentically human higher form of existence that man's creative and artistic nature, as they see it, naturally tends toward and for which material well-being is no more than a precondition. The end of economics means the beginning of aesthetics as the keynote of the life of productive activity.[35]

In Marxist theory the communist revolution is the supreme revolution of freedom since it does away not simply with this or that specific form of the division of labor but with all forms, and so with bondage as such. By the same token, this is the last revolution. With production no longer based upon a division of labor in society, there will be no kind of social relations of production that could become a fetter upon the productive powers, and thereby precipitate a further revolutionary upheaval. Accordingly, the communist revolution will bring to an end the historical growth process of humanity —the "pre-history of human society" as Marx called it in a well-known passage.[36] It will mark the maturation of the species, the time when man finally becomes fully human. In his early manuscripts Marx used the terms "humanism" and "transcendence of human self-alienation" to express this idea. Later the German philosophical terminology was abandoned, but the idea was not. The communist revolution continued to be conceived as a revolution of human self-realization.

This self-realization is understood by Marx in both collective and individual terms. On the one hand, it means the completion of the whole historical process of self-development of the species, the becoming of human society. At this point "socialized humanity" (*vergesellschaftete Menschheit*) emerges out of what had been, all through recorded history, a self-divided and inwardly warring hu-

---

[34] *Anti-Dühring*, pp. 420–421.

[35] For a fuller exposition of this theme in Marxist thought, see *Philosophy and Myth in Karl Marx*, chapter XIII.

[36] "Preface to *The Critique of Political Economy*," Marx and Engels, *Selected Works*, Vol. I, p. 364.

man collectivity.[37] The communist revolution, an act of appropriation by the vast majority of the totality of material means of production, is the means by which this final transformation is supposed to take place. The reasoning turns on Marx's view, mentioned earlier, that industry, the total complex of material instruments or powers of production, represents the "productive organs of men in society." Seen in this perspective, the communist revolution is the act by which man in the mass reappropriates his own organs of productive activity, of which he has been dispossessed in history owing to the division of labor in its various forms. By this collective act—runs Marx's argument—the individuals of whom the mass is composed regain their creative potentialities: "The appropriation of a totality of instruments of production is, for this very reason, the development of a totality of capacities in the individuals themselves."[38] This is the basis on which Marx advances the thesis that the change of material circumstances brought about by revolutionary praxis coincides with "change of self."[39]

It follows that man must realize himself on the scale of the species before he can do so as an individual, that there is no self-realization without social revolution. Before the communist revolution, no one can be truly human; afterwards, all can and will become so. Then and then only will free creativity become the characteristic human mode of production, will labor become "not only a means of life but life's prime want."[40] Then only will the human society of production become one in which "productive labor, instead of being a means to the subjection of men, will become a means to their emancipation, by giving each individual the opportunity to develop and exercise all his faculties, physical and mental, in all directions; in which, therefore, productive labor will become a pleasure instead of a burden."[41] Liberated from the acquisitive urge that has always in the past motivated the production process, and also from the slavery of specialization that this has engendered, men will finally become freely creative individuals, accomplished in a multitude of life activities, who produce without

---

[37] "Theses on Feuerbach," *The German Ideology,* p. 199.
[38] *The German Ideology,* p. 66.
[39] "Theses on Feuerbach," *The German Ideology,* p. 198.
[40] "Critique of the Gotha Program," Marx and Engels, *Selected Works,* Vol. II, p. 23.
[41] *Anti-Dühring,* p. 438.

being driven to it by the forces of need and greed and who arrange their world according to the laws of beauty.

That the Marxian revolutionary idea has a moral meaning is clear enough. But this dimension would, it seems, be more accurately described as religious than as ethical in nature. Moral teachers desire man to be virtuous according to one or another understanding of virtue; religious ones—Marx among them—want him to be redeemed. In this connection it must be said that there is a close relation between revolution and religion. Though the founders of revolutionary movements need not be men of religion, the founders of religions tend in their way to be revolutionaries. They envisage for man a goal of supreme worth that involves his total self-transformation, the revolutionizing of himself as it were, and they give him directions concerning the way to the goal. Marx does the same, and on this account may be characterized as a revolutionist of religious formation. The goal had variously been called the Kingdom of God, Paradise, Nirvana, Satori, Salvation; he called it Communism. When he wrote in his eleventh thesis that the point was to change the world, the message was that changing the world outside of man, by revolutionary praxis, was the way to change man himself, totally. There is little question about the religious quality of Marx's vision of the goal. The question that would have to be raised, in an examination of the religious aspect of his thought, is whether he offered valid directions as to the way.

11

MARX ON REVOLUTIONIZING THE MODE OF PRODUCTION

DAVID BRAYBROOKE

In his account, "The Marxian Revolutionary Idea," Robert C. Tucker does a thoroughly convincing job of showing that, for Karl Marx, "the revolution of communism is . . . essentially a change in the mode of production." If one does not recognize, with Tucker, that reorganizing the ways in which men carry on productive labor in society was to be the paramount feature of the revolution that Marx expected and called for, whereas raising the standard of living of the working class was at most a secondary objective, one will not easily understand Marx's intransigent contempt for temporizing provisions asked and offered under the heading of "social justice." One will also be misled by Marx's recurrent preoccupation with violent means for overthrowing the bourgeois state and the bourgeois class structure. Marx may have thought of violence as both eschatologically fitting and instrumentally indispensable; but the use of violence, I think, does not have the same indisputable claim as the matters that Tucker stresses to ranking among the logically essential conditions of accomplishing the revolution. (If it did, would Marx ever have speculated, even fleetingly, about the possibility of accomplishing the revolution without violence in a few countries with exceptionally favorable political histories?)[1]

Suppose, concurring in the judicious stresses of Tucker's exposition, that we treat transforming the mode of production as an essential feature of the proletarian revolution; and suppose (in accordance with Tucker's judicious neglect of the subject) that we relegate the use of violence to a subordinate place outside the list of essential features. Then, I think, Marx's case for the revolution's being necessary to regenerate human life in society in the respects important to him—which are respects of continuing interest to ourselves—becomes a great deal more compelling than is commonly allowed, more compelling even than Tucker allows, though he has done much to put us in a position to make due allowance.

Tucker says, "[Marx] believes—wrongly as it turns out—that a proletarian revolution will be necessitated by the impossibility of fully developing the productive potentials of modern machine industry within the confines of wage labor as the mode of production." (p. 228.) Possibly Tucker disagrees with Marx about the general doctrine of historical determinism; but we need not raise that issue. I take it that the quotation warrants our saying that Tucker disbelieves (while Marx believed) the following proposition: *A proletarian revolution is required in order to fully develop the productive potentials of modern industry.*

But can Tucker—or anyone else—have grounds for disbelieving this proposition? If, as Tucker rightly argues, transforming the mode

[1] See the well-known remarks about England, the United States, and (more tentatively) Holland, which Marx made in a speech delivered in the last-named country in 1872—quoted by Hans Kelsen in *The Political Theory of Bolshevism* (Berkeley and Los Angeles: 1948), pp. 40–41, following (according to Kelsen's citation) Karl Kautsky, *The Dictatorship of the Proletariat,* 2nd ed. (Manchester: 1920), pp. 9ff. See also Marx's letter to Hyndman of December 8, 1880, in H. H. Hyndman, *The Record of an Adventurous Life* (London: 1911), p. 283, which Karl Popper quotes on pp. 155 and 341 of *The Open Society,* Vol. II, 3rd ed. (London: 1957). Cf. Engels' pronouncements in favor of parliamentary activity in his introduction to the 1895 edition of *Class Struggles in France;* cited to make another point by John Plamenatz, *German Marxism and Russian Communism* (London: 1954), pp. 164–167. See K. Marx and F. Engels, *Selected Works* (Moscow: 1951), Vol. I, pp. 124–125.

of production is an essential feature of the proletarian revolution, then the proposition is either analytically necessary, in which case no one can ever have grounds for disbelieving it; or else it must be interpreted as embodying a complex of empirical theses, which (as I shall argue) no one yet has the evidence to disprove. What Tucker has uncovered is not a Marx that has been refuted by history, but a Marx that has not been empirically investigated.

The analytically necessary interpretation of the proposition can be made visible in this way: substitute the phrase "abolition of the division of labor" for "a proletarian revolution"; and substitute the phrase "the possibility of abolishing the division of labor" for "the productive potentials of modern machine industry." These substitutions can be vindicated (though not vindicated to the exclusion of other substitutions) by various statements of Marx's and Tucker's. If transforming the mode of production is an essential feature of the proletarian revolution, and abolishing the division of labor is an essential feature of the transformation, then abolishing the division of labor is a logically necessary element of the proletarian revolution, required wherever the revolution itself is required. Moreover, it is by Tucker's account the chief element in Marx's conception of the revolution. Must not, correspondingly, the opportunity to carry out the abolition be reckoned among the leading elements of the productive potentialities of modern machine industry as Marx conceived them? Technological progress "brings with it the possibility of a thoroughly human way of life in production."

When the substitutions are made, the proposition that Tucker says he disbelieves reads thus: "Abolition of the division of labor is required in order to fully develop the possibility of abolishing the division of labor." From a formal point of view, this is not a wholly explicit tautology; but it is explicit enough for our purposes. Once it is made visible, it can hardly be disbelieved, even by someone who (unlike Marx) would discount the opportunity offered by modern machine industry to abolish the division of labor. Abolishing the division of labor would be a necessary condition of realizing the possibility of abolishing it, however vanishing that possibility might be.

People who do not share the delight that I and other philosophers take in verbal gymnastics may be inclined to think that the point just made is a trivial one. But I must say that it is not a trivial point, even though I am not going to spend any more time on it. Much too much of Marx's philosophy, I suspect, is empty and intoxicating rhetoric—intoxicating because of the air of grandiose prophecy, but empty in so far as the prophecies do no more than circulate air. The detection of tautologies, in the manner of contemporary analytical philosophy, is a useful means of exposing the empty spaces in Marx's thought.

I hurry on, however, to recognize that the proposition, "A proletarian revolution is required in order to fully develop the productive potentials of modern machine industry," invites empirical interpretations as well as tautological ones. In dealing with Marx, we have after all not only to explain his extravagances but also to consider seriously the many unusual and arresting connections which he claims to detect among matters of fact.

At least three interesting empirical theses can be extracted from the proposition. They have never been disproven. Certainly they have not been disproven by the rising standard of living which (contrary to Marx's expectations) the capitalistic countries have enjoyed since Marx's time. Increased consumption was not to be the, main point of the proletarian revolution and it is not a good ground for disbelieving Marx's contentions about the main point, the transformation required in the mode of production.

I shall not try to do more than state the three theses that I would extract, attaching to each of them a brief comment designed to indicate their footing in Marx's doctrines and to evoke their fascination as matters for empirical investigation.

Thesis I: "Abolition of the division of labor is required in order to realize the possibility offered by modern machine industry of eliminating alienation as a psychological condition."

To make sense of the notion of abolishing the division of labor, one must suppose that Marx meant not the disappearance of specialized tasks but an end to the system whereby men are bound to specialized jobs, often for life. This, as Tucker shows, is the bondage that Marx decried; and it is in this bondage that men experience alienation. No doubt alienation, being a metaphysical condition, cannot be reduced to a psychological issue; but it is a condition with psychological features, whose presence or absence can be observed. Tucker cites Marx as saying that under capitalism, the means for developing production "mutilate the worker into a fragment of a human being, degrade him to become a mere appurtenance of the machine, make his work such a torment that its essential meaning is destroyed."[2]

Can the torment of alienation be eliminated without abolishing the division of labor? The division of labor persists; the torment continues. Is there not some connection? People in our society, even relatively fortunately placed people in academic or professional jobs, often wonder painfully if the degree of specialization to which they have been forced has not made their work trivial, or at least too narrow to engage humane interests. Less reflective people show that they feel their work is pointless by working inattentively; by watching the clock; by walking off the job.

On the other hand, as a result of the drastic reduction in the work week since Marx's time, many people now have the opportunity to engage in multiple pursuits. A man is a lathe operator at the factory; but also, in season, a boatman or fisherman or gardener; on winter evenings, a cabinetmaker in his own home workshop, an officer of the PTA. Has not such a man benefited from a reduction in the division of labor, and does he not manifest the benefits in cheerful work habits, a happier view of society, less class consciousness, and reduced militancy?

Thesis II: "Abolition of the division of labor is required in order to realize the potentialities of modern machine industry for producing socially useful goods."

The opportunity to increase output may not have been Marx's chief concern among the revolutionary potentialities of modern industry; but he certainly did not undervalue the opportunity. The world revolution would be pointless without the means of abundance; without them alienation cannot be eliminated—"only *want* is made general."[3] Furthermore, the amount, and especially the character, of output under capitalism reflects the alienation of labor. Unplanned and purposeless, the system floods the market for novelties and "conversation pieces" with a host of obscene trivialities while millions of people, even in the richest of capitalistic countries,

---

[2] For an extended discussion of the psychological aspects, and other empirical aspects, of alienation, see David Braybrooke, "Diagnosis and Remedy in Marx's Doctrine of Alienation," *Social Research,* 25, 3 (Autumn 1958), 325–345. I still feel the skepticism expressed in that article about Marx's remedies for alienation; but I now feel that the skepticism was perhaps expressed too destructively.

[3] *The German Ideology* (New York: 1947), p. 24.

fester in rural and urban slums. Is this not in some degree a consequence of the split that the division of labor entails between the production side and the consumption side of human life in society? While specialization is pushed farther and farther in the drive for competitive efficiency on the production side, privilege and caprice riot unrestrained on the consumption side.

Abolition of the division of labor was, in Marx's eyes, an inevitably associated feature of the same over-all social transformation that would bring in economic planning to coordinate both the production and the consumption sides with human needs. If planning is required to change the character of social output, so is abolishing the division of labor. There is also a more direct connection. General participation in economic planning is itself an important feature of Marx's implied program for abolishing the division of labor.[4] People whose tasks did not include the crucial task of assigning work to themselves would still be alienated, divided off by occupational specialization from the opportunity of expressing their own purposes in the tasks that they do. At the same time, it is Marx's contention that general participation in planning is a necessary condition for achieving an allocation of resources that fulfills genuine social purposes and gives urgent social needs due priority.

All sorts of difficulties can—and, in honest inquiry, must—be made about accepting this thesis. But are we in any position to dismiss the thesis out of hand?

Thesis III: "Abolition of private property in the means of production is required in order to realize the potentialities of modern machine industry for abolishing the division of labor."

Abolishing the private-property system has as firm a place on the agenda of the proletarian revolution as abolishing the division of labor. Moreover, Marx intimates, they do not have distinct places; doing the one involves doing the other, the private property system and the division of labor hang together.[5] And do they not? On the

---

[4] Under capitalism, "The social power, i.e., the multiplied productive force, which arises through the cooperation of different individuals as it is determined within the division of labour, appears to these individuals, since their cooperation is not voluntary but natural, not as their own united power but as an alien force existing outside them, of the origin and end of which they are ignorant, which they thus cannot control" (*German Ideology*, p. 24). "Naturally" is explicated on page 72 of the same book as "not subordinated to a general plan of freely combined individuals."

[5] Cf. pp. 224–225: "The social relations of production," hitherto "successive forms of the division of labor in production," are also interpreted

one hand, every step in the abolition of private property counts as a step toward economic planning; and the introduction of planning is a feature of the program for abolishing the division of labor. (If the planning does not turn out to be democratic, participant planning, perhaps the abolition of private property was only illusory, a device by which a new class obtained power and privileges.) On the other hand, perpetuating the private-property system perpetuates the division of labor. Under this system, men cannot insist on providing themselves with a variety of jobs assigned by a common plan. Instead, because the nearest that the private-property system comes to assuring them of any work at all is to give them a precarious chance of employment in their specializations, men cling to specializations with desperate strength.

Consider the railroad firemen, clinging to their outworn jobs. Under the private-property system, do the people who introduce technological innovations take sufficient responsibility for the fate of the men displaced? Does anyone take sufficient responsibility? Under socialism, would not the responsibility be firmly assumed by the community?

I have not meant to give any illusion of proving either this thesis or the two preceding ones. I remain a skeptic about the empirical case for a proletarian revolution. Against the considerations that I have brought forward to suggest that the three empirical theses might be true, one could easily raise considerations suggesting that they might be false. The truth that may lie in the theses can perhaps be saved only by multiplied distinctions and drastic reformulations. It can be established only by careful and extended social research.

Nevertheless, I hope I have shown that Marx's complex general thesis about a revolution in the mode of production being required in order to provide men with "a thoroughly human way of life" still deserves attention. It remains an arresting challenge to bourgeois complacency, though not to the complacency of the *bourgeoisie* alone. Neither West nor East has yet given enough thought to Karl Marx.

---

as "property relations." I think that Tucker perhaps conflates these ideas too rapidly, but at the same time I think that their mutual dependence in Marx's doctrine gives some warrant for conflating them.

DATE DUE

SEP 25 '76			

DEMCO 38-297